This Kind of Woman

This Kind of Woman

TEN STORIES BY JAPANESE WOMEN WRITERS, 1960–1976

Edited by Yukiko Tanaka and Elizabeth Hanson

With translations by Mona Nagai, Susan Downing Videen,
Akiko Willing, Elizabeth Hanson, and Yukiko Tanaka

Stanford University Press   Stanford, California 1982

Stanford University Press, Stanford, California
© 1982 by the Board of Trustees of the Leland Stanford Junior University

Printed in the United States of America
LC 81-51332
ISBN 0-8047-1130-5

All stories appear by permission of their authors: Kurahashi Yumiko ("Partei"
[Parutai]), Setouchi Harumi ("Lingering Affection" [Miren]), Kōno Taeko
("The Last Time" [Saigo no toki]), Enchi Fumiko ("Boxcar of Chrysanthe-
mums" [Kikuguruma]), Ōba Minako ("The Three Crabs" [Sanbiki no kani]),
Tsumura Setsuko ("Luminous Watch" [Yakōdokei]), Tomioka Taeko ("Family
in Hell" [Meido no kazoku]), Yamamoto Michiko ("The Man Who Cut the
Grass" [Kusa o karu otoko]), Takahashi Takako ("Doll Love" [Ningyō ai]),
and Tsushima Yūko ("A Bed of Grass" [Kusa no fushido]).

Preface

In the summer of 1979, when we first began translating pieces of short fiction by Japanese women writers, we intended simply to submit some of the stories to magazines for publication. The positive reactions of friends and colleagues to our project encouraged us to consider an anthology, however, and we plunged into the task of selecting and translating a collection of fiction that not only would represent something about the lives of women in modern Japan but also would show the high quality of writing by women, so little of which has been translated into English.

Initially we planned to begin the anthology with a story written by Hirabayashi Taiko in 1946, the first year after the end of the war and thus a logical starting point for a collection of postwar fiction. Later we decided that the 1960's were the beginning of a new era of women writers, so we chose Kurahashi Yumiko's story "Partei," published in 1960, to be the first in the anthology. We retained the title of the Hirabayashi story, "This Kind of Woman," as the title of our book.

In selecting stories for this collection our concern has been to choose works of fiction that are of "short story" length, that are of the highest literary quality, and that represent a wide range of experience and subject matter. No such collection can be considered definitive. We are aware that there are endless possibilities for an anthology of fiction, limited only by the interests and imagination of the compilers. We present this book as a sampling—the first English volume with the work of ten Japanese women writers between its covers—in the hope that it will encourage interest in the fine work done by these and other women authors in Japan. For the reader not familiar with Japanese names, we should perhaps note that the forms of all names in the volume follow Japanese practice: last (family) name first, then given name.

This book is the result of the effort and talents of many individuals, who worked long hours on what was at first a speculative project. We would like to thank our contributors, Mona Nagai, Susan Videen, and Akiko Willing, for their superb and painstaking translations; Yasuda Yuriko for her invaluable help in contacting the authors in Japan; Judith Tyson and Liz Monk for reading over parts of the manuscript and making suggestions; and our editors at Stanford University Press, J. G. Bell, Joy Dickinson, and Peter Kahn, for their enthusiasm as well as their perceptive and intelligent comments on the translations and the introduction.

Y.T.
E.H.

Contents

Introduction

Yukiko Tanaka

Women in Japan, as in many other places, have been taught for centuries to strive for modesty and selflessness and to spend their lives serving the needs of their parents, husbands, and children. The ideal woman has been submissive, reticent, and happy to make the home and family her entire world, and a certain shyness and fear in relation to the outside world have been considered virtues rather than handicaps. As a result, any woman who chose to write was opening herself up to the criticism of directly challenging the feminine ideal, since writing is an act of self-assertion and the antithesis of the selfless submission prescribed by Japanese culture. Women writers have needed great courage to surmount the many obstacles to their attempts at such self-assertion. Yet in some ways those obstacles may have led them to try harder, because telling about themselves in writing, particularly fiction, has been one way of freeing themselves from the imprisoning image forced on them by men.

In the late nineteenth and early twentieth centuries, at the beginning of Japan's modern age, women writers existed on the periphery of the literary world and had very little social, economic, or emotional support for their attempts to write and publish. They often imitated male writers, who had been creating the dominant literary tradition, rather than develop their own forms of expression. The social changes that Japan has experienced in the last hundred years, however, have increased the opportunities for women to express themselves, and the number of women writers has increased greatly since the Second World War. Many important and successful women writers have now emerged, particularly since the 1960's, indicating the start of a new phase in the history of literature by women.

Unfortunately, only a few of these writers have had their work translated into English. The ten stories in this anthology were published between 1960 and 1976 and were chosen not only for their high quality but also because they show the experiences, thoughts, and feelings of a variety of women whose lives reflect the changes in Japanese society. These stories display a wide range of female experience: some are tinged with respect for traditional ideals, some with a tone of protest, and some with a new element of search. Although the role of "good wife and wise mother" may persist as an ideal, the stories in this anthology show that Japanese women have as many conflicting emotions, frustrations, and questions—and as much anger—as women in other countries who are trying to adapt to new freedoms and understand what it means to be female.

In order to appreciate the basic assumptions about the woman's role that are either challenged or incorporated in the stories in this anthology, a brief look at the historical status of Japanese women may be necessary for the Western reader. During the 1,200 years of recorded Japanese history, women have been portrayed both in servitude and in power. The women represented in the earliest recorded myths were generally strong, free, and assertive, and they frequently sparred with their male counterparts. Between the sixth and ninth centuries female rulers were not unusual. With the emergence of clan politics during the Heian period (794–1185), however, women began to be used by fathers and brothers who wanted to further their political careers through marriage liaisons with powerful families. The daughter of an aristocrat stayed in her father's home even after marriage, and was not allowed out in public, although her husband was free to come and go as he wished. Women were discouraged from learning the Chinese language, which was the official written language at the time, and instead had to content themselves with the use of the Japanese phonetic syllabary, referred to as "female letters." Heian women were allowed to own and inherit property, but they needed men to help them manage their affairs because they were not allowed to move about freely in the world.

As the society changed from an aristocratic to a feudal one, an image of women as strong, free, and resourceful began to emerge again. Lady Shizuka, an extremely popular figure in *The Chronicles of Yoshitsune*, for instance, did not win her reputation merely on account of her exquisite beauty and tragic life. She accompanied Yoshitsune in his futile attempt to escape from the hands of his jealous brother Yoritomo, head of the Minamoto clan and de facto military dictator of Japan from 1185. When captured, she not only unhesitatingly showed her passionate love for and loyalty to Yoshitsune but openly displayed her contempt for the followers of Yoritomo. Fiercely loyal and spirited women like her—the antithesis of the languid court ladies of *The Tale of Genji*—abound in twelfth- and thirteenth-century war tales. This image of women was qualified, however, by the beliefs of Buddhism, which were beginning to exercise a strong influence on every sector of Japanese society by the middle of the twelfth century. Buddhism taught that the nature of woman is inherently evil and that the only salvation for her is to be reborn a man. These beliefs, combined with the samurai ethic that developed during the Japanese feudal period, established the feminine ideal of submission, obedience, and humility.

During the Tokugawa period (1600–1868), when neo-Confucian thought was strongly influential and the essential doctrine for all people was "to do one's duty according to one's place," women were expected to serve their husbands as vassals would a lord. A woman was supposed to show total submission and dedication to her father when she was a child, to her husband and in-laws when she married, and to her sons when they reached manhood. The male head of the household had control of the female members of the family; a woman could not marry, nor could a widow leave her in-laws' home to start a new life, without permission from this family head. Women no longer could own property, and they could be divorced by their husbands but could not themselves initiate divorce proceedings.

Boys and girls were separated after the age of seven. Women were discouraged not only from associating with the opposite sex, but from leaving the house to go into public places. Women were considered to be stupid and jealous by nature—defects that could be checked only by constant self-inspection and self-reproach. Ironically, however, "stupid" women were expected to manage the household and keep the family finances in proper order. It was considered virtuous for a girl to allow herself to be sold into service or prostitution to help an impoverished father.

Many of the feelings about women that existed during the Tokugawa period continued through the Meiji era (1868–1912), when Japan ended over 250 years of isolation from the world and began to modernize. Under the Meiji law codes, women were once again allowed to own property but were still subject to the family head. Divorce laws still favored husbands. Women could ask for a divorce, but not on grounds of infidelity; by contrast, a woman convicted of

xii   Introduction

adultery could be sentenced to two years in jail. In any divorce, the
husband was granted custody of the children, even if his own wrong-
doing was the cause of the divorce. The Meiji government also supported education for women—but only to produce women who
would be first and foremost "good wives and wise mothers," and
who would thus produce male leaders to contribute to the success of
the nation. A woman's main function was still considered to be bearing male offspring for her husband and his family.

After the Second World War, women gained many rights denied
them in earlier times, including the right to vote. The new Constitution of 1946 defined marriage as an agreement between two individuals, not families, with wife and husband having equal rights to
own property, ask for a divorce, and choose where they would live.
Public schools were made coeducational, with equal opportunity for
men and women.

It is difficult to determine precisely how emancipated Japanese
women are today. Certainly there have been many changes in laws
as well as customs since feudal days, but in many ways Japanese
women seem to lag behind their counterparts in other industrialized
nations in their opportunities to pursue a career and participate on
an equal basis with men in society. In 1974, 30.8 percent of female
high school graduates and 31.6 percent of male graduates went on
to higher education. However, women account for only 20 percent
of the enrollment at four-year universities, as compared with 90 percent at junior colleges.* Moreover, junior colleges in Japan mean an
end to the educational process and are not used to prepare students
for other four-year degree programs, as in the United States. The
subjects offered are usually limited to home economics and courses
for kindergarten or nursery school teachers.

Nearly half of all women over the age of 15 work, 73 percent in
clerical, service, or factory jobs. Women are 40 percent of the Japanese labor force, yet they are hired at lower salaries than males and
are cut off from opportunities for advancement, since companies
anticipate that women will quit working when they marry and so do
not consider them for managerial positions. Thus it is impossible for
women to enter the mainstream of business on an equal level with
men.

Joyce Lebra in *Women in Changing Japan* concludes that there has

* Joyce Lebra, Joy Paulson, and Elizabeth Powers, eds., *Women in Changing Japan* (Stanford, Calif., 1978), p. 21.

been no fundamental questioning of the traditional role of "good wife and wise mother." A marriage based primarily on mutual love is an ideal introduced to Japan from the West, and like the concept of individual freedom, it is both attractive and yet difficult for many Japanese to realize. One might say that whereas in the United States the foremost reason men and women marry is to share companionship and love, in Japan the primary reason is to create a home and a family that includes children. Japanese believe strongly that happiness for a woman lies in marrying well, that she can achieve status best through the success of her husband, and that he needs his wife's support to be able to function well in the demanding world of work. Thus women who work outside the home continue to do most of the housework in order to provide this support.

Some more recent statistics, however, show that in fact women may have begun to question certain of these expectations. Recent government statistics report that 25 percent of single women had no intention of marrying, compared to 14 percent in 1972. Of the 62 percent who wanted to marry, only 12 percent expected that marriage would bring happiness, compared to 34 percent in 1972. Fifty-six percent of divorced women did not want to remarry, an increase of 11 percent from a decade ago.*

Since no definitive history of postwar Japanese literature has been written, some information on general trends in fiction may help the reader place the stories in this anthology in their historical context.

The end of the war meant for the Japanese the end of everything once held valuable; it was the starting point for a new society and a new way of life. Though the country was in chaos economically and politically, and the people were without food, fuel, and shelter, writers who had been silenced or who had chosen not to publish during the years of military domination of the government began to be heard from again. The American Occupation government did not censor fiction as severely as it did newspaper reporting, so they wrote for the new magazines that sprang up one after another, despite the severe paper shortage.

The release of pent-up intellectual energy was first seen in the activity of older, established male writers such as Tanizaki Junichirō, Shiga Naoya, and Nagai Kafū. Younger writers, more deeply affected by the war experience, needed some time to recover from their inner

* Robert Whymont, "Letter from Tokyo," *Manchester Guardian Weekly,* April 6, 1980.

confusion before they started writing. Those who had gone along in one way or another with the aggressive nationalism of the 1930's and early 1940's found themselves in an incapacitating state of shock, and their sense of loss as well as of guilt left them temporarily silent. Left-wing writers, by contrast, felt a sense of liberation and resumed writing actively; they were considered the hope of the new age.

Several women—Miyamoto Yuriko, Hirabayashi Taiko, and Sata Ineko—were among these latter writers. They wrote strongly auto-biographical stories about their own experiences and feelings, and through their fiction they expressed their thoughts about socialism and about what it was like to be a woman in a time when basic changes were taking place in society. Their heroines were independent and had great aspirations to grow and live fuller lives; they reflected their authors' feelings that their personal drama was part of the larger drama involving all of society. The heroines' outgoing expression of love toward their men, coupled with their serious attitude toward their own lives and their sense of indignation about the weak and the oppressed, gives a rather refreshing image of Japanese women. These characters represent an aspect of the Japanese ideal of the woman as loyal, sympathetic, and maternal, with enduring strength.

Other younger writers in the immediate postwar era won considerable fame not only because of their writing, which revealed deep skepticism and despair, but also because of the way they lived. Their characters attacked the ways of law-abiding citizens and acted irresponsibly and insensitively. These writers, among whom Dazai Osamu is the best known, abused alcohol and drugs, indulged in sexual promiscuity, and typically ended their lives with suicide. The earlier fiction of Hayashi Fumiko, a well-known woman writer of this era, is based on her own stormy life, which was characterized by poverty, rootlessness, and a free, reckless life-style. Her heroines share much in their feelings and philosophy with Dazai's hedonistic characters, but Hayashi's stories reflect a certain optimism similar to what one finds in the works of the leftist women writers. She died several years after the end of the war, at the height of her career.

Many young writers who began to write and publish in the 1950's were influenced in their younger years by Marxist philosophy; in their fiction they expressed concern for issues such as the human condition, love, and the existence of God. Their experiences of war—often firsthand on the battlefield—were central to their writing.

More than anything else, they questioned whether or not human beings are free. Yet the highly philosophical and ideological overtones of the fiction written by men in the first decade of the postwar period are curiously absent in works by women writers of this time. In fact, only a few new women writers—such as Sono Ayako and Ariyoshi Sawako— started publishing in the 1950's. Unlike their predecessors, they wrote historical epics with female central characters, or novels treating current social problems in a detached manner.

The disintegration of belief in the existence of some knowable reality was the starting point for a generation of writers like Mishima Yukio, who were adolescents during the last years of the war. With his *Confession of a Mask*, published in 1949, Mishima achieved instant fame, and by 1954 his reputation was firmly established. By contrast, the women writers Tsumura Setsuko and Ōba Minako, who were also in their late teens during the war, did not publish until the 1960's.

By the time Japan officially became an independent nation again in 1952, the social and political climate had already changed dramatically. Owing to U.S. involvement in the Korean War, the country had recovered from the devastation of 1945 with a speed no one had expected. Soon people began to enjoy a life of affluence that included many new conveniences and material comforts. The middle class was expanding, and technological advances became visible in every part of daily life. A new type of hero appeared in fiction—a man of action rather than an introverted intellectual—and sex was treated for the first time candidly and directly. Existential philosophy appealed to wide audiences in the late 1950's and 1960's, particularly to young people. Ōe Kenzaburō and Kurahasi Yumiko were influenced by Sartre and Camus, and the characters in their fiction faced existential crises and were plagued with various obsessions.

In 1960, Kurahashi Yumiko, a graduate student of French literature, won instant recognition with her story "Partei," the second story she had ever written. Although her sudden celebrity was something of an isolated incident, the 1960's was the beginning of an era when women writers became increasingly important. Toward the end of the decade, their work was well represented in—and sometimes even dominated—literary magazines. Not only were greater numbers of women writing than ever before, but the quality of their fiction was generally high.

Kurahashi's early stories are satirical; they criticize the grotesque pettiness of people who blindly believe in their power and authority, and point up the emptiness of ideology. For Kurahashi, to write stories is to fabricate, to construct a world that is not familiar to us in our daily life—or in her words, an "anti-world." She herself claimed that "Partei" was the product of an attempt to imitate Camus and Sartre. In other words, it was not the vague desire to give her own life and experiences an artistic expression that motivated Kurahashi to write. As brilliant as her literary debut was, however, public taste in 1960 was not ready for her avant-garde writing.

Realism had been the predominant mode of prose narrative in modern Japanese literature until the Second World War, and the basic urge for those who wanted to write came from the youthful yearning for expression of the inner self. Writers in this realistic tradition continue to be important today, with a number of women prominent among them. They record incidents from their lives, and their personalities are clearly reflected in their stories—with all their weaknesses and their strengths. At the same time, their work is a sort of testimony to their era. To these writers the sense of actuality is the most important element in their literary expression. Perhaps Setouchi Harumi is the prime representative of the younger generation of women writers of this autobiographical school. She consistently looks for creative impetus to her own life, and time and again she treats events from her not-so-spectacular life in her fiction. Reading her stories, however, one learns that she writes in an attempt to gain a sense of self, and thereby of freedom and independence.

Though Enchi Fumiko is a contemporary of Sata and Hirabayashi, her actual debut as a fiction writer was in 1953. After switching from drama to fiction and writing for several years, she received recognition for a depressing story about a middle-aged woman, who, after years of poverty and caring for her selfish husband, dies without getting anything whatsoever from her life, not even reconciliation with herself. Enchi, not an autobiographical writer, has written many novels and stories about unhappy women who live lives of self-denial. They are depicted, however, as having more complex personalities than their male counterparts, with more inner strength. Often her women, like the heroine of "Boxcar of Chrysanthemums," are a mystery not only in men's eyes but also in women's. "Boxcar of Chrysanthemums" describes how the narrator, a woman very much like the author, comes to recognize in the central character, Rie, the passive strength of the ideal Japanese woman. The mystery of Rie is slowly and gradually understood by the narrator after she has heard about her occasionally over a 20-year period, and it is the im-

age of a mother in Rie—gentle, forgiving, and forever self-sacrific-
ing—that is finally disclosed. The reader, along with the narrator,
comes to accept the fact that there is more diversity in human lives
than one might imagine and that women's minds are indeed complex.
Yet the world in which Rie lives (the prewar world) is presented as
black and white, and the relationship between Rie and her society is
rigid and well defined. It is a society with definite sets of values and
morality, deviation from which is understood either as a mistake or
as a rebellious protest, and only occasionally—as in the case of Rie—
as a rare but highly commendable act.

By the mid-1960's, Japan had achieved its postwar aim of becoming an economic success, but the result was nothing like the utopia
envisioned by the socialists at the end of the war. Although women
had gained new rights and freedom, a spiritual crisis began to develop in the midst of abundance. There was a prevailing sense of
emptiness and loss of direction that was the result of rapidly changing values, severe crowding in urban areas, and progress attained at
the price of destruction of the natural environment. Fiction reflected
this situation: some writers tried to show it by focusing on everyday
family life and recording the barely perceptible changes that were
slowly corroding traditional values and human relationships; others
wrote about the problem of freedom and alienation in a society that
had become increasingly complex and difficult to grasp. Disillusion-
ment and inner confusion recur as basic themes in much of recent
fiction.

Japan's highly industrialized, urban, and affluent society may or
may not be related to the increase in the number of women writers
since the mid-1960's. Critics have tried to explain this phenomenon
of the current prominence of women writers by concluding that perhaps the very ambiguity of complex modern life can be best portrayed by women, who are "temperamentally" suited to describing
subtle details of their immediate surroundings and narrowly focused
events. Whether it is a matter of temperament or something else is
an issue that requires more space than is available here, but it is evident that women who began to write actively in the mid-1960's share
some basic concerns: their women characters question the traditional
role assigned to women and try to examine the morality they grew
up accepting; they doubt the meaning of their lives and reflect upon
their sense of self; and they are more aware of their secret yearnings
and unfulfilled dreams than women in earlier fiction.

With a few exceptions, all the writers whose stories are included in this anthology draw on their actual experiences, as their predecessors did; the differences between these writers and the earlier women writers discussed above are not only in the number of autobiographical elements in their fiction but also in the basic notion of what fiction writing is. Recent writers more or less share Kurahashi's view that a story is a fabrication, and that they can and should express their opinions and ideas as well as their self-awareness as women. They try to reflect a woman's point of view and sensitivity more freely in an imaginary world. Images of women represented in their stories, though they vary, are clearly different from those presented by their predecessors and have much to tell us about contemporary Japanese women.

The main characters in "Lingering Affection" by Setouchi Harumi, "Luminous Watch" by Tsumura Setsuko, and "The Last Time" by Kōno Taeko have all failed in their first relationships with men and have doubts of one kind or another about the meaning of marriage as a bond between a man and a woman. Each story describes different situations and problems, but all reveal the consciousness of women who, though they do not wish actively to reject the traditional framework, cannot passively accept their own situations. All of them are capable women, far from being "shallow," "illogical," or "unstable."

The men in these stories are weak and ineffective, want to maintain the status quo, and cannot face the truth about themselves. The women, by contrast, have an urge to reexamine their relationships with men and their sense of identity as women and individuals. They do not consciously choose their life-styles, however, and as a result they cannot understand what their real problems are; they are ill at ease with themselves and feel that they are being pulled in two directions. Their lives are at an impasse.

Tomoko, a financially self-sufficient professional woman who is the central character in "Lingering Affection," demonstrates this conflict most dramatically. Though she has maintained a love affair with a married man for many years and gets some emotional sustenance from it, she sees the relationship as a "mere habit." She becomes extremely uneasy with her awareness of the dual life she leads and experiences violent emotion, yet it is not the issue of love alone that torments her. She is preoccupied with concern over how she might appear in the eyes of the man's wife as well as those of society in general. And yet she involves herself in another love affair, this time with a younger man, and makes her life even more conflicted.

Tomoko approaches both of her lovers with a sort of maternal protectiveness and with a deep desire to nurture them with her own abundant life force—the easiest way for her to express her female qualities. Even though Tomoko has an unorthodox life-style, her basic pattern is that of a wife sensitive to the needs of her husband.

What is it that Tomoko looks for in this double triangle of love affairs, which she seems to have created for reasons unknown even to herself? At one point she realizes that what she is drawn to is the intoxicating secrecy and the thrill of deception. Tomoko's deviation from the norm is not only a protest against a society that rigidly prescribes a woman's role but also a way for her to acknowledge her own sense of self. Once the union of a man and woman becomes a "home," it commonly turns out to be something altogether different from what it was meant to be. Men and women like Tomoko and her lover, therefore, try to sustain the initial impetus of love in a relationship outside of marriage.

The woman in "Luminous Watch" also approaches a man with the protective instincts of a mother. Here again, a normal marriage and family life do not form the background for the story. In order to support herself and her daughter after her husband leaves her for another woman, Michiyo washes *tabi*, the kind of white socks worn with kimonos. It is hard work that pays poorly, but it is more respectable and in accord with her sense of the feminine role than becoming a bar hostess, the easiest way for women without education and skills to earn a living. Michiyo even takes pride in doing her laundry work well; her strong need to sustain the traditional image of womanliness determines the work she chooses.

When Michiyo meets a total stranger who sits in the park alone day after day, her maternal instinct is aroused, mixed with a longing for a man's companionship. She is shocked, however, when she realizes that she has invited a man to her apartment; she discovers a woman within herself of which she had been unaware. Unfortunately, however, this newly discovered self cannot find a means of expression.

"Luminous Watch" presents a picture of an ordinary middle-class woman who suddenly finds herself outside the family structure, yet who does not let herself get swept away easily. At the end of the story the reader sees her living as she did before, but as a sadder woman.

Setouchi and Tsumura, like earlier women writers, tend to focus on the discontent the female characters feel with various social conditions, their lives, and themselves, or on the ways women cope with both external and internal obstacles. Kōno Taeko writes about women who feel ill at ease with their own female identity, and she takes up for the first time as a fictional motif the meaning of being born female. "The Last Time" concerns a woman who has become uneasy about being a wife, and who confronts the questions about what marriage is and ought to be in a way that she has not done before.

A sense of sudden discovery comes to Noriko in "The Last Time" when she realizes that she will have to die within 26 hours. It is a discovery involving not only Noriko's perception of herself but also her relationship with her husband. Until then she has had very little doubt about her marriage; she and her husband are sexually compatible and considerate of each other; she felt in fact that she was quite happy. She is disturbed by the sudden realization that she has perhaps been unconsciously deceiving herself, that being a tolerant wife who is always eager to serve and please her husband is a superficial and empty role. And yet it is not that someone has forced her into such a role. She feels that her unknowing self-deception has slowly eroded her true self, and she feels uneasy about being a wife. Being legally married, sharing a house, having a sexual relationship, and loving each other, Noriko says, are not sufficient for a true marriage. She tries to explain to herself what a real marriage is, but in the end it remains ambiguous in her mind as well as in the reader's.

In her story "Partei" (the title refers to the Communist Party), Kurahashi Yumiko asks far more radical questions about existing rules, morality, and the basic relations between men and women. Woman's place is not in this world but outside it; thus the heroine of "Partei" thinks of leaving the party as soon as she finds out that her application has been accepted.

Although dealing with the questions of existential philosophy that were imported from France and were fashionable among young Japanese writers in the 1950's, "Partei" contains elements that tie it to the other stories discussed here. The woman character shows a sense of dread not only at the human condition but also at the female one. In one of her essays Kurahashi says that she must pretend to accept and obey the rules of the world so that at the same time she can change the content in such a clever, subtle way that no one will be able to detect what has been done. In writing fiction, she is actively attempting to redefine the female condition according to her own ideas, not those of the male-dominated society; fiction writing is a means for her to explore and experiment with her ideas about being a woman in the world.

Ōba Minako's female characters, most of them comfortably married, are at odds with the traditional view of feminine roles, just as Kurahashi's are, and share a similar sense of dread at being a woman. In Ōba's "The Three Crabs," Yuri, a housewife and the central character of the story, recognizes the self-hatred—poison, she calls it—that enables her to see the pettiness and shallowness in the other women gathered at her party. She looks critically at middle-class sensibility and values and refuses to go along with prescribed roles. She tries to escape a sense of meaninglessness—which she expresses as the nausea of morning sickness, a uniquely female experience—but she has no clearly conceived plan for doing this. She acts on impulse and eventually returns home, defeated and undoubtedly filled with even more self-disgust. Even though her attempt to escape was destined to fail, she has tried something that women in earlier stories never thought of. Yuri represents a middle-class housewife whose discontent lies not in a specific situation or relationship but in something more essential: being a woman who has awakened to the discrepancy between her role and her sense of self.

The narrator-protagonist in "Doll Love" by Takahashi Takako plays a role that is the exact reverse of that traditionally prescribed for women—to wait passively for a man to love her. "Doll Love" is the Pygmalion story written from a woman artist's point of view—a woman gives life to a younger man. The heroine loses her sense of identity in the end, however, as the price for asserting herself and demanding that prescriptive roles be altered. This is a characteristic of Takahashi's women characters; they are often lonely housewives cut off from human relationships and driven to obsessive behavior that approaches madness. Like Ōba's protagonists, they are suppressing real needs in their routine lives as housewives.

Takahashi often writes of women who feel that there is no clear distinction between themselves and others and who have a deep-seated sense of alienation and self-loathing. These women entertain sadistic, violent fantasies and direct hostility toward those who are close to them. Everything related to the life force is negated, and nature seems filled with ill will. Female sexuality, with its regenerative qualities, is abhorrent to Takahashi's women; their conscious or unconscious death wish seeks the destruction of the existing order in which the woman feels alien. Takahashi writes of women who are discontented and cannot be happy unless they discover their true selves, and yet the discovery of this true self is dangerous because it can lead to the destruction of relationships with others.

Yamamoto Michiko's "The Man Who Cut the Grass" presents a

childless suburban housewife, Mayo, precariously balanced on the edge of a nervous breakdown. Nothing happens to her in real life, and each day passes in exactly the same way. Her sexual fantasies are locked inside, just as she locks herself in her house. Only the physical landscape is unsettled, with the tall wild grasses swaying in the wind. Mayo's vague sense of guilt, which is associated with a dark fascination with mystery and crime, breaks the monotonous drudgery of her life and bridges the past and present. Her guilt has sexual overtones that stem from an experience she had during puberty. Mayo's life as a suburban housewife is filled with ennui, but it is overshadowed by a special kind of guilt tied to her female identity.

Writers like Ōba, Takahashi, and Yamamoto differ from the earlier writers in their tendency to turn inward and write of a closed world within themselves. Their female characters share a fair amount of self-hatred, are basically hostile toward society, and are cut off from other people. These negative characteristics are associated in some way with the fact that they are women suffering a profound discontent, not so much with the socio-cultural condition of women as with the female condition itself—that is, with everything about being a woman. They challenge the popular notion that women are creatures of flesh rather than spirit, abundant in life force, but with scant chance of transcending their physical limitations. The characters in these stories search for ways to bring their femaleness and their existence as individuals into harmony somehow, but in order to do this they must first of all try to define themselves. In the process of such definition they must explore their own interiors.

Tsushima Yūko and Tomioka Taeko try to convey their understanding of the feminine situation not by merely exploring their characters' inner landscapes, but by presenting real problems with which the female protagonist is forced to cope. Their stories present the drama of feminine experience, emphasizing how their protagonists fail. Rather than confront and deny their sex and sexuality, however, the protagonists recognize the powerlessness of all modern mankind. It is through confronting their feminine predicament that they try to restore in themselves a sense of wholeness.

In the stories by Tsushima and Tomioka, the end of a relationship with a man forces a young woman to examine her past, her feelings about her family ties, and her own female identity; ultimately, she asks the basic question of whether she needs a man in order to define herself. The young woman in "A Bed of Grass" by Tsushima returns to her mother's house after her marriage fails, even though she once left the same home to free herself from the control of her mother. She remembers the days of her childhood, when she was rapturously happy playing with her retarded brother, a boy who never grew up and who never was conscious of her as a female; and she gradually faces the complexity of adult life and her fears of the unknown, including men, who were once rough boys that she watched from a distance on the school playground. She sees herself as weak, or having a tendency to identify herself with the weak; the story explores the problem of a woman's self-image and ideas about herself, concepts that she begins to internalize as a girl and that become the source of her victimization.

"A Bed of Grass" also analyzes the relationship between the narrator-protagonist and another young woman, Kumi, who is raising an illegitimate daughter. Through the intimate relationship between these two women, Tsushima shows a new aspect of the search for a feminine identity. The two young women, living with images of a dominating mother, a selfish husband, and a father who deserted his family, share a sense of self-loathing and a feeling of insecurity about themselves as women. Kumi is the narrator-protagonist's alter ego, and Kumi's isolation, her poor self-image, and the rebellious toughness that enables her to cope with reality are all shared by the protagonist as well. As a result of her close relationship with Kumi, the narrator-protagonist gradually comes into contact with a more basic and intrinsically feminine nature within herself and finally accepts her femininity, with its strengths as well as its limitations and vulnerability. Only then can she rid herself of fear and a deeply repressed anger.

In Tomioka's "Family in Hell," a girl leaves her mother's house to try to live a life that is not much more than playing house, but the boy, her partner, is as elusive as the young man in "A Bed of Grass" and takes off, leaving her behind. In both Tsushima's and Tomioka's stories, the heroine's relationship with her man is not the central focus; to understand what the relationship means to her, she first has to look at her own family, particularly her feelings about her mother. Thus the main motif of "Family in Hell" is how the heroine Nahoko comes to question family ties and separate herself as an individual; her task is to transcend the forces that have formed and defined her. These family relationships are presented as monstrous, formidable, comic, and perplexing, yet as phenomena that have their own logic and credibility.

Tomioka's woman looks at herself with more analytical detachment than do the other women in the stories in this anthology. Before she can see through the man who has forsaken her and see herself outside the "dark hole" where she has been playing house, Nahoko must first understand how she is trapped in the network of human relationships. She sees reality as an accumulation of facts, memories, and emotions that cannot be understood with the rational mind alone. Tomioka suggests that this same reality, with its preconceived notions, expectations, and judgments, traps all women. In "Family in Hell," before Nahoko can set herself free from the constraints of society, her own past, and the human relationships she is involved in, she must understand and then eventually express herself, thus objectifying herself not only in her own eyes but in the eyes of the world.

For those who have not read Japanese narrative prose, a few words on its language and form may prove useful.

The Japanese term *shōsetsu* refers to both novels and short stories. The *shōsetsu* was invented in the early twentieth century when Japanese writers rejected traditional tales and romances in search of a narrative form that would suit their need to express themselves freely in the modern world. There is some distinction made between *chōhen* (full-length) and *tampen* (short-length) narratives, but a clear line is not drawn between the two categories. Whereas most Japanese *chōhen shōsetsu* are shorter than the average English novel, *tampen shōsetsu* are often longer than one would expect a short story to be. Moreover, *tampen shōsetsu* often lack the structural characteristics one expects in a short story, such as unity of plot, place, and tone.

One of the initial tasks of the pioneers of the *shōsetsu* was to bridge the gap between written and spoken Japanese. At first the writing in the *shōsetsu* was stiff and artificial, but over the years it has become more natural and closer to the spoken language. The *shōsetsu* has some problems when analyzed with Western critical approaches: it has very little plot, characters are usually not fully developed, and the voice of the narrator is almost always that of the author. These characteristics do not mean that Japanese writers have not yet mastered the art of fiction; rather, they are related to the Japanese tendency to put emphasis on suggestion and evocative power rather than description and eloquence.

The stories compiled in this anthology show changes over the span of eighty years since women started writing *shōsetsu*. Not only in subject matter and style but also in the writer's approach to fiction, they are recognizably different from those written by earlier writers. The writers of the stories collected here do not believe that the power of their personalities and the uniqueness of their experiences allow them to write with little regard for dramatization. The narrators of these stories are not the authors thinly disguised—as in previous autobiographical stories—even when the stories faithfully relate the authors' actual experiences. The authors are conscious of their art, of style and the effect of language. The greater artistic control and objectivity give their stories an ironic tone that was absent in the earlier works. Younger writers also treat more clearly outlined themes in their stories and try to present characters—their circumstances and their thoughts—in a way that invites the reader to understand them intellectually as well as emotionally.

A hundred years ago, becoming a writer of *shōsetsu* meant accepting a status almost equivalent to that of a low-class entertainer, but today fiction writing is considered a respectable occupation. Japanese writers often publish their stories, and sometimes even novels, first in magazines. Literary magazines under the aegis of major publishing houses have a readership beyond small circles of scholars and critics, and they try to encourage younger writers and discover new talent. There are many literary prizes for newcomers as well as established writers, and some young writers come to enjoy both fame and some economic reward after a relatively brief period of apprenticeship, and are thus able to devote all their time to writing.

In the prewar era, the stereotypical woman writer was single or divorced and childless, and was thought to live a free and immoral life, giving up home and family for her career. Today, however, women are able in some cases to combine their writing with family responsibilities, and although successful woman writers in Japan have many different backgrounds and family situations, one may say that it is no longer necessary for a woman to sacrifice her personal life for the sake of her writing.

This Kind of Woman

Partei

KURAHASHI YUMIKO

Translated by Yukiko Tanaka and Elizabeth Hanson

Kurahashi Yumiko (b. 1935) was the eldest daughter of a dentist. Her generation was the first to receive secondary education under the new system established after the Second World War that provided equal opportunity for boys and girls. She ignored her father's wish that she become a dentist and entered Meiji University to study French literature. In 1960, before graduating, she made a brilliant literary debut with "Partei," the second story she had ever written. Kurahashi said that reading and studying Franz Kafka, Albert Camus, and Jean-Paul Sartre made her want to write fiction. In "Partei" she imitated these European anti-realist writers, ignoring the traditional style of her literary predecessors in Japan.

While she was still a student, she established herself as one of the brightest and most promising writers of the new generation and wrote prolifically. Her avant-garde fiction, however, was not always understood, and often received unfavorable reviews. In 1966 she went to America as a Fulbright fellow and spent a year taking creative writing courses at the University of Iowa and traveling to various parts of the United States with her husband. After her return to Japan, her fiction became more realistic; at the same time, she started to use traditional themes and myths to give structure to her stories.

Kurahashi, her husband, and their two children went to Portugal in 1972 with the idea of settling there, but their stay ended after two years because of political unrest. In 1975 and 1976, eight volumes of her collected works were published.

Kurahashi herself said that "Partei" is an "imitation of Sartre," and its style is strongly reminiscent of translations of French existential writing. It also can be read as a satire on the young intellectuals, particularly university students, who strongly identified with Communist ideology. Kurahashi uses the German word "Partei," written in the Japanese syllabary used for foreign words, as her title. The narrator also regularly uses a word that can be romanized as "onto" but that probably is the Japanese pronunciation of the French word honte ("shame"); this expression is used to suggest the sense of despair and alienation found in existential philosophy.

ONE DAY you asked me if I'd made up my mind. You had tried to bring up the subject several times before, and besides, this time you were unusually frank. So I told you I had decided, since I felt I too should be frank. Joining the Party, you began to explain, meant relinquishing one's personal life, including love relationships, and subordinating oneself to the Party's principles. I couldn't see the expression in your eyes because your glasses were glittering too brightly. Your teeth clattered like two poorly constructed skeletons when you brought them together; no doubt you were unnaturally excited. I couldn't help but give an animal-like laugh. Then you took my hands. Yours were warm and damp, as always. I found them rather unpleasant. You seemed to want to make certain of my decision, so I had to reassure you with slightly exaggerated gestures and words.

You told me one by one the procedures necessary to receive formal permission to join the Party. To tell the truth, I was hardly listening. The enthusiasm you showed for these procedural matters I found ridiculous. Preparing one's "life history," you said, was the most important. You put a thick pile of documents in front of me and said this was your own life history. Sitting in a heap before me, the worn, crumpled pages were soiled from being handled, which seemed to be proof that they had been passed around among the Party members for rigorous examination. When I thought of your life being handled by so many strangers—even if they were called an "organization," to me they were still strangers—I felt an embarrassment that was almost painful. I thought you, too, would probably have realized how ridiculous this life history was, if your face and even your eyes hadn't been so covered with "belief" that spread over you like a birthmark.

We were in a room. It was a dirty room with walls that were beginning to crack, deep within the maze of an extraordinarily large building. Since the time when you first brought me to this room, I had noticed that my existence had become strangely abstract. I rarely laughed, I always spoke logically, and the few times

I did laugh, it was with a fixed heartiness. I felt no sadness, for it was silly to do so in this building. In fact, once I stepped into this "dormitory," as the building was called, "reality" was transformed into a smelly, slimy world. The rooms, large and small, were divided by thick walls, but because these walls connected the rooms like ligaments, I had the impression of an aggregate of cells filled with stale air. That day too I was in one of those cells, talking with you while ignoring the "students" around us doing their various kinds of work. I had once told you my impression of the room, saying that the air was abnormal, too thick and somehow abstract. But after you had asked me a number of questions, you dismissed my impression.

After all, you said, I did not have enough experience with the Party. This was the source of my lack of confidence, you said, trying to comfort me. Well, then, I said, the best solution seems to be to get used to things. Still, I couldn't seem to get used to this place. There were too many people, and I was irritated by their noise and dirt, and by the peculiar, unpleasant odor from the lower part of the body that is produced when human beings live in a group. It had bothered me for some time that the "Imperial Rescript to the Army and Navy" was scribbled on the walls and ceiling. I asked you as a kind of warning if you didn't agree that this sort of thing was inappropriate for the dormitory. Occasionally a student who lived there began to shout the Party's song. Then similar songs would come through the walls from other rooms here and there; I thought that I could never get used to such a place.

Until that time, I can say that I had been almost perfectly in love with you. Although I wasn't sure what "perfect" meant, you had continually assured me of the existence of that "perfection." From the first time we met, you had shown an interest in me, and I felt the same way about you. After a short time I had said that I loved you and you had confessed the same. Then you had cried copiously. You said that the fact that you, a member of the Party, had cried such human tears was because of me and my love. This more or less flattered me at the time. When I thought about it, however, it made very little sense. First of all, it seemed strange that it was possible to be a Party member and become emotional at the same time. Soon after that, at your suggestion, we had declared to our fellow students that we were in love, and had received their congratulations. I had flushed with humiliation. Nevertheless, I think that the reason I had loved you for a comparatively long

time—or more accurately, had believed in my love—was because I had spent my days within these abstract walls. It probably would not have happened that way if we had been someplace where the air was lighter—if we had made a big fuss about sharing the ordinary details of everyday life.

In any event, it was extremely difficult for me to write my life history so that it included these things about us. This was simply because I felt almost no interest in my own past. You had advised me to pick details of my past as faithfully as possible, to summarize them, and to connect one to another in some logical order, so that everything could somehow be related to my motivation to join the Party. I knew from experience the contradictions of the world, having lost my parents when I was born and having experienced poverty and betrayal. You explained that because of these things I not only had sufficient motivation to join the Party but also had developed the various characteristics needed in a Party member.

Several days later, however, I told you I couldn't write a life history. You started to construct the story of my past, beginning with my childhood, and you argued that it was "inevitable" that I join the Party. Your persistence was remarkable, and I felt both admiration and wonder that my past could be molded in such a splendid way. But at last I interrupted you. That's not the point, I said. No matter how much you brushed and creased my past, it did not mean that "therefore" I "had to" join the Party. I felt nauseated at the thought of using my past to restrict and defend myself. I wanted to escape from the past and throw myself into the future I had chosen the Party and had resolved to let the Party restrict m' freedom. I had not arrived at this decision for any clear reason ' through some cause-and-effect relationship. Wasn't it enough if t Party accepted this decision? But you disagreed. You called my ar' ment "intuitionalism" and said this is a dangerous ideology. ' informed me again that for an individual to join the Party, an jective "inevitablity" acknowledged by the Party was require'

I left the dormitory feeling somewhat discouraged. I rode a for two hours to get to my own room, then did nothing but When the morning sun was casting its rays of orange-colore' I left for the dormitory again, still wearing my same swea' ened clothes. I worked quite hard. That afternoon I was to you to K City to visit a few "unions." I would have rat with another student, but since the decision had already b there was nothing I could do.

We arrived in K City about two in the afternoon. The sun came weakly through the cloudy sky, and it was muggy. Looking down from the bridge, I could see the freight rails running under several overpasses and spreading out radially, so that they were drawn into and connected many "factories." The city was crowded and it extended to the sea. The factories, which were made from patched sheets of black iron, were heaped together so that when you looked at them as a group, they resembled a crude but imposing icon. We changed trains many times and went up and down iron staircases. Since the factories were originally built on irregularly divided lots, additions were built not only on the sides but above and below the buildings. As a result, these additions sometimes crossed into other lots or leaned against the buildings of other factories. We got lost several times and went into factories that were not assigned to us. Even when we found the factory we wanted, it was difficult to find the union. The gatekeepers would ask our names and what our jobs were, and each time we had to come up with fake names. Looking back it seems ludicrous that someone would ask our names, but the gatekeepers were satisfied with the ones we gave and handed us entry passes.

We had a hard time locating the union once we were inside the factory. Sometimes the union was not in the factory itself but in some barracks exposed to the salt wind blowing in from the sea over the nearby trash dump. Most of the time, however, the union was part of the dim factory building, and the union officials looked at us with eyes that glowed yellow in the dark. I thought they looked exactly like owls, but this metaphor made you cross. Actually they were quite gentlemanly and didn't give me the impression of being "workers."

Our mission was to explain and publicize the "workers' school" we were going to open and also to feel out the current condition of the union. You smiled continually and made yourself agreeable to the union officers, but I couldn't do this. As we were leaving the factory, however, you told me that you yourself did not completely trust those union members. You said we must not, under any circumstances, lose our class awareness. This was because they might be union members and they might not; they might not even be workers. Reality is always complex, you said, and our practical experience is the only touchstone we have for determining who is a real worker and who is not. Of course for me, such a thing was incomprehensible as well as impossible.

I must explain a bit about the circle I belonged to then. It was one of the groups generally referred to as a "settlement"; ours was called the "workers' school settlement," and our main task was to infiltrate the workers in K City. The students who did the same work were called "fellows." To me, this name had a certain dampness to it. It was like your hands, warm and sweaty. When I used this word, I usually felt as if I were a member of an organization that preached brotherly love in the name of God. But what concerned me was the relationship between the fellows of the workers' school and the Party. I didn't doubt that there were some Party members among the "fellows," but it was not easy to tell who they were. The fellows, without exception, had the look of Party members, and in fact I think they all wanted to join the Party. In public, however, all of them acted as if they were not members. I thought that they did this to maintain a public appearance that made it easy even for regular students to participate in the workers' school. The Party members I knew were you and S, a big shot in the "regional committee." His piercing, snake-like eyes and his professional eloquence were enough to tell me that he was an important Party member. It seems that he had been infatuated with me for some time.

Even after the workers' school began, you lectured to me about my life history and pressed me to hurry and finish it. When I said I was having a hard time with it, you asked why. This irritated me, so I said I was having trouble for the same reasons I had mentioned before. Then you criticized me for being impractical and too conscience-ridden, and you brought up the "M Incident" out of the blue. Innocent "comrades" had been sentenced to death in a courthouse surrounded by armed policemen and tanks, you said, trying to stir my sense of justice. I understand very well the injustice, I couldn't stop myself from saying, but unfortunately I am not terribly interested in such things right now. What I am concerned about now is joining the Party; on this point it seems you and I agree. I want to achieve this goal with a clear-headed state of consciousness, so no matter how furious the M Incident makes me, I don't want this to be my motivation for joining the Party. After all, things that are not transparent have always made me feel *honte* . . .

We organized a small, personal "study group," starting with workers we had met at the workers' school. At that time my first responsibility was managing the operation of the workers' school, particularly recruiting the instructors for the school. Second, I worked as a tutor for the study group, and third, I collected information on the condition of the unions. I soon became friendly with the workers who came to our study group. They had thick-jointed limbs, were bowlegged, and had dark, hot skin. They talked only of practical matters, of things that were so concrete that I felt faint. I conducted the study group in the attic storage area of a bookstore, a room that faced the sea at the top of a narrow fire escape.

One day I ran into a worker who attended my study group and he treated me to a meal. The worker was better dressed than I was and seemed to have more money, so I accepted gratefully but felt a little embarrassed. I went with the worker to the attic of the bookstore and waited, but no one else came that day. This often happens, the worker said, and we sat there for a while, hugging our knees. It was hot. I was the one who suggested that it would be a good idea to take our clothes off, and the worker agreed. The ocean seen through the window had brown waves and was coughing up the odors of oil, metal, and other, organic substances. The smoke from the factories made the sky a cloudy red, and the setting sun, the color of a ripe persimmon, seemed to have stopped in the middle of the smoke. I saw that the worker's skin had a reddish hue like ingot steel, and I began to feel an interest in him like that I might feel for a strange animal.

There is essentially nothing to say about the incident that followed. I touched the worker's body without knowing why and found that it was made of hard muscles; the worker was startled, then became excited and took me right away. Breathing roughly, he did his best to make me love him. Rather than being actually hurt, I felt uncomfortable, as if I were being pushed open as far as I would go. The worker was alien even as he was inside of me, and I was irritated by the feeling of distance, as if we were two animals of different species that had accidentally met and copulated on the spot. However, I was able to remain almost perfectly clear-headed. I was even generous toward the worker. I would have responded to him at any time after that, and I myself even wanted it to happen again. The worker was cleaner than he had looked. But he was very hard and heavy, and difficult to deal with, because he had nothing to say; his existence was nothing more than his simple, down-to-earth life. After this incident, I began to nurture the hope that one day I would understand what a worker was.

I asked your opinion of this hope. You answered promptly that it was a good thing, that I should try to understand the worker in a more aggressive way. Then you mentioned S as an example of a comrade who combined the qualities of student and worker. I disagreed. S is neither, I said, and that is the cause of his filthy, amphibian-like repulsiveness. Then I left to find a substitute lecturer for the workers' school. One possible lecturer lived in a house that was crowded together with many others and was difficult to find.

Typically, my search for lecturers followed a predictable pattern. I might meet A for some reason and ask him to talk to our group. He would say that unfortunately he was not free at that time and would suggest B as an appropriate alternative. When I would finally locate B and make the same request, he would also refuse and give me the name of C. Thus I would spend several days trailing after these "progressive intellectuals" as if I were following sweet-potato vines. I must say that I never built up any unrealistic hopes. They were busy and the workers' school paid the lecturers a miserable fee, so I thought their bashful refusals were understandable.

Nevertheless, I would go on tirelessly explaining the significance of the workers' school, and they would listen with attentive expressions. Although we were overly eager in pretending to be eager, we didn't believe anything that was being said. They seemed to be afraid of something, and I had to swallow down a taste that was as sour as vinegar, while I was acting like a missionary. Finally in this case I ran into a progressive poet who had some free time and convinced him to come and lecture.

On the day of his lecture he came on time. Another poet, whom I did not know, also appeared to lecture. It seemed that one of my fellows who had been separately trailing another sweet-potato vine had located this second poet. I was flustered, but divided the pay between the two of them and had them both speak. They nestled together like two birds and spoke in turn about "literary circles in the workplace."

I remember that S severely "criticized" me for this. He told me that I lacked the ability to handle practical matters, and then asked me suddenly how my life history was coming along. I was silent. All this time he had been looking at me as if I were some "object," and since he made no effort to conceal his desire, I felt uncomfortable. S then said, in order to attract me, that he would help me write it. Of course I declined. He then attacked your "opportunism," saying that it was your fault as well as mine that I was as timid and slow as a rabbit.

One day after the rainy season had begun, I finally finished my life history and took it to your room to show it to you. I had simply put down facts in chronological order. Still, as it included rather detailed descriptions of my life, it was so thick that it did not compare unfavorably with your life history. You read it, shaking your head at every word in your usual annoying way. I was fed up. Tiny particles of water caused by the rain filled the room, intensifying the usual odor. I had grown used to this environment little by little, so while you were reading my life history, I walked around the room, energetically exchanging opinions on revolution with other students.

You suddenly interrupted me when I was speaking of "the revolution." You pointed out that, judging from my own life history, it seemed I had an insufficient grasp of the inevitability of revolution. I exploded and said I wished you would stop saying such inane things. I said that "revolution" was not something that existed outside of myself. If revolution was external, how could the "inevitability" of something outside myself affect my freedom and ability to choose? I would join the Party not because the revolution is inevitable but because I want to choose the revolution, I said. I had chosen to restrict my freedom so that ultimately I would be even more free. My participation would make the revolution inevitable for me.

At this you became argumentative; you took up each of my words and hurled them back at me, trying to cut off my arguments with your hard, glassy eyes and with the cigarette smoke you blew out incessantly. Why don't you understand? we both yelled at almost exactly the same moment.

Without mending this schism of disagreement between us, you accepted my life history as a legitimate "instrument" of the Party, recommended me yourself, and took care of all the necessary procedures within the Party cell. My life history would be passed from one person to another, dirtied by spit and handling, and would gradually rise to higher levels of the organization. As it moved farther from me, it would become less mine and would be treated as something with real substance. When I thought of this, I felt both pleased and anxious. I wanted very much to see how the decision was made. I thought the process must be like that of a ticket-vending machine: it takes a coin, automatically swallows it, moves its gears elaborately, and finally spits out a ticket.

One day in August when the strong rays of the sun had burned everything to a whitish color, I felt queasy several times. After the workers' school was finished and the workers had gone home, I was extremely tired but went to S's place to discuss a few things and finish some remaining business. S asked me if I was going back to the dormitory. When I told him it depended on how soon I could get things done, he smiled as if satisfied. I added that I was very tired and found it painful to think of going all the way home from K City. S ran his yellowish eyes, which had the "activist's" special look of constant fatigue, over my body and asked if I had been feeling poorly lately. It was an appropriate suggestion. My stomach below my waist had begun to swell visibly, and judging from my frequent attacks of nausea and my swollen legs, I had to acknowledge immediately that I was pregnant.

S asked who the father was, and I told him I didn't know. Then I added that it might be the worker and, trying to suppress my embarrassment, I held my breath and made an ugly face. I explained, mumbling, that it had not happened very often. This seemed to excite S even more. He pushed me down on top of some books that were scattered around, and while hurriedly trying to take me, he said it made no difference now anyway . . . Afterward he suggested several possible remedies but for some reason I couldn't get interested and didn't say anything, enduring the nausea. What happened to my life history? I asked. An ambiguous smile appeared on his face, and he seemed to want to evade the question. He said he himself was not certain, but that he guessed that I would soon receive a Party membership card.

For several days after this my increasing sense of *honte* made me sweat profusely, even when I wasn't moving, and the world seemed to be rocking back and forth. Each time, my head hit a slimy, abstract wall and rubbed against it. I knew that what seemed to be a wall was in fact myself. I was shut inside walls made by the past I had chosen, and I was nearly suffocating in the hot air. This dazed state was ludicrous. I could probably call it comical. There were times, however, when I did occasionally break out of the walls and go into the outside world, and the lightness of the air there startled me.

About that time, several new students joined our circle as "settlers." On your suggestion we had planned a week-long "retreat" by the M River in K City. At first I had felt some interest in this retreat because it reminded me of "military life," with its communal activity and regimented routines that extended from meals to evacuation of the bowels. It seemed that when living with a group of people, one would cease to be aware of *honte* and would get used to the peculiar odor of human beings. The retreat confirmed this. With you at their center, the group exuded honesty, friendship, brotherly love—in short, "fellowship," as they like to call it, a feeling that embarrassed me. Even so sometimes they all seemed to me, myself included, like a group of dogs bound together by a leash of *honte*.

When we gathered on the riverbank, it seemed like a garden party; several couples formed amid the pleasant drawing-room conversation that the comrades exchanged. You held my hand, and I tried to talk to you about *honte*, surrounded by the warm wind from the river and the insects that swarmed around me. It was no use. The others were absorbed in singing and dancing on the wet grass. We returned to the building that we were using for the retreat and took turns telling of our past experiences late into the night. When one student was finished, it was my turn. I said I had nothing I wanted to tell about my past. You suggested, showing your eager generosity, that I tell about some problem that most concerned me now.

When I mentioned the Party, each person's expression changed as if covered with a metal mask, and they all stared out into space with vacant, unfocused gazes. Perhaps I shouldn't have spoken about the Party in the way I did. You looked me firmly in the eyes, and I was furious. I pointed out in a strong tone how disgusting it was to see the members of the circle adopting blank expressions at the mention of the Party. I said that we should clarify our relationship to the Party once and for all. You said that this was a difficult issue and hinted that we should drop the subject. I persisted. Many new students had joined the group and become fellows, I said. This gave meaning to their lives and they expended tremendous amounts of energy for it, although this interest did resemble the interest in sports they had enjoyed as students. The longing and sense of inferiority they felt in relation to the Party was muddied by contact with this group and the Party itself . . . I think I expressed myself more coherently than this, although I don't clearly remember. I do recall that someone criticized me for being "sectarian."

This did not bother me, however, and I continued to speak; I said that I did not quite understand the significance of these activities and that when I began to consider the point at which my participation touched reality, I felt completely confused. In other words, for the time being I had no hope, and I was doing nothing more than scratching at a frozen sky in the midst of starless darkness, trying to leave some streaks of light there. I could not believe for a minute that these streaks would lead to the possibility of a revolution. I believed only that the organization that limited my freedom also gave me a freedom I could not have attained myself.

As the night deepened and the air became chilly, salt from the day's perspiration began to appear on earth-colored skin. The other fellows seemed sleepy, which made their faces look somehow symbolic. The white specks of sweat on their faces looked like stars decorating clay figures . . . The sounds of the slaps they used to combat the constant attacks of mosquitoes made the gathering seem like some mysterious ceremony. This is indeed a secret ritual, I thought. There was no doubt that what was important here was not to understand but to go through the formalities of attempting to understand. In fact no one understood what I had said, and I hadn't expected that they would.

Eventually you began calmly to criticize me, your glasses glittering. With some hesitation, you described me with the term "petit bourgeois." My anger rose from my neck and filled my head, and I turned bright red. I was quite accustomed to the scrutiny of others and to being labeled by them, but this time I couldn't stand it. This convenient term "petit bourgeois" was too absurd. I couldn't think what to say and remained silent. You thought I had accepted this criticism and began to speak lucidly. We participated in the workers' school, you said, so that we could understand the workers and draw on the vitality that was part of their daily lives. This participation would tie us together through humanistic love as fellows and thus we would be able to escape isolation and loneliness . . . I was impressed with the way you had summarized things. I told you that it was indeed a clever explanation, and I had nothing to say against it, but that it was a way of thinking I couldn't understand. I wondered why you had carefully avoided "revolution" and had instead advocated the loose ideas of "service" and "brotherly love." When I saw that no one responded, I realized that the clay figures had probably fallen into an earthen-like sleep. They were leaning against each other, their bodies chilled from the sweat; some were holding their knees and others had their legs stretched out, exposing the dirty soles of their feet.

The next day we divided into several groups and went out to do union surveys. I went with you to visit the union of S Oil; a worker in the public information division began to speak to me with great interest when he saw me. I thought I had seen this worker somewhere before, but decided it was not important. I stood up immediately to leave, but the worker followed me to near an oil tank that was marked "off limits" and said that he couldn't forget me. I asked him detailed questions in order to find out why he knew me, and he claimed to be one of the workers who had come to the study group, and he said he had had a sexual relationship with me. He said he wanted to marry me. I declined his offer curtly. I did not understand what he meant, and the expression that he wanted to set up a "household" with me was puzzling. He also said he wanted the child. I replied that I was capable of having the child but that I had no intention of doing so and planned to have an abortion. You had been waiting for me outside the gate and asked if I had been "educating" a worker. This thought made me laugh. You insisted that I help bring the worker into the Party.

The next day you found me in the washroom and said that you wanted me to go somewhere with you. The Party had sent orders for a certain duty, you said. First we went to the dormitory and removed anything that might show our identity. Then we went to the entrance of a busy shop-lined street and hawked the Party newspaper. You explained that this was part of the publicity activities needed for the election and the anti-A-bomb demonstration, both of which were coming up soon. Imitating you, I shouted slogans in a harsh voice that became more and more out of tune as I continued. Things didn't go well. We didn't sell a single copy of the paper; they curled up and turned yellow in the strong sunshine. You maintained a dauntless attitude, however, and didn't even try to wipe off the sweat that was rolling down your face.

Shortly after noon we were arrested. The police officer explained that what we had been doing was a possible violation of both the election code and the traffic code, and he requested politely that we go to the main police station with him. We went with him, dragging our apple boxes and carrying the newspapers under our arms. You signaled me repeatedly to run away, but I didn't obey.

The room we were put in had a bare floor and was poorly constructed; it was shabby like some servants' quarters. You remained silent and I said nothing either. Several police officers surrounded us and began to ask questions about the Party. This interrogation was very tedious. It began with the formalities of asking our names and addresses and what we did, then developed into leading questions, irrelevant and mixed with conjecture, regarding the Party; when we said nothing, they went back and began to ask our names and addresses again. I was able to indulge freely in my own thoughts during this repetitive interrogation, which was like listening to a monotonous symphony. It wasn't necessary for me to give them a false name; I was a perfectly nameless suspect with some relationship to an organization but without any distinguishing characteristics or connecting strings, a single smooth particle.

The police officers handled us as if they had expected our attitude and they said they wanted to take fingerprints. You asked why. They looked at each other and smiled. They must not have known themselves. Thinking that taking fingerprints was a stupid, useless thing to do, I made my hands into fists. When I did this they lifted me onto the table, holding my arms down firmly. They tried to force my fingers open with a screwdriver, and the edge of it dug into the space between my nails and my flesh. My fingers opened one by one. I had begun to enjoy resisting and the police seemed to feel the same. Smiling, they finished their task and shut us into a small room about the size of a lavatory.

About the time it got dark, a large man brought us dinner. You did some arm and leg exercises to increase your appetite, then stuck your face into the aluminum container and began to eat. While you were eating you suggested that I do the same; you said that we would probably be released the next day. I said I didn't particularly want that to happen but if it did, there was nothing I could do. You looked rather surprised and then, moved, took my hand in yours. You praised me grandiosely for not betraying the Party, despite the "torture" I had undergone, and you called me "comrade" for the first time. You insisted that I was a person who truly loved the Party. I disagreed and ended the discussion simply by saying that under the circumstances, it was impossible to betray anyone. Nevertheless, the term "comrade" made me feel very uncomfortable, as if I were being forced into a container. I said I wished you would stop calling me that since I had decided not to join the Party. I noticed then for the first time that you were extremely wall-eyed. I was convulsed by a fit of laughter. What had you been seeing all this time? You are comedy itself, I said, rolling around, and while I was laughing I vomited.

You were completely taken aback, but when I stopped vomiting and told you, tears still in my eyes, that I was pregnant, you brought your pupils to the center of your face and stared at me. Then you took off your glasses and began to cry. Although I didn't have much to say to you, I announced that I didn't love you and did not in any way love the worker, S, or the Party. When I had finished I felt alone. Neither your sobbing nor the smell of my vomit bothered me. I was extremely clear-headed, but I forbade myself to direct this clarity toward analyzing the situation or establishing a cause-and-effect relationship. I should strip my actions of all motives and rationalizing. I should not have written a life history, and I thought I should try to get it back as soon as possible. This had been my first *honte*, but in an effort to get rid of it, I should not make more *honte*.

The Party no doubt existed somewhere, functioning with its strange, complex mechanism, expanding and shrinking, swallowing individuals like me and then spitting them out. This existence, however, was extremely abstract. To me it seemed like a kind of religious organization, developing as it did from a body of commandments and secret rituals. Its purpose was salvation, and to be saved was to believe. I didn't believe in anything, however. I didn't believe in the "inevitability of revolution" or in the objective significance of what I had been doing. I had simply decided to choose the Party, and I had done so without any belief.

Perhaps I would apply the same attitude to any future decisions. I soon fell asleep, and when I awoke, the room in the jailhouse was unexpectedly bright. You were still sleeping, exhausted. The coarse flesh of your cheeks, your fat neck, and your glasses were all there in front of me, and now they meant nothing to me.

A while later, food was provided, I went to the bathroom, and we were taken to the police chief's office. After some simple interrogation—the questions were almost an exact repeat of the day before—we were released. You raged that we should be given a written apology, but the chief explained that it was impossible for their office to publicly apologize to a nameless "nobody."

You went to K City to return to the "boardinghouse," stirring up some kind of hope again, and I stayed in my own apartment for several months. The room seemed unfriendly, and for a while I hesitated to touch the furniture and walls. On my desk I found an envelope without a sender's address. Inside it was a notification to the effect that I had been accepted into the Party, and a red membership card. After inspecting it carefully, I threw it away.

I decided to begin the procedures necessary for leaving the Party.

Lingering Affection

SETOUCHI HARUMI

Translated by Mona Nagai and Akiko Willing

Setouchi Harumi (b. 1922), the daughter of a merchant, grew up on the island of Shikoku. She was a sickly child and read poetry and fiction extensively at an early age. She entered Tokyo Women's College when she was eighteen and studied Japanese literature. In 1943, the year she graduated from college, she married a teacher nine years her senior and went with him to China, where a daughter was born. The family left China in the summer of 1946, and after a year they moved to Tokyo. The marriage, however, was dissolved in 1948 when Setouchi fell in love with a former student of her husband.

Leaving her husband and daughter was the starting point of Setouchi's long struggle to establish herself as a writer. While writing children's literature to make a living, she also wrote fictionalized biographies of women writers who had notorious reputations because of their passionate devotion to art and a free life-style. Setouchi seemed to find in these women's struggles with traditional Japanese society a yearning for fulfillment as free individuals and a search for the true self similar to her own.

Setouchi was not recognized as a serious fiction writer until 1963, when her "Natsu no Owari" ("The End of Summer") won the Women Writers' Prize. A great deal of her writing takes the form of shi-shōsetsu, a confessional style in which the main character is the author. This is a very popular literary form in Japan, allowing the author to present his or her own life for the reader's judgment.

"Lingering Affection" is one of several confessional stories Setouchi has written telling of her own complicated love affairs with two men, one an older, unsuccessful writer who cannot give up writing, the other a younger man for whom she once gave up her marriage. Setouchi's soap-opera-like themes are no doubt partly responsible for her popularity. She has become a Buddhist priestess and now lives in Kyoto, where she devotes her time to her writing and to her religious training.

ON THE TOP LAYER of the bureau drawer was a man's ikat kimono that had just arrived from the tailor that morning. The white of the basting stitches stood out sharply against the color of the indigo dye that had settled in a deep, rich shade. Restraining her desire to see Shingo wearing it, Tomoko pulled from beneath it a well-worn garment spotted and stained from everyday use.

Tomoko had resolved that these clothes, as well as the others expected from the tailor, would no longer be worn by Shingo in this room. She wanted to deliver them directly to Shingo's wife just as they were, with the basting thread still in. Including underclothes, the load would probably take up more than three wicker hampers. Tomoko had not yet thought of exactly how she would hand them over to Shingo's wife.

When was it that she had begun, in a roundabout way, putting in order his various kimonos and other clothing? It seemed that she had started after that visit to Shingo's house just a couple of months ago, at the end of summer; but at the same time it seemed it had been going on in the depths of her unconscious feelings for nearly a year now, a quiet preparation for their parting.

The padded winter kimono should be sent to the cleaners soon, the short *hanten* coat should go too—Tomoko's mind spun busily.

In her concern for the cleanliness and order of Shingo's clothes, not wanting them to expose to Shingo's wife the grimy evidence of his life with her, there was something of a shallow feminine concern for appearances.

Tomoko had her own notion of Shingo's wife's reaction upon encountering this mountain of clothing, but in her imagination she underestimated how this raw evidence of her husband's affair thrust before her would renew that bitterness she must have felt so keenly.

About the same time that Shingo started coming to her apartment, Tomoko was casually told a story by a friend who had married an office worker.

"It's really disgusting. The girls at my husband's company go so far as to wash his lunchbox for him. Isn't that worse than if he

didn't finish his lunch because it wasn't appetizing enough or whatever, after you'd fixed it for him so lovingly? It was so offensive I
threw away the whole thing—the lunchbox, the cloth it was wrapped
in, and all."

Tomoko stared at her friend, who looked as if she had said nothing
remarkable. Tomoko too had known married life, for not quite five
years, but whether or not it was because of her husband's fidelity,
she had never experienced this terrible jealousy. Nor with the lovers
after her marriage had she even once taken an affair so seriously
that such jealousy arose.

Listening to her friend, Tomoko wondered whether despite her
own readiness to fall in love repeatedly against her better judgment,
her blood was uncommonly thin, or her passions disappointingly
shallow.

From all Tomoko could tell, Shingo's wife did not seem to be a
woman of such violent temperament that she would be moved by
jealousy or moral fastidiousness to burn up or tear to shreds or sell
off the clothing her husband's mistress had provided him, those
garments saturated with the odor of their life together. If she were
a woman of such moral fastidiousness, she couldn't possibly have
tolerated her husband's affair without a word of complaint for eight
long years, Tomoko supposed conveniently. Of course, that was no
more than Tomoko's one-sided conjecture to suit herself. She had
no way of understanding what really went on in the heart of a
woman whom she had never met or even seen a picture of.

Two months ago when Tomoko impulsively went to Shingo's
house near the sea, his wife and their only daughter had been out.
The manner of her visit was so abrupt that it was more of an assault
than a visit.

The relationship between Tomoko, Shingo, and Shingo's wife,
which had already continued for eight years, seemed as though it
would go on forever just as it was, if they left it alone. From the
beginning it was based on a compromise between Shingo's wife
and Tomoko in which each tolerated the other's existence; and the
dust of eight years had settled so thickly upon it that now it was
impossible to detect whose endurance and sacrifice had enabled
the triangle to be formed in the first place. Normal sensitivity and
emotions had become dulled, and there seemed no way out of the
stalemate that had developed. Moreover, on Tomoko's side, the
reappearance of her former lover Ryōta had twisted the messy relationship into further bizarre complications, and Tomoko was confused and exhausted.

Tomoko's real motive in going to Shingo's house, as a last resort, was the hope that by actually confronting the wife who had thus far remained faceless and formless in Shingo's shadow, she would gain some clue to a decision that would lead her out of the impasse of this awkward situation.

Shingo, home alone at the time, was more than a little surprised by Tomoko's sudden visit. But the impact on Tomoko was greater. Although she herself had sought it, she was shattered by confirming with her own eyes, at last, Shingo's home and the circumstances of his married life. It crushed her beyond imagination.

For a while things she had seen at their house kept appearing in her dreams: a pair of women's yellow vinyl sandals flung carelessly in the entrance hall and, hanging against the wall, Shingo's wife's brown-and-white print dress that Tomoko felt glaring at her from behind. There were also times when she awoke from nightmares of faceless people—Shingo's wife and daughter.

Nor could she forget the chilling impression of ominous desolation when she had finally arrived at Shingo's house, weary from trying to find her way there, covered with dust and sweat.

In the dusty evergreen shrub growing by the entrance, in the way the patchy brushwood hedge was withering, and in the dried, cracked yard where even the weeds were stunted and sickly, Tomoko thought she saw the dreadful years of loneliness in the heart of Shingo's wife, and she stood there paralyzed and despondent.

Tomoko forgot the blithe hopes she had set out with and sighed with relief that Shingo's wife was not at home.

Crying so hard her face became swollen, she had no sooner started talking in vague terms about ending their relationship than abruptly, like one possessed, she confessed the secret of her relationship with Ryōta, which until then she had rigorously concealed from Shingo. With that, she hurriedly left as if driven away by a vision of his wife's imminent return.

Late that night, after she had finally arrived at her own apartment, she wrote a letter to Shingo's wife for the first time. After apologizing for her silence and the rudeness of the past eight years, Tomoko begged her assistance in separating from Shingo. She used up half her new writing pad trying to write the letter.

She did not notice when dawn came. Feeling refreshed, as if she had vomited up all the poisons in her body, she slept deeply for the first time in days. When she awoke, the white midday sunlight was already flooding her pillow.

She reached from the bed for the letter she had left lying on the

desk and began to reread it. Although she had certainly not intended
to exaggerate or lie, now as she read the letter after a night's sleep
she was surprised to find that parts of it were not to her liking.

"Please forgive me," the letter said repeatedly, and each time
Tomoko saw these words she shuddered. It was true she had been
filled with remorse for Shingo's wife the night before, but this
morning she felt she could not allow herself to apologize in such a
servile, pitiful manner. Whatever the circumstances, part of the
responsibility went to Shingo's wife as well for silently tolerating
her husband's affair for eight years, Tomoko argued with increasing
vehemence, knowing it was a false accusation.

She spent a long time tearing the letter to shreds. She spent even
longer resentfully burning it in the ashtray, scrap by scrap.

She could accept that she had confessed to Shingo about Ryōta,
but why had she ended up saying, as she left, "Tell her everything—that I came here today, and everything I said. It doesn't matter if you tell her about Ryōta too." Tomoko felt like grinding her
teeth in chagrin at her thoughtlessness and naive optimism.

Did Shingo's wife deride him, "See there, just as one would expect, she's a loose woman"? Or did Shingo by chance conceal from
his wife Tomoko's affair with Ryōta, saving her and thus himself
from disgrace, as in the past he had never even once spoken of his
wife in a disparaging way? Tomoko agonized alone, and in the
misery and ugliness of the situation felt herself spinning in all directions.

In this anguish, she breathlessly awaited a move by Shingo and
his wife.

Two days later in the afternoon Tomoko sat at her desk by the
window writing an article. Now that she was at last becoming
recognized as a professional textile dyer she was beginning to receive occasional requests for articles on the subject.

"Looks like it's going to rain."

Shingo's sudden voice startled Tomoko and made her jump from
her seat. The pen slipped and made a clumsy mark on the manuscript she was writing, an article on stencil and block printing for a
women's magazine.

The noiselessness of a cat had always characterized Shingo's way
of walking. When, in their long relationship, had she begun wel-
coming her lover in such an inelegant manner? By now Tomoko
could no longer remember.

Her surprise at his appearance had become noticeably stronger ever since she started her secret affair with Ryōta and her guilty conscience led to this new habit of startled reaction. Even after she had looked up at Shingo's face she could hardly calm her throbbing heart, and would gasp wordlessly through dry lips.

Now, even though she had confided the affair to Shingo, the awkwardness of this momentary alarm that was so extreme it seemed abnormal still remained.

"Oh, you scared me," Tomoko said as she turned around. Shingo was standing right behind her, looking just like a man refreshed and cared for by his wife. With his tie still on, he was taking out his cigarettes.

"Is the laundry all right?" Shingo spoke in a quiet voice, glancing out toward the clothesline. It had started drizzling from the dark overcast sky. As Tomoko stood up, Shingo went over to the television and turned it on to a baseball game. Then, stretching his long neck, he tugged at his necktie roughly as if it annoyed him. This was his customary behavior whenever he made himself at home in this room. Tomoko was stunned by Shingo's totally unchanged manner and wondered if her visit to his house had been a dream. At least, the fact that she had gone to his home seemed to have had no significant effect on him.

"What did she say—about my visit?"

"Uhmm . . ."

"Was she relieved? Is she pleased?"

"Well, yes, probably."

"Did you tell her everything?"

"Yes."

"Does she despise me?"

"No, not really . . ."

This was about all she could coax out of the reticent Shingo concerning his wife's reaction.

What could they be intending to do? Though feeling somewhat relieved at Shingo's coming to her place as usual and acting just as before, Tomoko experienced an empty sort of exasperation as if she had been fended off. The exasperation gradually grew into a feeling of humiliation, and with it an emotion resembling rage built up deep inside her. Before she knew it, she was burning with a rage directed at Shingo's wife alone. Where were her feelings—this wife who sent her husband to Tomoko's apartment just as before, after Tomoko had gone to the extreme of visiting their house in an attempt to resolve the bizarre situation?

Tomoko began to feel as if Shingo's wife were a huge tile wall towering directly in front of her. Its hard smooth surface offered no hold and allowed no possibility of even clawing one's way upward. Once obstructed by that wall, Tomoko would lose sight of Shingo's heart as well. She felt mortified and bitter at having played the fool, rushing over to their house without considering the consequences and accomplishing nothing except her own disgrace.

Shingo would continue to divide his week between the two women, going back and forth between them regularly like the pendulum of a clock. It took more than Tomoko's turning up uninvited at his home or confessing her betrayal with Ryōta to disturb Shingo's routine.

Tomoko now felt the weight and meaning of the eight long years that had gone by. It was so much easier and more comfortable to go on with the habits entwined with those years than to make an effort to break them. With tears gathering in her eyes as if her strength had failed her, she was shocked to notice that she too was already half-filled with the relief of ennui.

Shingo had changed into a kimono Tomoko had gotten out for him, and had tied a sash comfortably around his hips. They sat facing each other, sipping tea from their special matching cups, and Tomoko began to feel that hours shared like this, familiar and warm like the warmth of the teacup between her palms, would continue indefinitely in the future as well.

But her innermost thought that they must eventually part, whatever Shingo's attitude might be, continued to spread its roots tenaciously. And as the roots spread, her hours with Shingo seemed even more precious than before; strangely, her heart in complete devotion seemed to draw closer to him.

As in the early days of their courtship, they would sometimes go out for long walks even during daylight hours, strolling closely side by side; other times they went into the coffee shop in front of the station as if they were a couple of young people again; they even entertained themselves browsing through street fairs. These pastimes became more frequent than ever.

When most men of his age were either at work in their offices or busy tending to their shops, the casually dressed Shingo, walking like a man of leisure with a woman at his side, was conspicuous in the street. Tomoko, too, attracted attention. She did not look sophisticated enough to be taken as a woman of the pleasure world, but for an ordinary respectable woman her dress was too chic, with the sash of her kimono knotted a bit lower than usual and stylishly loose.

Whether something that seemed not quite proper was suggested by the bearing and mood of an unfortunate man who had spent the last thirty-odd years writing novels that did not sell, and a woman in her late thirties who, earning her living as a professional textile dyer, had willingly immersed herself in the man's unhappiness, or whether a singular eroticism drifted through the atmosphere surrounding the two of them as a couple, people in the streets often stared at them or turned to look after they had passed.

Whenever this happened Tomoko would deliberately act demure and, gazing straight ahead, speak in a voice only Shingo could hear.

"Look, the one who just passed. She turned around to look at my sash," or "See the housewife over there? She's eyeing you and blushing . . . Are you all that handsome?"

With this kind of frivolity Tomoko would force a wry smile from Shingo and enliven their stroll.

Shingo carried himself soundlessly, his tall, impassive figure close beside Tomoko as if to shield her from the stares of passersby as well as from the dust stirred up by buses and trucks crowding the full width of the road.

One day when they went out on one of these walks, a woman unexpectedly bowed to them at the entrance to their narrow street. After returning the bow automatically, Tomoko realized that she was the woman who lived in the house with the black wooden fence at the entrance to the lane leading to Tomoko's apartment.

She recalled an incident in which her landlord's good-natured daughter-in-law had told her that the woman was a former hostess at a dance club. "But now she's someone's mistress," she had added inadvertently; and then, realizing her slip of the tongue, she had quickly averted her eyes in a fluster, blushing so deeply Tomoko felt sorry for her.

After they had come out to the main road, Tomoko wondered what the woman was doing. All she could figure out was that the woman, standing directly in front of the house with her arms crossed behind her back, was staring at her own house.

"That house where the woman was just now . . ." Breaking their usual pattern, Shingo started a conversation. "When I passed by yesterday, she was wiping the fence with a damp cloth. Some children had scrawled 'HAUNTED HOUSE,' and she was trying to erase it."

Tomoko and Shingo let out a muffled laugh. It was indeed a de-

crepit, gloomy house, and the shabby branch of a scraggly pine
hanging over the rotting gate made the place look all the more
dismal.

Two days later demolition of the woman's house began. Tomoko
learned that the woman had quietly moved out the day before. She
thought about the silent exchange of bows the day before the
woman left, after years without a single word between them. Perhaps the woman had meant it as a farewell gesture. Tomoko tried
to remember the face of this woman who had seemed so inconspicu-
ous it was hard to believe she had once been a favorite dance partner
at the Florida Club, but all she could call to mind was the pale, broad
forehead.

So, that's one way to change your life, too. Tomoko stood for a
while near the house, for some reason feeling deeply moved by it
all.

Under the half-rotten board fence that was being torn down before her eyes, clusters of asters lay crushed, coloring the ground in
a profuse blooming of light blue.

There were times when she was filled with an odd hope that
Shingo's wife might come see her in secret, leaving Shingo at home
alone, unaware. She even thought she could almost hear the tone
of Shingo's wife's voice saying, "Let's do our best to keep him
locked up in the house by the sea."

Tomoko felt that if that happened, she and his wife would come
to understand each other more deeply than they understood anyone else.

It was as if she could hear the poignant sighs of the two women
who had maintained a peculiar relationship of passive complicity
and inertia centered around Shingo for the last eight years. At the
same time, when her daydream faded away she was unable to grasp
an opportunity for leaving Shingo, let alone hate him; and she felt
instead like hating only Shingo's wife with all her strength. However, in her sanguine nature there was neither the passion nor the
perseverance to hate anyone for more than a few days. Her idyllic
hope that Shingo's wife might come to visit was also, of course,
thoroughly disappointed.

And, as before, only time passed swiftly in the stalemate of their
relationship.

When the call came from his wife, Shingo was away from Tomoko's apartment on a trip, which was unusual for him. A job as-

signment—something that seldom came his way—reached him at Tomoko's apartment, which he had started using as his base in Tokyo. He was asked to go to Shinshu to report on the estate of a certain poet.

When the listless voice of the operator informed her that there was a call from the seaside town, Tomoko automatically covered the mouthpiece with the palm of her right hand. Her heart started pounding.

It was not uncommon for Shingo's wife to call. But conveniently, calls from her town could not be dialed directly. When it was Tomoko who answered the phone, as soon as she heard the operator's voice she would quickly cover the mouthpiece with her hand and call Shingo in a shrill voice, "Hurry up! It's from her." Then she would hastily go stand in the kitchen or the toilet and stay away until the call was over. It was not from any genteel reason such as etiquette that she did this; rather, her very senses rejected staying in the room while Shingo was talking to his wife. And then, out of thoughtfulness toward him, she did not want him to feel constrained in his conversation by her presence.

Once in a while Shingo himself took the call. When this happened Tomoko did not always realize that it was a call from his wife until he had spoken a few words into the phone. She would suddenly perceive in his voice a certain peremptory tone or a note of carelessness he would never use to outsiders, which would send her hurrying out of the room as if shoved from behind. It was not until half an hour or so afterward that she would realize that the tone of Shingo's voice by which she had recognized that the call was from his wife was exactly the same one he used with her as well.

Because of this way of handling the calls, Tomoko had not only never seen Shingo's wife, she had not even heard her voice in all the eight years.

After the operator spoke, a noise like the sound of waves came through the line. Tomoko held the receiver pressed so hard against her ear it almost hurt, her mind still wavering. She felt an irresistible curiosity to hear Shingo's wife's voice, but it was mixed with an instinctive aversion that made her want to run away, and her nerves became taut with agitation.

"Hello." Finally the other party was on the line.

It was a slightly high voice, full of life.

Tomoko automatically responded with a conscientious reply as if she were a grade-school pupil. The voice at the other end stopped cold. From the depth of a heavy silence the confusion and dismay of the caller could be felt with an almost eerie presence. She must have assumed that as usual Shingo would answer the phone.

"Is this Miss Aizawa's residence?" a tense voice asked with stiff formality.

"Yes."

"This is Mr. Kosugi's wife speaking. Is my husband there?"

"Mr. Kosugi is away in Shinshū. He left yesterday on a job assignment that came up unexpectedly. I understand he will be returning tomorrow."

Finding herself speaking about Shingo in formal terms that she never used to him personally, Tomoko smiled half bitterly in recognition that Shingo was indeed this woman's husband.

"I see . . . How inconvenient . . ." Mrs. Kosugi's voice suddenly lost its careful control. It appeared that she mistook Tomoko for domestic help. Shingo had no doubt told his wife about the young girl from the neighborhood, just out of junior high school, who came in three times a week to help Tomoko with the housework. Once, the girl had carelessly burned a hole with the iron in a new shirt of synthetic fiber that Shingo's wife had him wear.

Tomoko's voice was naturally high-pitched, and sounded even more so over the telephone, so that it was not unusual for her to be mistaken for a young girl.

"Well, when he returns, could you give him a message for me? Tell him that his niece back home is ill in the hospital, and ask him to send her a get-well gift."

Tomoko had known for some time that Shingo had a niece back in his hometown who kept house for his elderly mother. The girl's parents, Shingo's older brother and his wife, had both died at a young age within a short time of each other. Tomoko understood that Shingo had a nervous dread that the same illness which took the girl's parents might someday show up in the girl as well.

"All right? Was that clear, or shall I repeat it?"

"No, I have the message."

Shingo's wife then said she might as well ask her to take down the address of the hospital, and began to dictate slowly with a pause after each word. Repeating after her like a parrot, Tomoko busily jotted down the address of a hospital in a mountain town in Tōhoku.

As they continued, the voice at the other end began to lose its composure and distinctly started to quaver.

"In care of Yūki Hospital—Yūki as in . . ."

"Yūki silk?"

Suddenly a strong, resolute voice, so different in tone from before, came reverberating down the line, as if to accuse her.

"Is this Miss Aizawa? You are, aren't you?"

"Yes, I am . . . Pardon me for not introducing myself first."

After a moment of ominous solid silence, laughter rose from both sides, it seemed, and filled the receiver. It was a peculiarly empty and somewhat treacherous laughter that trailed on aimlessly. Just as Tomoko's eyes were glaring with anger while her voice feigned laughter, it was obvious what sort of fierce expression Shingo's wife wore as she joined in.

After the laughing subsided, a cold feeling remained. Adding one further item of business—the suggestion that a box of cookies and a pretty nightgown might be best for the gift—Shingo's wife hung up.

Picturing Shingo in a department store trying to choose a nightgown for a young lady, Tomoko muttered sullenly in his direction, "Suit yourself."

Her throat was parched with thirst when she put down the receiver. She went running noisily to the kitchen for a drink of water.

When Shingo came back from Shinshu, Tomoko excitedly told him about the call.

"I took the call. There wasn't any choice."

A rare blush tinged Shingo's unexpressive face.

"What did she want?" He spoke in a tone of voice that had something like a note of amorous pleading in it. Even after she had given him the message from his wife, Tomoko did not stop.

"She thought I was Toki-chan, you know. Then, in the middle of the conversation she realized who I was, and even though there was nothing funny we started laughing really loudly, both of us."

Now Shingo laughed too, voicelessly, as if at a loss what to do.

"When I made that trip to your house, why did I return without meeting her? That was the whole point of going: just to meet her. I should've waited there until she came back and met her. Why are you so afraid of us two meeting?"

"It's not that I'm especially . . . afraid . . ."

"But you're always acting so nervous about it. That time, too, you took such pains to prevent us from meeting."

"If you want to meet her, well, go ahead."

It wasn't that he was sulking. He was just so utterly lacking in resistance, and his noncommittal answers offered Tomoko's simple personality no possibility of confrontation.

"Ask her when you go back. I'm sure she's starting to get this uneasy feeling too." That was the way Tomoko expressed what was in her heart.

The fact that after eight years she had finally heard the actual voice of Shingo's wife, and furthermore, that they had both broken into loud laughter, gave even Tomoko, whose sensitivity had been dulled in this affair, a strong shock. It was even greater than that time she had read Shingo's carelessly mislaid letter from his wife and discovered in it sentiments unexpectedly youthful and tender, and had felt as if her own skin received the raw touch of the woman's flesh.

One day Tomoko received an unexpected phone call from Ryōta. She started out hesitantly to meet him at the coffee shop in front of the station. Their parting two months ago had followed a quarrel so bitter that no amicable meeting in the future seemed possible, and one could say it was the impact of that which spurred Tomoko to go dashing over to the house by the sea.

Ryōta was waiting in a booth by the window, like a meek lover.

"I have moved," Ryōta said politely in a reserved manner he might use with a stranger. He meant that he had moved out of their secret room in a residential district one station away on the train line. Everything about the small room—its ceiling full of knotholes, the cigarette burns, even the glinting shadow of the new foliage of a persimmon tree reflected in the windowpane—had become as deeply familiar to Tomoko as her own room, in the hours she spent there with Ryōta.

These memories, which she had tried to turn away from during the past two months, were instantly revived by Ryōta's words. And then suddenly, with unexpected clarity, they awoke in her the memory of her unrestrained sensuality in that room.

Hurriedly she averted her eyes from Ryōta's face. By moving out of that room Ryōta was demonstrating that their affair was over, not just by words but by his action.

"You've moved? That's good . . ."

Tomoko thought her voice sounded casual. A genuine gladness began rising inside her, happiness that at least Ryōta, even if it were he alone, could break loose from their ugly, strangely tangled relationship.

His new lodging uptown was as much as an hour away, and was hardly better than an inexpensive boardinghouse for students. The first clause in the rental agreement stated "Women strictly forbidden," Ryōta told her with a slightly cynical smile. "It seems that I was wrong," he went on. "Now I see that I was just being conceited to think I could pull you out of that weird relationship. We were only hurting each other. It turned out to be my lone battle . . . flailing at the wind. You didn't change at all. Both of you, all three of you, maybe . . ."

"Maybe."

Each time a train passed outside the window the coffee shop was drowned in the deafening roar and their conversation was broken.

Ryōta's eyes were softly radiant, glistening brown, and Tomoko gazed at him, profoundly moved. She could sense him recalling their secret hours of the past year with a longing as if to caress each memory.

"I paid a visit to Shingo's house."

Ryōta's face showed astonishment and disbelief. Then abruptly the blood rose on his face as swiftly as if he were getting drunk. Tomoko too felt carried away and a torrent of words poured out.

"And then?" Ryōta asked impatiently when she finished her story.

"What do you mean?"

"I mean, what happened after that? You certainly didn't go all that way just to have a chat, did you? You confessed everything, and talked about it, and then what sort of concrete plans did you come up with? That's what I'm asking."

As was his habit whenever he felt exasperated, Ryōta unconsciously kept lighting a new cigarette after only a couple of puffs on the previous one.

"Just as before—the same as it's always been. What can I say . . . They . . ."

" 'They'?"

As if he couldn't find words to continue, Ryōta fell silent, his dry lips twitching with emotion. An expression of tenderness as much as sorrow spread over his features. In a low, flat voice he murmured as if searching for the words and discovering them, one by one, in the depths of his heart.

"Really, it seems that you don't want to leave him . . . not at all. I can't see it any other way. You're quite strange. In other matters you show ordinary good sense and discretion, and yet for some reason when it comes to this problem, you somehow seem to lose your will completely."

Tomoko answered in a low, gloomy voice. "I can't talk about

breaking up when I'm face to face with Shingo because of the habit of these eight years we've shared. Habits are far more power-ful than love—for the first time I understand that completely. And the reason Shingo can't leave her is also habit, much stronger for the many more years they've had together than he's spent with me. Those habits, in that house and within their family, just can't be changed."

Tomoko thought that of all the faces she had shown Ryōta the one she now wore was the most aged and unattractive; but she did not even feel like putting on a better one.

In a sluggish voice she half whispered, "Don't come anymore, please. You be the first . . ."

Seeing Ryōta's face stiffen and lose color, Tomoko stood up. She felt miserable that she could say all too easily to Ryōta the words she could not say to Shingo.

When she recovered, she was alone, walking along a muddy river on the edge of a field. Across the river towered an apartment build-ing, its white walls quietly reflecting the afternoon sun. The sparkle of the sun's rays and the depth of the cloudless blue sky shouldered by the high-rise apartments were suffused with the weariness of autumn, which was already well along.

When Tomoko and Shingo first moved into their present apart-ment, in place of this multi-unit building had stood an enormous private residence, which had been appropriated by the foreign oc-cupation forces and remained in their hands. The grounds of the mansion had been visible directly in front of Tomoko's northern window, its gently sloping lawn like undulating hills; and a full view of the white Western-style building that resembled an English castle was framed by the small window.

One May morning Shingo and Tomoko, with their faces close to the window, were looking out at the roof garden of the mansion. They could see a fat man, a foreigner, apparently having a great deal of trouble trying to hoist a carp streamer for Boys' Day up the flagpole. A young boy whose blond hair blazed in the sun like a flame was flitting and hovering around the man, impatient for the carps to be up. At their distance Tomoko and Shingo could not have caught the expressions on the faces of these two, and yet it was as if they could hear the heartbeat echoing between them, who seemed to be father and son, and they too held their breath, waiting for the streamer to be up.

The cloth carps, limp and drooping, started gliding up the pole, and in no time the three red carps inhaled the wind and swelled to full size; one above the other in the dazzling, clear blue sky, they began to swim with leisurely grace.

The boy flung his short plump pink arms upward and jumped up and down around the pole. His blond hair reflected the sunlight like a crown. Breathing as one, Tomoko and Shingo confirmed the quiet, deep response that passed between them at this sight.

As she looked up at the nondescript apartment building straight ahead of her, its windows colorfully decorated by laundry, Tomoko was reliving that fine May day, still vivid in her memory. It seemed to her that such bright moments with Shingo were still, beyond number, tucked away in the depths of her heart. The realization pressed upon her that, just as the stately old mansion had become an apartment building, and the scene of the carps swimming above it could never be brought back, so her long hours with Shingo were now past.

This path by the muddy river was also a place she had frequented with Ryōta. He would always accompany her this far on her way home from his room. From this riverside path to the base of the cliff on which Tomoko's apartment stood, a cultivated field stretched for about one and a half acres, an uncommon sight in this old area of the city.

Across the field in the distance one could see Tomoko's second-floor apartment high on the cliff. Once in a while a light showed in her window. These were the nights Shingo waited alone for her in the apartment.

Seeing that light over Ryōta's shoulder when they were in each other's arms, Tomoko would feel a shiver as if her back were being stroked with a feathery flame, and would plunge her nails into Ryōta's back.

While she was giving her lips to Ryōta, her eyes were drawn in by the light, and her heart trembled in the presence of Shingo in the shadows beyond that light. Hearing Ryōta whisper his customary farewell, "Take care of yourself," Tomoko would break into an impatient run and dash full speed to where Shingo was waiting.

Still with downcast eyes, Tomoko almost cried out. Wasn't what had sustained her affair with Ryōta the excitement—at the same time fear—of concealing a secret of betrayal from Shingo? And she perceived that now that she had confessed to Shingo, that thrill and intoxication would never return.

A fervent desire that she might truly want to be alone welled up inside Tomoko and, bubbling over, became a fountain of tears gushing from her eyes.

Days passed like this and autumn gradually deepened. In Tomoko's room as well the preparations for winter, if nothing else, progressed steadily and surely. On the days when Shingo was at his home, Tomoko immersed herself all day long in putting Shingo's winter clothes in order. By undertaking such specific preparations for their parting, she covered up the fretfulness she felt at not being able to initiate any concrete discussion of their separation. Before long she ran out of kimonos and undergarments to send to the cleaners, and any time now she could send Shingo's clothing to his house. But, as always, they made no progress at all in talking about breaking up.

In the past, when Tomoko was working in the same room as Shingo, his presence, as transparent as if he had melted into the air, did not tax her nerves. On the contrary, the fact that he was in the same room gave Tomoko peace of mind, and it was with his presence at her back that she could, with a sense of security, plunge deeply into her work.

There was no change whatsoever in Shingo's bearing or behavior, so still that it was as if he were not even breathing. His calm presence, which at one time had acted as unspoken support and encouragement to Tomoko, now began to weigh upon her like a heavy pressure.

Working at her desk all day but not coming up with a single design, she hurled the paint brush that had failed her onto the floor and burst out crying.

"What's wrong?"

At Shingo's mild voice, she writhed all the more, and all she could do was wail hysterically at the top of her voice.

"There isn't enough air! It's too hard to breathe in here! You breathe all the air, even my share. I'm suffocating!"

This was a plea wrung from the bottom of her heart, but Shingo only tried to soothe her in a calm, unperturbed voice.

"You don't exercise enough. You should go out for a walk more often. You're not having trouble with digestion again, are you?"

One morning Tomoko left on a trip alone. Shingo as usual had gone back to his house the previous day and would be staying there for three days. It had become unbearable for Tomoko to go on

as she had been, waiting for Shingo in a room where, in the closets
as well as the bureau, everything lay in readiness for their separation.

She boarded at random a train for Nikkō. As it crossed a drab,
monotonous plain, Tomoko came to realize fully how exhausted
her nerves were.

Harvesting had started here and there in the interminable golden
sea of rice fields along the tracks. Has autumn already ripened this
much, she thought, and, pressing her forehead against the window,
continued to gaze at the monotonous scenery, never tiring of it.

Beside a brook a flowing line of dragonflies swarmed swiftly
through the air, flashing past her eyes as bright as a stretch of red
cellophane ribbon.

She had been so swallowed up in the oppressive premonition that
their affair was coming to an end that the passage of seasons and
the changing attire of the landscape had gone unnoticed, and the
two or three months that had slipped by this way came back to her
now as an endless stretch of time.

When she stood at the deserted Nikkō station, with its dark grove
of cedars beside it, a wave of chilly air not yet encountered in Tokyo
soaked her skin. A number of sightseeing couples from abroad got
off the same train. This was her first visit to the region but, not feeling inclined to see Tōshōgu Shrine, she boarded a bus immediately
at the station. She intended to go straight to a lodge among white
birch trees in inner Nikkō, which she had been told about at an information center before her departure.

There were unexpectedly few passengers on the bus. In the windows, as the bus ascended, autumn foliage blazed like a flame. Each
time the bus turned a corner of the winding road, twisting so often
that Tomoko felt dizzy, a different view opened before them, and
the woven design of autumn leaves that adorned the mountains was
kaleidoscopically transformed, as if magnificent Persian carpets were
being displayed one after another.

Starting in the vicinity of Chūzenji Lake, gradually passengers
got off the bus, and by the time Tomoko got off alone on the wide
road at the entrance to the lodge, only two or three passengers remained. On both sides of the road silver-gray pampas grass stretched
like the sea, and amid this were gentian, valerian, gypsy rose, burnet,
and other flowers trembling in the wind.

The wind that came blowing across the field and set the grass
and flowers sparkling was not an autumn wind; it already had in it

the hard coldness and light of winter. Beyond the sea of pampas grass stood massive Mt. Nantaizan holding up the azure sky of the plateau.

Not a soul passed by. In the stillness of deep silence, the chirping of birds echoed now and then as if they had suddenly remembered to sing. Standing all alone in the middle of the paved road that went on endlessly, white and bare in the sea of pampas grass, Tomoko was suddenly captured by the illusion that she had come here seeking a place to die. It was, unexpectedly, a sweet sentiment that eased her heart.

Inside the small North European–style hotel surrounded by white birch trees, logs were burning scarlet in the fireplace. Here, too, there were unexpectedly few guests. Tomoko was the only one traveling alone. In Tomoko's eyes the couples sitting at their tables discreetly by themselves all appeared to be lovers carrying on clandestine affairs. Once they decided on their table, these couples always sat in the same places for all their meals.

Among them, a couple sitting at a table by the window farthest from the fireplace particularly attracted Tomoko's eyes. They were a beautiful girl who could not have been more than sixteen or seventeen and a man with the air of a university professor. The girl was mysteriously beautiful when she was silent, but her way of eating and talking was vulgar. Her voice when she laughed had a transparent beauty, yet her features then were unrefined.

Every time they entered the dining room, the man helped the girl into her chair courteously, the way foreigners do. Each time he came round behind her and put his hands on the chair, the girl would immediately assume a prim air and gracefully take her seat or stand up. It was like watching some kind of ceremony, and in a strange way it was very beautiful. On these occasions, an innocent pride shone in the girl's earnest expression, making her look strikingly pure.

Tomoko stayed at the hotel for four days. Each time she went to the dining room, she saw different faces. Only the girl and the older man were always there.

On the morning of the third day, Tomoko at last wrote a letter to Shingo.

"I came here on a spur-of-the-moment decision. I feel as though I've already been here as long as a week, but in fact it's only the third day. I've been doing nothing but sleeping, so much so that it's as if my body is going to melt away. It's peaceful here. It's the kind of quiet that makes me think I might want to die if I had come here with someone.

"I can't think.

"Only, I now feel I can write to you about things which I couldn't say to you in person no matter how hard I tried.

"Please, I beg you, let us part. It's not that I have any self-confidence about what will happen afterward. But I feel it's not right to go on the way we are. Just imagining my future without you makes my legs weak. But I think it's our responsibility to try at least. Even if it means using Ryōta's love. I ask both of you to help me, please."

Without rereading it, she sealed the letter. When she addressed it she wrote both Shingo's and his wife's names side by side.

Upon being told that she would have to go to a post office farther up by the lake in order to mail an express letter, Tomoko caught a bus to the lake.

At the bottom of the small lake, too, as everywhere else, the fire of autumn leaves flickered.

The post office was painted blue. As soon as she handed the letter over the counter, Tomoko left as if she were fleeing and began making her way back to the hotel along the road by the lake. Without waiting for the bus, she started walking haphazardly. She hoped to distract herself from the fatigue and misery that made her simply want to sit down and not move.

As she reached the hotel, after about forty minutes, she passed an ambulance that was coming from the front porch. An unusual commotion filled the area around the reception desk as well as the lobby. The woman at the kiosk, whom Tomoko was now on familiar terms with, came edging up. She was wearing an ikat kimono, and her rounded shoulders nearly touched Tomoko as she whispered, "They committed suicide. Those two."

Tomoko said nothing as the woman told her that it was the young girl and the gentleman. The hotel personnel found out because the couple had not appeared for breakfast; by then the two were already dead.

"They had only 1,200 yen with them. So it was all planned."

Tomoko heard that the couple had used morphine injections and that their faces in death were beautiful.

The following day Tomoko left the mountains.

The next afternoon she set out to look for an apartment with the aid of newspaper advertisements, acting on the conclusion she had reached in the mountains. She decided that, no matter what, she should move out of the apartment that had taken on so strongly the color of her life with Shingo.

As she was walking the straight road to the bus stop, she caught sight of Shingo striding toward her almost as if he were tumbling forward. A cold shiver ran down her spine and the words "cursed spirit" flashed across her mind, so eerie was the ghastly air that enveloped Shingo. His face had hardened into a dark, fierce expression Tomoko had never seen before. Passersby, too, were struck by his extraordinary mood, casting sidelong glances of fear and wonder, keeping their distance; and some turned to look again after they had passed. Shingo's eyes stared into space, and even when Tomoko had come so close they nearly collided he gave no sign of recognition.

Seeing Shingo like this, Tomoko felt the sharp pain of a thousand needles piercing her body. She thrust herself in front of him, blocking his way.

"Move!" he snapped.

Tomoko had never heard him abuse herself or anyone in a voice full of such intense rage, nor had she ever seen his face livid with hatred and anger. She could feel her own face stiffening in an ugly expression as she tried to suppress her terror.

"What are you doing?"

"Going on a trip."

"Did you get my letter?"

A look of contempt rose in his bloodshot eyes as if he wanted to spit on her.

"Why else would I be here? What the hell did you mean by 'even if it takes using Ryōta as the excuse'?"

Just this outburst—and yet it seemed to cleanse his system of the filth he had choked down. Tomoko said nothing.

Some of his usual calm had returned to his voice when he said, "I meant to leave without seeing you."

"I'm glad you didn't . . ."

"The bus broke down and we were held up about ten minutes. If it had arrived on time we'd have missed each other."

His voice was becoming even calmer. Still, his dismal expression did not change. His traveling clothes and suitcase were at Tomoko's apartment, and quite naturally she started walking back there with him.

As if his strength had suddenly failed him, Shingo lost control and staggered two or three steps. Forgetting people's eyes on them, Tomoko hurriedly supported him with her arms.

Back in her apartment she removed a charcoal-gray suit from the dry cleaner's plastic bag and helped Shingo put it on. This suit, too, had been put away with the others in readiness for their parting.

As she carefully packed his bag with various articles for the trip, she struggled against a fear that came surging up inside. If she let him go on this trip, he might never come back alive. The image of the man who had committed suicide with his lover in that mountain lodge floated through her mind. How could Shingo's wife let him leave alone, looking so desperate?

When the packing was finished she followed him out of the apartment.

"Maybe you shouldn't go?" These words nearly escaped her but, swallowing them with great effort, she said instead, "I'll come to see you off."

"How far?" Shingo's voice had its usual tone of sweet affection. Tomoko consciously resisted being lured by that seductive ambience, and this deliberate effort clashed with her emotional habit of catering to his every need.

"To Tokyo Station." She intended this reply as a directive to herself.

Shingo's face immediately relaxed and, nudging her shoulder, he said, "It's still early, let's go have some sake."

At once his face and voice were those of his usual self. At this Tomoko felt as if the murky poison that had saturated his being until a while ago were thoroughly transfused into her body instead. She suddenly felt fatigued, and now it was her turn to stumble out of control. Shingo's hands quickly reached out to support her.

By the time they arrived at Tokyo Station darkness had fallen, deepening the brilliance of the lights. The station just after the evening rush hour had a run-down, languid look. As if pursued by something close behind, people hurried along nervously all around Shingo and Tomoko.

"Where will you go?"

"As far as I can."

With a gesture of indifference Shingo bought a ticket to Kyoto. There were plenty of westbound trains at this time of day.

Nothing remained to be done. Standing in the center of the ticket area, Tomoko looked up at Shingo. Streams of people flooded around them, swarming past incessantly in a huge river. Like stones washed in the current they stood motionless, gazing at each other.

"Going now?"

He did not answer.

Recognizing in Shingo's eyes a sign of dread that only she could read, Tomoko felt something in her heart now mellow from the sake they had shared. In a voice filled with her usual tenderness, she finally said the words after all.

"Tonight, don't go?"

Color rose instantly on Shingo's cheeks, which had turned even paler than usual from drinking.

"Stay with me, even if it's just for tonight," he said.

Amid the footsteps of the passersby, their low whispers hung about them with a tender suggestiveness almost like lovers' talk.

There was only a room with twin beds available at the hotel next to the station. The spacious room, furnished more like a family home than a hotel, soothed their tired nerves. Like a traveler who had finally reached the end of a long journey, Tomoko sank into the couch without speaking a word, exhaustion now beginning to show on her face.

Shingo looked as if he had at last been restored to life. He ordered brandy to be brought up, adjusted the lamps, and busied himself around the room in other ways. When there was nothing else to be done, he quietly knelt on the floor at Tomoko's feet and buried his face in her lap.

"Thank you."

"Why do you say that?" Bending her face over Shingo's head, Tomoko felt a dam inside her give way and she burst into passionate crying.

Countless memories of the eight years she had spent with Shingo came flooding back, almost overwhelming her and sweeping her away. Rather than the happy times, it was her remembrance of the pain and sadness they had shared that now stirred her heart with yearning. She wondered whether what she was experiencing was similar to the instant before death when people are said to see their entire life flash before them.

The faces of the couple who had committed suicide flickered through her mind. Suddenly she was tempted by the alluring thought that she, too, might choose to die with Shingo, now, in this room. Yet she resisted, stammering between sobs the words she had repeated to herself so many times.

"We just have to stop seeing each other . . . There's no other way . . . You know that, too . . ."

Even after they lay down on their beds, they remained silent, as if any topic of conversation would be too frightening. Shingo reached out and took Tomoko's hand.

Their hands spoke countless words for them.

Tomoko knew that at one word from her Shingo would call off his trip. But she also knew that with that one word she would be thrown straight back into their old, habitual ways. The prospect of sending the reluctant Shingo on a trip aroused foreboding and fear. The strongest tie that had bound them for eight years, she now realized, was this very fear that if she let him out of her sight he might die.

The unlucky fate that had constantly thwarted his ambitions and hopes and had reduced him to so pathetic a state now that he was nearing fifty had always been, in Tomoko's heart, linked with the vision of his possible suicide. The dejected face she had encountered on the road yesterday was an expression of despair that she had never seen on him in the past, in all his adversity and humiliation.

Deep inside she felt that if her letter from the mountains had hurt Shingo so profoundly this was the best chance to test her resolve. This was where she had to hold fast. If she could somehow manage to hold fast until morning, the crisis would pass. And then she would gamble everything on Shingo's departure.

Never before had she been so filled with love for him, she thought. And yet in this supreme happiness of love there was no carnal desire. Shingo's hand too was free of any such suggestion. She was about to open her mouth when Shingo uttered the very words she was going to say.

"You'd better get some sleep, even if it's not much. I'll watch over you."

Through the slats of the venetian blinds the faint dawn light came stealing into the room. With this light in the corners of her eyes, she closed her eyelids. As she told herself that this was what Shingo most wanted of her now, she was already falling into a deep, engulfing sleep.

Days passed with no word from Shingo.

By the fifth day Tomoko was in such a state she found it impossible to accomplish a single task. Fear and anxiety wrung her heart.

"I think it's best if you go, after all."

"Yes . . ."

"Have a good time by yourself. It will be refreshing for you to get away from both of us."

Knowing that in his heart Shingo had been hoping and waiting for her to detain him, nevertheless she had coaxed and encouraged him into leaving that morning; and the cruelty of that contrivance on her part now tormented her.

"Well then . . . ," he had murmured, and looked at Tomoko with a weak smile—and then instantly he was lost in the sea of pushing and shoving people that swallowed him up and carried him around the corner of the passageway.

Her visions of Shingo lying dead in the middle of an isolated forest or at the bottom of a deep pool went on multiplying endlessly, overlapping and doubling, gradually taking over even her dreams.

This, then, was the true nature of the force that had connected her to Shingo for eight years, she thought, and she stared into the fear that deepened its shadow day after day.

At the extreme limit of anxiety, Tomoko resolved that the next day she would go visit Shingo's wife, putting aside her vanity and all sense of shame. That same afternoon, Shingo's postcard arrived.

Nine days had passed since Tomoko had seen him off.

The rounded, smallish handwriting that was so familiar trembled in her hands. In it were recorded his wanderings through the desolate coastal region of San'in. The fact that his living hand had written this postcard brought Tomoko such wild relief and joy that she almost cried out hysterically.

Shingo's dark, wind-blown figure emerged before her, as he stood with his back to her, on a sand dune she had never seen. In the background the somber Japan Sea, already colored by winter, stretched without end. Clutching the postcard in her hand, Tomoko rolled on the floor and wept aloud in short sobs.

When she had stopped crying she put aside the postcard and with the same hand pulled a newspaper toward her.

After a while, her eyes began to focus coldly and clearly on the print of the apartment ads.

The Last Time

KŌNO TAEKO

Translated by Yukiko Tanaka and Elizabeth Hanson

Kōno Taeko (b. 1926) was the daughter of an Osaka wholesale merchant. A sickly child, she suffered deprivations and discomfort in her early years and had difficulty adjusting to school. She was nineteen when the Second World War ended, and as with Ōba and Tsumura, her education was interrupted by compulsory work in a factory.

Kōno has said that with the end of the war she felt a new sense of freedom and had an urge to do something, but was not sure what. She joined one of the many literary groups in which would-be writers spend the years of their apprenticeship. Through their membership fees, such groups publish journals containing their members' writings. As Kōno became more serious about writing, she left home to go to Tokyo, where she took a full-time job and wrote at night. She went through several years of discouragement and ill health, however, before she was finally recognized. Just before winning the Akutagawa Prize in 1963, she resigned her job to devote herself completely to writing. Since then she has published a book every year and won many literary prizes. She is now considered one of the major writers of contemporary Japanese literature. She married a painter at the age of 39.

Shocking motifs—sadomasochistic relationships, a woman who kidnaps a young boy, wife-swapping—and the detailed description of small incidents from everyday life are carefully combined to good effect in Kōno's work. These elements create a sense of incongruity that forces the reader to take a second look at his own life. Underneath the seemingly normal routines of daily life, one may find hidden propensities for abnormal or pathological behavior. Kōno's fiction points out that reality and fantasy are not so clearly distinguishable from each other. Often the heroine of her stories seems to feel that something is missing in her relationships with the world and that something is wrong with her perception of her own sex. She is neither violently unhappy nor deeply involved in any relationship; she is almost always well-mannered and in good control of herself, and yet she cannot stop pursuing the reason for her sense of discordance.

"The Last Time" is the title story of Kōno's fifth collection of short stories, which won the Women's Literature Prize for 1966.

Even though everyone must die at one time or another, and even if it were her fate to die in one certain way, Noriko simply could not accept the sudden decree that she must die at that moment.

"Give me some time," she begged.

"Are you asking for time so that you can get yourself ready?"

"You don't really think anyone can prepare for his own death, do you?" she replied. "I'm not an old woman with a terminal illness. I'm a healthy middle-aged woman, and nothing is wrong with my mind, as far as I know. Besides, there is no old samurai blood in me, so I won't die with dignity unless you do an especially good job."

"You said you believe in spirits . . ."

"Yes, I do. But that doesn't mean I can accept my own death, does it?"

"Better than not believing at all."

"I wonder if it's better not to believe. Besides, I don't think a spirit has much real power. It can see into the human mind and affect it, but it can't see or do anything to the flesh or to physical objects. And it's also possible that the person a spirit is trying to reach might be somewhat insensitive and not catch a signal, or might be oversensitive and read too much into the signal and misunderstand it. If I were a spirit, this would frustrate me so that I would lose interest in trying to communicate. What I could see going on in the human mind might not be that worthwhile. It seems to me that a spirit must be full of frustration and resentment. I dread my death that much more when I think of being forced into such a painful existence. I envy those who can believe in nothingness after death." Then she cried out, "Oh, I wish my spirit and my body would never be separated! I wish they could stay together, even after I die!" This wish became so strong that for a moment she forgot about her plea for extra time.

"Oh, all right," she began again, "I don't want to die, but you say I have to. You can at least give me some time."

"You know you can't escape."

"I know. That's why I'm asking. At least two or three days . . ."

"That's out of the question."

"But I didn't come into this world all of a sudden. I don't want to die suddenly, either. There are various things . . ."

"What things?"

"Look at this," she said, stretching out the sleeves of her kimono. "I was on my way to my friend's funeral. If I had known I would have to die, I wouldn't have come like this."

"You look good enough. Don't you think that's much better than wearing an apron and sandals?"

"I don't think so. I'm wearing the color of the dead."

"The color of the dead is white. But black is too, for that matter. But if you yourself say that you're in the color of the dead, so much the better. People will think you had good taste, that you had prepared yourself."

"That's exactly what I object to. I don't want people to think I prepared myself for my death and then calmly died."

"What would you wear then, to look like you were resisting your own death?"

"I don't know. That's why I need time, to think about it and to change my clothes."

"One day."

"Give me two days."

"A day or two won't make any difference. No more than one day."

Noriko glanced at her wristwatch. It was seventeen after one. She heard the ticking of the watch grow louder.

"I'll see you here at one-seventeen tomorrow."

She heard the ticking sound again as soon as these words were spoken, and she flinched. At seventeen after one tomorrow I might be alive, but at one-thirty and one-forty I'll be dead, she thought. And one-thirty today will be here soon. Once that time passes, I'll never be able to experience that particular time of day again.

"Could you please make it twenty-six hours?" she asked. Even while she asked, the time was passing. The long hand of her wristwatch was pointing at nineteen.

"Well, then, at three-nineteen tomorrow." Her request for twenty-six hours had been granted. Noriko bowed and walked away.

"What's this, you're not going to the funeral? You don't care if your friend's spirit is sad?" the voice said to her back. She didn't turn around and walked even more quickly toward her house.

In front of a bakery at the corner of the main street where she had to turn to go to her house, she spotted a public telephone and went over to it. After she finished dialing her husband's office number and heard the phone ringing, she realized that it would seem rather odd to simply ask Asari what time he was coming home. Staring at the edge of the telephone, she thought she would have to pretend to be consulting him on the amount of the condolence gift. The switchboard operator answered.

"Mr. Asari of the sales section, please."

"Who is calling, please?" the switchboard operator asked. Noriko didn't respond.

"Who shall I say is calling, please?" The operator's voice rose. Noriko cut the connection and put the receiver back.

When she got home she put the key into the lock and her hand on the doorknob, then noticed the yellow milkbox on the wall by the door. It was half open, and she saw the two empty bottles she had put there after breakfast that morning. Starting with the day after tomorrow one bottle will be enough, she thought. She had always attached notes for the milkman to the bottleneck with a rubber band—notes that read, "One bottle until such and such a day, please," or "No milk until such and such a day, please."

As soon as she went into the house and took her shoes off, she realized she would have to attach a note to one of the empty milk bottles, saying, "One bottle from now on, please." She sat down at the dining table with a ballpoint pen in her hand. She took an envelope out of her purse, the envelope she had put the condolence money in when she had left the house, and tore off part of it. She started to write a note to the milkman: "Dear Milkman—Thank you for your daily delivery of milk . . ." When she had written as far as "From now on," her hand stopped. I am going to say goodbye to my husband secretly, she thought. If I write a note like this and if he finds it attached to the milk bottle. . . . I'll have to wait to do this until after he leaves to go to work tomorrow.

It seemed that many other things would come up that she would simply have to wait to take care of. For instance, what about the key lying on the tatami floor next to her purse? She always left the key in the drain spout near the back door when she knew Asari would be home before she was. Occasionally she forgot, and he couldn't get in. This time for certain this must not happen, but she couldn't leave the key in the usual spot until the next day when she left the house for the last time. Noriko tore another piece of paper from the envelope and wrote "key" and "the milkman" and put it in the little box on her dresser where she kept her powder puff. She would surely open this box just before the last moment.

Then she untied her obi, took off her kimono, and changed into a sweater and skirt. She opened the windows and sliding doors of all the rooms, and the small house was filled with spring sunshine and a fresh breeze. For a moment she thought she would spread the kimono out and leave it there for a while, but her wristwatch showed that the time was one-fifty-seven. If I air this mourning kimono—I only wore it for a short time—I won't have time to finish doing more important things before three-nineteen tomorrow, she thought. She was certain she would regret that, so decided to put the mourning kimono away. While she was folding it, she glanced at the undergarments, thinking that she would discard them. Fortunately the garbage truck would come the next day.

When she had put the kimono away, she took the neckband off the kimono slip, wrapped it with the undershirt in a newspaper, and put them in a large plastic bag that she used for garbage. I'll put everything I want to throw away in here, she thought. The garbage truck comes at eleven. Tomorrow morning when I get up I'll change the underwear that I'm wearing now and put it in here, too. She took a set of clean underwear from the dresser and put it on top of the quilt in the closet. She realized then that she couldn't leave behind the last nightgown she would ever wear and decided to put it into the plastic bag too. She then put a set of Asari's clean underwear and a pair of his pajamas on top of the quilt. From the other side of the closet she took two pillows and changed the covers. Then she took out the quilts one by one and stripped off the sheets. She put all the quilts and pillows back in the closet, placed two clean folded sheets on the top, and closed the door.

She looked at the pile of dirty linen; she didn't want to leave it as it was, but it would be a waste of her scarce time to wash it. The laundryman might come around the next morning to take an order, but again, he might not. She considered calling him, but she wasn't sure if she would be able to wait at home for him to come.

"I have to get rid of these things right now. I have to take care of them all right now," Noriko told herself. There were six sets of sheets and pillowcases and another set for guests. Since she herself would be gone it would be all right to get rid of two sets. She hesitated to throw away one of Asari's three sets of pajamas, but considering the little time left, it had to be done. She noticed the socks she had taken off, and when she added them to the other dirty linen, the plastic bag bulged. But she was sure her husband wouldn't notice a garbage bag, nor would he want to examine it if he did. She tied the bag, took it outside, and put it next to the garbage can. There were more things to throw away, but she couldn't take care of them until the next day.

Noriko got a sheet of letter paper from her husband's desk and started to make a list. "My pillowcase, sheets, and pajamas; the clothes I'm wearing—the skirt and sweater," and for her husband she first wrote "underwear," then thought for a moment and added, "socks and handkerchief." She couldn't think of a place to put the list, a place where Asari wouldn't find it, yet where she would be sure to see it before the garbage truck came. The more she thought about it, the harder it was to find the right spot. She decided to put it temporarily in the canister where she kept dried fish. Asari would still be in the house the next morning when she opened the can, since she always opened it when preparing the miso soup. She would have to think of a better place at that time; another idea might come to her before then.

While she was busy putting things away, Noriko kept thinking about what to wear the next day when she would leave the house for the last time. More than anything, she wanted to die with a struggle; she wanted to leave the clear impression that she had not been resigned to dying. She wanted to spew out blood as horribly as possible and leave as much bloodstain as she could. She would struggle until the last breath, thrashing about and smearing the blood with both hands and legs, not only on her body but all around her. She realized then that the crimson blood wouldn't stand out against mourning black. She was glad she wasn't going to die in the black kimono.

She thought of a white outfit that she had had made two years before. She hadn't worn it that year because it seemed to have yellowed, but anyway, white was still white. The blood would look vivid against it. Then she recalled suddenly that white was in fact a color for the dead. I was about to make the mistake of dying in a color for the dead, the last thing I wanted, she thought. She decided against the white; the only suitable dress for her death would be an eggshell-colored outfit. It was a rather casual, two-piece jersey knit that she had worn only two or three times. Even though she knew it was in the dress closet, she thought she had better make sure, so she opened the closet door.

The eggshell-colored dress was hanging there, and she thought it would set off the color of blood nicely. There were other clothes in the closet: a purple winter suit, a raincoat and an overcoat, and a pale green spring outfit. A blouse and a sweater were hanging on the same hanger. None of the clothes had been cleaned since she had worn them. She would have to take care of them all.

She would also have to take care of the things in the shoe cabinet. I need only one pair of shoes now, she thought. She had worn all the shoes and didn't want to leave any of them. But since Asari used the closet too, she would have to wait until he had left for work the next morning to dispose of the dress and shoes so he wouldn't notice a difference. She noted she would have to add "closet" and "shoe cabinet" to her list, and she was heading for the kitchen to get the note from the dried-fish canister when she stopped. I have been a legitimate wife in this house, she thought. If I get rid of everything that's mine, the house will look as if a daughter has left to get married or a maid has run away. She didn't go to the kitchen but went back to the closet and hung a tortoiseshell necklace on top of the egg-colored dress. Then she glanced at the shoe cabinet in the entryway. Her brown shoes and Asari's shoes were clean.

Noriko realized that it hadn't occurred to her to get rid of the clothes and shoes until she had opened the closet door, and this made her exceedingly uneasy. Unless I attend to matters carefully, I'll have to die without doing many things that are important to me, she thought. The more she worried, the stronger the pressure of the tasks became. The amount of work was so overwhelming that she couldn't determine what each individual task would be.

It was already three. The front door of the public bathhouse must have just opened, she thought. Noriko would go inside and take one of the wooden buckets that were piled up on the tile; she imagined the hollow sound the bucket would make when she put it down in front of a faucet. The sun would be shining at an angle through the high window with its white-painted frame. She could picture the sunlight falling on the bright bottom of the bathing tub. She thought of her last bath; she wanted to hear the sound the wooden bucket made and see the light reflecting on the water.

But there were more urgent tasks than bathing, Noriko realized. She went upstairs and took from the closet a wicker chest that was underneath some large cushions. She took out three cotton kimonos, all Asari's, and put the chest back. As she stood up she looked at the kimonos in her arms. In a month or so, it would be time for cotton kimonos. He will notice these if I put them in his chest downstairs with his underwear, she thought. Suddenly Noriko thought it would be nice if she could talk to her husband when he was wearing one of these kimonos for the first time on an early summer evening.

She wanted to whisper to him from somewhere inside this cotton kimono.

She sat at her husband's desk, picked up a fountain pen, and spread out a piece of letter paper. She looked at Asari's kimono on the floor. She couldn't picture Asari wearing it on his way to and from the bathhouse. Instead she imagined him leaving to go to a movie on one of those evenings when he didn't drink with his dinner. Once every ten days or so, Asari would come home and say, while changing his clothes, "I don't want it tonight," meaning he didn't want sake with his dinner. If she would say, "That's good," or "You're being good," he would snap back irritably, "I didn't say I wouldn't drink at *all* until I went to bed." If she merely said "Yes" or "All right," he would say reproachfully, "You're so indifferent."

On evenings when he went without liquor, he tended to be in a bad mood. Once, on one of those evenings, Asari asked her where the hammer was. Noriko upset him by saying without thinking, "It's in the cupboard where I keep the sake." He didn't know what to do with himself on such evenings and ended up going to the neighborhood movie house. Asari rarely invited her along on these occasions, and she didn't particularly want to go. Whenever he said he was going out after having a quick supper without any liquor, she felt relieved, and cheerfully helped him get ready. It seemed to Noriko by the look of his shoulders as he left that he was mad at himself for refusing to drink. Noriko put movie tickets in his kimono sleeves rather than money so that he wouldn't be tempted. She felt sorry for him but at the same time wanted to laugh.

She wrote on the piece of paper: "Good evening, dear. So you put on your cotton kimono? You look cool and comfortable. Are you going to the Showaza Theater? They may be showing one of those sexy comedies you like."

She signed the paper, folded it twice, and put it into the sleeve of the cotton kimono on the top of the pile. The kimono had a pattern of dark blue lines on white. The idea of her talking to Asari like this after her death made her think that she should greet him again in winter when he put on his overcoat. She wrote another note: "It's gotten rather cold. I bet you'll stop for a drink on your way home tonight. Here's some money for that. I wish I could say that this is from my own savings. As you've told me, and as you seem to believe, I'm not good at saving money. You're right. This is the money I had left—the last of my monthly allowance, together with the money I was going to take with me to the funeral. Since you're kind of fussy about money spent for anything other than to buy yourself drinks, you must have been wondering about this money. Weren't you ransacking the drawer, looking for it the other day? You finally found it. I'm sorry there's no interest payment on it. Well then, say hello to the friends you'll meet tonight."

She tore off the sheet of paper she had been writing on to wrap around the money and put it aside on the desk. As she picked up the pen again, she wondered if she should spend her time writing her will rather than these notes. But she knew she wouldn't forget the will. There was no reason to hurry. Besides, if there wasn't enough time, it would be all right to write a will only to Asari, and she could take care of that easily. Noriko thought it was far more important to write the notes than to write a will.

"Are you going on a business trip?" she would greet Asari from a note in his suitcase. "You work hard. Shall I go with you? Maybe not. I really ought to stay home. Instead, think of me a little when you leave the house. That'll make you remember to lock the door and to check for fire hazards before you leave. Have a good trip."

Her next chance to speak to him would be when he wrote New Year's cards. She would appear from a pile of old cards that he would certainly look through before starting to write the new ones.

"I hope you'll remarry and be happy. I won't greet you anymore. Goodbye." She would then disappear from Asari's life.

As soon as she finished this note, she realized there was no guarantee that Asari wouldn't get married before the end of the year. Even if the new wife didn't find Noriko's message in the kimono sleeve, she might when Noriko appeared from the overcoat pocket. It wasn't unlikely.

Asari wouldn't have much trouble finding a partner, being a childless man of forty with a steady job, even if he did have a poor chance for promotion and drank a bit too much. She thought he wouldn't waste much time. As losing Noriko would clearly prove, he hadn't been lucky with his wives. In fact, Noriko was his second wife. Judging from his past and his personality, Asari wouldn't desperately seek another marriage, but at the same time he wouldn't give up the idea altogether. It wasn't that he would feel he had to get married; he would go ahead and do so without thinking too much about it.

When Noriko had met Asari for the first time seven or eight years before, he hadn't tried to conceal anything about his first wife. Asari had divorced his wife, a woman who was conscious of her traditional Japanese taste, three or four years before; he had said it had been a rather short marriage. Noriko didn't know the first wife's

name because before Noriko had her name registered as Asari's
wife, he had had his first wife's name removed from the registration
document.

Noriko knew, because Asari himself had told her, that he had had
some affairs with women before his marriage to her and after his
divorce. It seemed he had had one particular woman. When Noriko
came to live with Asari, she had discovered various articles that
were foreign-made and seemed strange possessions for a woman
with traditional taste—a red fountain pen and pencil set, a small
wicker bag, and a scarf. Asari wasn't concerned that Noriko had
seen these things, and neither was Noriko herself. In fact she had
used some of them, although the fountain pen she used to write the
notes with was her own.

Once, a year or two after she married Asari, Noriko was looking
for some wrapping paper and found a piece of department store
paper with a name and address still attached. The address on the
label was the old address where Asari had lived with his first wife.
He had supposedly divorced her three or four years before meeting
Noriko, but the postmark was for about a year before they had met.

"I want to show you something interesting," Noriko said and
took the wrapping paper to Asari.

"God, where did you find this?" When Asari saw the sticker on
the paper, he stared at it.

"Does it bring back memories?" Noriko said and smiled. "It was
in the closet in a pile of wrapping paper."

"That's strange. That's funny."

"Yes, it really is strange. Particularly here . . ." She pointed
to the date on the paper. Asari didn't seem to know what to say.

"That's right. I see now," he said emphatically. "Look here. It's
from my brother."

"Yes, that's right. He was already in Hakata then."

"I didn't let him know I had moved because I was busy and . . .
he mailed this to my old address."

"Then?"

"It was forwarded and I got it at the new place."

Noriko started to laugh. "Did it take two or three years? Does
the post office still forward things after two or three years? Well,
all right, don't worry. I'll let it go."

"You sound like the secret police." Asari grinned and handed the
paper to her with a deliberate air, as if he wanted to show his indifference.

Considering the number of items left behind, Noriko suspected

the owner of those foreign-made objects was a woman Asari had
had an affair with after his divorce. If her marriage to him wasn't
as many years after his divorce as he had said, she would have to
accept the fact that Asari had, in a very short period of time, been
divorced, lived with another person, and then married Noriko.
Nonetheless, as far as Noriko knew, Asari had been discreet in his
affairs with women. True, she suspected a few times that he had
been to "those places" with some naughtier friends. Maybe he had
fooled her, but she had basically trusted him.

Perhaps because of this trust, she had never felt jealousy toward
the women in his past. She herself had had a lover, but she had
broken off completely with him. She and Asari had no right to complain about each other's past affairs; neither were they worth dwell-
ing on.

Noriko felt rather close to both women, Asari's former wife and
the owner of the foreign-made objects. After realizing that the three
of them had been with Asari one after another in relatively short
succession, shorter than she had first thought, the sense of closeness
increased. She imagined herself as a woman in a primitive country
who lived in harmony with several other women and shared her
husband with them.

Asari seemed to understand this feeling and once said to her,
"Hey, I found something. Can you use it?" He didn't say it had belonged to his former lover, but it was clearly one of her possessions.

"Looks like it's still in good shape. Yes, I want it." Noriko gladly
accepted it. She felt then that she had had a rather pleasant encounter
with the owner, just as she had felt when she discovered the wrapping paper.

Noriko realized now that she was beginning to have a similar
feeling of closeness toward the woman Asari would be involved
with in the future. She felt that his next wife wouldn't object if
she appeared from Asari's belongings and greeted them. The new
wife would enjoy reading the notes with Asari. She might even say,
"I like her best of the three women in your past." Noriko had an
urge to speak to her. Since Asari hadn't been cautious enough to
discard the wrapping paper, he probably wouldn't put things away
before his next wife came to live in the house. She had no trouble
deciding what to say in her note.

"Hello, I'm glad to meet you like this . . . ," she started to write.
"I feel like talking with you, since there are so many things I'd like
to share with you. First, let's start with the bad things about him.
He won't buy you anything unless you keep asking. As you might

realize by now, he's tight with money. For some reason he's particularly reluctant to pay for our clothes. He's shrewd and tries to talk you out of buying them, saying, 'You shouldn't get that. Let's wait until we figure out what style suits you best.' You should make him buy you as many clothes as you want, including those he never bought for me. Also, please go ahead and use what I've left, although I'm not sure if it's what you need. I myself used things that belonged to his other women. I'd be happy if you could use mine."

Noriko thought Asari might renew the legal document required for a marriage license and therefore his future wife wouldn't know her name. She signed her note, "The deceased wife."

She put the note on the desk; later she would put it in the box of glassware she used in the summertime. She started to write another note to the same person.

"Seems like you've settled in quite well. You're so good to him, and that makes him happy. I hope you'll make him happier . . ."

As soon as she had finished writing, Noriko pictured the way Asari and his well-adjusted wife would be living. The living room was cluttered, and they were cramped for space. They were renting out the upstairs, and Asari's desk was in the living room. Various things were piled on and beside the desk. There was a kimono hanging on the wall. On the table there was some food, an odd combination of curried rice and squid cooked with radish. The two were eating silently with their eyes on the television.

"This singer looks like that man upstairs," the wife said. Asari didn't reply. The wife continued. "Speaking of that man, he's going to get married soon. I just have this feeling."

"Why?"

"I don't know, but . . . He's got nerve, sitting up there and paying such low rent. He's such a hick, anyway."

"But it was your idea, remember?"

"I know. We need to save money for our house. We'll never be able to buy one if we depend on your salary."

"The rent doesn't add much, does it?"

"Yes it does. We couldn't build a house if we didn't get it. Your pay isn't so good. Besides, you like to drink."

Asari, who wasn't drinking, grimaced with his eyes still on the television and his hand moving the chopsticks. But the wife didn't hesitate and went on.

"Last month's liquor bill was more than 8,000 yen, you know."

"So what?"

Asari now turned his face toward his wife. They argued violently for a while. Later in the bedroom, however, the wife said, "Honey, it would be really nice if we had our own house."

Asari answered, "If there's some land within an hour and a half of work, I'm willing."

Noriko had never complained about Asari's salary; since they had no children, she had been able to manage without much difficulty. They had always lived in a rented house, and getting their own house no longer occupied her mind. This was because Asari kept presenting a grandiose, dream-like plan for their new house, and as a result, both of them had silently accepted that they would always live in a rented house. Noriko realized that she had never really discussed having their own house with Asari. So could they be called a couple? Suddenly she was forced to look back at her life with Asari in a way that she had never done before. Noriko went back to her note to the future wife.

"Thinking about it now, maybe Asari and I were not truly a husband and wife; we were nothing more than a particular man and woman who were together. I shared a life with Asari longer than other women had—for six years we lived together and were legally married. At least I believed that we loved each other. Still, our life was that of a man and woman living together. People wonder if couples who don't share a sexual life are a real husband and wife, but we weren't a real couple in the opposite sense. I hope that you'll be a real couple. Please let him have a real married life. He doesn't seem to have ever experienced that. The reason why I say we haven't been a real wife and husband . . ."

The pen dropped from Noriko's hand. The truth about her life with Asari, which she had just come to realize, steadily closed in on her until she couldn't see it anymore. It's true, we weren't a wife and husband but merely a man and woman who lived together, Noriko said to herself. She recalled that they were sometimes like a brother and his sister, sometimes like an older sister and her brother; at other times, they were like a mother and child or father and child. Whatever they were, they were never a married couple, and there was no doubt that their life together hadn't been a marriage.

The first thing that came to mind when she looked back at her life with Asari was that she had enjoyed it. As long as that was the case, Noriko wondered, was it really important that they hadn't been a couple? Nevertheless, Noriko couldn't help but feel dismayed that she had come to believe they were a couple when in fact they hadn't been.

That she and Asari were simply a man and woman and incapable of living as a married couple—or becoming one—was because of Asari in a sense, Noriko thought, but also because of her. They had not married at a young age, it wasn't their first marriage, and they had no children—all of these things contributed to the fact that their life was simply that of a man and woman, but none of these was the basic reason. Noriko thought the cause might be the propensity the two of them had for one to suggest the use of objects owned by former lovers, and for the other to gladly accept, but she wasn't sure. She was suddenly forced to see the proof that their life together had not been a real marriage.

Noriko had always treated Asari rather well. Not even once did he have to go get a towel when he washed; she gave him clean underwear every day; she always served all kinds of dishes; and his sheets were always clean. She was tolerant about his drinking. She didn't get angry even when he came home after midnight and wanted to drink more, or when he became rowdy and threw up, keeping her from sleeping. She didn't look particularly unhappy the following morning. When Asari, who had never known a hangover, emerged the next morning looking even more refreshed than usual, Noriko found that without even trying, she felt refreshed herself. When he wanted to go out for a drink with his friends, she let him have all the money she could spare instead of trying to discourage him.

Yet most wives didn't seem to possess such tolerance and such a willingness to serve. On such mornings, wouldn't most couples refuse to speak, one of them with a hangover and the other pouting? That Asari had never known a hangover might not have been because of his constitution alone.

Noriko now realized that generously giving money to Asari when he went out drinking would have been inconceivable for a real wife, and that at those times the two of them were like a spoiled son and doting mother. There were also times when they became like a father and child, with the child doing the housework.

"Do you have some money left?" Noriko often asked Asari as he left to go to work on payday.

"You don't have any left?"

"No."

"You have to be more careful. Well, I can get some meat or something on my way home. Or would you rather come and meet me for dinner? For lunch you can manage with this." Asari would search in his pockets and leave her a couple of hundred-yen coins.

That Noriko had no interest in secretly saving money as most wives did, and that Asari didn't get into trouble with other women, were because they were nothing more than just a woman and man who loved each other. If they had loved each other as a wife and a husband, they would have been excited and tempted by the prospect of secret savings and flirtations.

There was hardly any cause for quarreling between Noriko and Asari, and since they still loved each other, there were no arguments in their day-to-day life. When she thought of Asari as stingy and said so, she was perhaps exaggerating. She was probably just looking for a taste of a true married couple's life. Their life was extremely calm unless Asari lost his temper because he was drinking too much or was irritable because he wouldn't allow himself to drink. Noriko had been happy. Although she wasn't enough of an optimist to believe that her happiness would last until she died, it had never occurred to her that she would be forced to reevaluate her life in her last hours.

"Hey, I'm home," Asari said as he opened the door. "There's a strange letter in the mailbox." As he spoke, he threw the evening paper Noriko had forgotten to bring in at her feet and pointed toward the gate. Noriko bumped against Asari's shoulder while he was taking off his shoes, slipped into her sandals and ran out toward the gate, but when she opened the mailbox, she found only a salt-shaker with a red top.

When she went back into the house with the saltshaker, Asari stopped untying his necktie for a moment and made a motion of shaking salt over his body, saying, "You didn't do it?"

Noriko had learned from her parents the custom of shaking salt on oneself in front of the house after returning from a funeral. It was an act of purification. Her parents had always done this. One summer's evening her mother had called at the door, "I'm home . . . Can someone bring me some salt?" Her mother was supposed to have gone to a theater that evening, however, not a funeral.

"What's the matter?" Noriko went out and saw that her mother's face was quite pale.

"Salt. Quick. I need some salt," her mother had said. Noriko had fetched a jar of coarse salt from the kitchen. Her mother took a handful and sprinkled it over her shoulders and around her hem several times. She went into the house and, sitting down, said that on the way home a young woman had committed suicide by throwing herself in front of the train.

"She was about your age," her mother said to Noriko, who had just turned twenty. "She wasn't married, they said. I couldn't look at her, of course, but heard them saying, 'The legs are there, and that's an arm . . . that must be a piece of flesh.' And it smelled awful."

Noriko never forgot to follow the salt ritual, probably because of this experience—her mother's pale face as she stood outside the door, the young woman who was about her age whose limbs had been instantaneously separated and turned into lumps of flesh. Noriko had thought that something had taken possession of her mother when she saw her pale ghastly face, but when she saw her under a bright light this quality disappeared. If her mother had come straight into the house, that ghastliness might have come in with her and stayed in the air.

So whenever Asari returned from a funeral, Noriko would say, "Wait, don't come in," and would hurry to get the salt.

"Don't bother. It's silly," Asari would say, going in nonchalantly and taking his shoes off. Noriko would take him back outside and sprinkle him with salt. Her parents had always used coarse salt for the ritual, but coarse salt was no longer available. Noriko felt that something was lacking but used refined salt anyway to ease her mind.

One day after returning from a funeral and being sprinkled with salt from a saltshaker, Asari said, "What'll happen if you die before me? Who is going to do this when I come back from your funeral? Will you do it from somewhere in the sky?"

Whenever she came back and had to perform the ritual on herself, she put a saltshaker in the mailbox before leaving the house. She had done this that day . . .

"I wasn't thinking," she said, putting the saltshaker back on the table and forcing a smile. "Do you want to go to the bath first, or later?"

"Which would be better for you?" Asari asked, changing into his kimono.

"Whichever you want."

"Well, I'll go to the bath later. I'm hungry." Then he said, "I don't need it tonight."

Noriko didn't want him to abstain from drinking that night. She didn't want him to go to the Showaza Theater by himself. On the other hand, if he stayed home he would be in a bad mood. If he did drink excessively, he might lose his temper, which would be worse.

"All right, for the time being," she said. This was her stock response to Asari when he didn't want to drink. Tonight she put a special feeling into the expression. She hoped he wouldn't go to the Showaza Theater but would have something to drink—though not too much—before going to bed and would talk with her. In the end Asari's abstinence that night did turn out to be "for the time being," and it wasn't his fault.

"Can I have some beer? I'm very thirsty." It was Noriko who said this. She imitated the hesitant expression Asari used when he wanted to drink in spite of his initial decision.

"All right, since it's a request from one who rarely drinks, I'll make an exception and keep you company."

"Then we'll go at my pace."

"What do you mean, 'your pace?' "

"Well, you know what I mean."

"All right. I understand."

When Noriko brought in the beer bottle, Asari reached out and opened it and poured for her, saying, "Let me pour for you. Since you've forgotten to sprinkle yourself with salt, beer is a good way to purify yourself."

Without a word Noriko watched Asari pour beer into a glass. He stopped when the glass was half full.

"Don't be stingy," she said.

"You can't drink much. I'll give you more when you finish that."

Noriko took the bottle and poured for Asari. When she put the bottle down and looked up, she saw him gulping his beer.

"Don't you want to toast this rare occasion of my drinking with you?"

"You're right," he said, but put the glass down and picked up his chopsticks. Noriko drank a swallow.

"How old was your friend who died?"

"Same age I am."

"An old lady like that . . ." Asari said, then put his hand over his mouth, pretending this was a slip of the tongue. "That's what she gets for driving."

"She gave me a ride once."

"That was silly. You have to watch yourself. What if the accident had happened then? You'd be dead, and I wouldn't have anyone to sprinkle salt on me."

Noriko picked up her glass and had another sip and another. "It was safer then," she said. "She had a sticker on the window that said 'I just got my license. Thank you for your cooperation.' "

"No one notices those stickers."

"But she was very careful. That's what I mean."

"Anyway, I don't want you to ever ride in a car with a woman driver."

"Is it all right if a man is driving? Is it all right to ride with a man, even if we go far away?"

"I'm serious."

"I know."

"Okay, then. But it must be awfully hard to die suddenly."

"Do you want me to say goodbye to you?"

"No, what I meant was, if I die myself. Of course it would be the same if you died."

"I see. What sorts of things would you do if you knew you had to die? Is there another woman?"

"Maybe there is . . . Actually there was a time when I thought a lot about it. What'll happen, I asked myself, if I die suddenly? My father died around the time I graduated from school. We divided the property between Mother and us children. I got some land in Setagaya, and Mother wanted me to have a house built there so she could live with me when I got married. I didn't get married for a long time. Instead I sold the land and spent all the money."

"You've told me about that."

"But Mother didn't know what I did. Every time I went back home, she told me to go ahead and build a house and get married and she would help me with the money. Meanwhile the cost of land went up. I had sold it cheaply long before, and the money was gone. I used to drink a lot more then. I ended up having no money to pay the rent and had to go to pawn shops. My clothes drawers were all empty. You know, I remember once I had eighteen pawn tickets at the same time. Several times after I'd been drunk I'd wake up on a bench in some train station and ask myself, 'What'll happen if I die like this?' Then I had a vision of the pawn tickets fluttering in front of me. I felt terrible thinking about how awful my mother would feel if she knew I had drunk up the price of the land and let the rent debts build up and was left with nothing but pawn tickets. I thought I'd like to have time at least to take care of those pawn tickets."

"What would you want to do if you were going to die now?"

"Well, first of all, this, I think." He lifted his glass and drank some beer. Noriko picked up her glass too. There was hardly any beer left in it. When she had emptied the glass, the bubbles sank to the bottom and began to disappear, and Asari's face, about the size of a bean, appeared at the bottom of the crystal glass.

"Do you want more?" Asari asked. She put her glass in front of him. The beer flowed in vigorously.

"Oh, not that much."

"You called me stingy," Asari said, lifting the bottle with deliberate slowness. The glass was nearly full. Noriko drank two swallows one after another.

"Are you all right?"

"Yes," she answered, holding the glass and pretending to drink more. She gazed at the picture that appeared in the bottom of the glass. It was a distant, shining, miniature picture with a twinkling quality. In this picture Asari was sitting in front of a cute little table that was scattered with various dishes. He seemed small enough to sit on the palm of a hand. If I tell him that my life ends at three-nineteen tomorrow afternoon, what will he do? she wondered. Will he kill me before that time comes?

"I see what you're doing." He looked into his glass. "You look so small."

"You do too. Isn't it pretty, though?" she said. "But didn't you think of leaving a will then?" she continued after a pause.

"No, I didn't think about it," he said and put his glass down. She did the same.

"I wished then that Mother would die soon, to save her from seeing my miserable end. That was the only unselfish thought I ever had."

"How about some sake?" he asked then. Once he had started drinking sake he usually found it difficult to stop.

"If we are going at my pace, then it's time to stop drinking. How about eating now?"

"Okay, if you say so." Asari didn't object.

"What will we be like when we're old if we keep going like this?" Noriko asked while they were eating.

"What do you mean?"

"I mean how will we be living?"

"Same as we do now, of course."

"You mean that for the next twenty or thirty years we'll go on living together like a newlywed couple or like friends who get together for a cup of tea?" Noriko meant to say that such a life was not a true married life, but he didn't understand her.

"I like what you say, that sounds good!" Asari said and looked at the clock. "Hey, it's not too late for the Showaza Theater. I'll take you along if you want to go." Asari picked up a book of movie tickets from the letter rack and opened the little red cover. "Only one ticket left. How about buying another book and making it a gift for me after you use a ticket tonight?" Noriko agreed.

They walked along a street bordered by a hedge, beyond which there were houses with lit-up windows. The light was calm, like a spring evening, and gave Noriko an impression of security and assurance. She remembered that once when she had been terribly lonely, deserted by a former lover, the light from other people's houses had always looked warm and comforting. When she had returned to her place, turned on the light, and looked at her small, shabby room, she used to think that her light wouldn't seem warm and comforting even to people who were dying of hunger and cold. As she walked with Asari and looked at the light, she wondered if the light from their living room gave the same sense of stability. Or did it give the shallow glow of the light that comes from an inn or a dormitory?

They walked to the main shopping street and crossed the railroad tracks. The Showaza, to which Asari escaped on nights when he wasn't drinking, was a small theater on the other side of the station that showed only foreign movies.

"What's on tonight, I wonder?" Asari said, looking at the posters in the window. They advertised a Western and an Italian movie.

"A book of tickets, please." Noriko handed over a 500-yen bill that she had inserted in the front of her sash.

"I thought you were going to buy a few books for me," said Asari, standing next to her.

Inside the theater she looked over Asari's shoulder and saw the backs of the audience. After her eyes had adjusted to the darkness, she spotted several empty seats.

"Let's go over there." Asari went ahead of her. When they had settled into their seats and looked up at the screen, the Italian film was on. There was a scene of quiet countryside in subdued and beautiful colors. This scene then changed into one of a train station. A sickly woman appeared on the screen; she was accompanied by her husband. They were returning from a health resort. Shortly after they arrived at their house, the husband's friend came to visit. From the conversation between the men while the woman was out of the room, it appeared that the love between the woman and her husband had cooled off, that their hearts no longer beat so strongly.

Noriko thought that her heart and Asari's still had their vigor. Day to day, she was able to sense the beating of his heart, and he, she was sure, was able to sense the beating of hers. But she was uncertain about the light that leaked from their home. A legal bond, a shared household, sexual love, and emotional love were supposed to be the four pillars of marriage. But just as no one would say that four pillars alone were enough to make a house, those four conditions were not enough to construct a true marriage. Noriko felt that she and Asari had not put up a roof or painted the walls. They hadn't built anything together. Even if one pillar became shaky, as long as the walls and roof were intact, a house was still a house. She felt that they hadn't been building anything from their days together, but instead had been living one day at a time.

We haven't known the true pleasures or the difficulties of married life, she went on thinking. If I had realized that we were in fact simply living together as a man and woman and had followed through accordingly, then we would have had a different way of living altogether. They might have been criticized by the world, and the tranquillity of their life might have been destroyed, but they might also have felt a keener, fuller joy. Noriko thought if she were to write a note to Asari before she died, she would have to include a paragraph that said, "What I regret most is that I have to die without finding out how we would have lived if we had realized we were no more than a man and a woman living together."

The movie was still depicting how hopelessly estranged the wife and husband were. There seemed to be no possibility for reconciliation. Now and then one of them would try but would end up being disappointed, and as a result the two would grow farther apart.

"Your wife is not well; she needs a great deal of support from you," the husband in the movie was advised by his friend. The husband tried to do this. "You look wonderful this morning, my dear. Your cheeks are rosy. You're practically well now," he would say.

The wife took this as her husband's criticism of her illness but pretended that she felt fine. He told her that they would be able to go to a party they were invited to.

Several days later, their little boy became ill; they nursed him through the night.

"Mommy and Daddy are here, son," the husband said to the sick boy.

The wife, her husband's arm around her, said, "How many days do you want to stay out of school, honey? You can ask your father.

He seems to be able to cure people, so surely he can make your illness last longer."

The husband withdrew his hand from her shoulder.

"I want to get better soon," the son said.

"All right, I'll make you get well very soon."

On the day of the party, the wife, ready to go out, came into the husband's room. He'd forgotten about their going out, and hurriedly started to shave.

There was no fighting between this husband and wife. There were no incidents that might have caused them to divorce, and so their days continued. There were only the short, ironic conversations that affirmed their mutual feelings of isolation.

Noriko turned her stiff neck to see Asari sitting next to her. He was watching intently, his face bathed in the light from the screen. Would he understand if I told him now about my doubts, that our marriage hasn't been real? she wondered. They were quite different from the couple in the movie. Since they had been living together as a man and woman who loved each other, they had come to accept each other's words, whatever they were, only in a positive sense. For instance, when she had told him earlier at the dinner table that their relationship was that of a newlywed couple or friends who drink tea together, Asari had agreed with her, saying, "I like what you say." The couple in the movie moved farther away from each other by always responding negatively, but she and Asari had been partners in a crime of distortion by always responding positively to each other.

If I were to say to Asari, "Please listen to me. I don't think it is necessarily a good thing that we've never quarreled," he would undoubtedly say, "It's a fine thing. No doubt about it. Don't you worry," Noriko thought. Then I probably wouldn't feel like correcting his misunderstanding, just as the couple in the movie wouldn't attempt to correct their errors . . .

It was only ten o'clock when they arrived home after the second movie, a Western.

"I think I'll go to the bath," Asari said. Noriko stopped herself from saying that she would go with him.

"That's a good idea, why don't you?" she said. When he left, she went upstairs and sat down at the desk.

"I want to tell you that I have deep regrets and that I couldn't be free from remorse if I were to die now," she started to write. She expressed her doubt that their marriage had been real, although they were united not only legally but in their hearts and bodies. "The reason is . . . ," she continued, then listed her reasons for feeling this way.

"On my way to the funeral," she went on writing, "I looked at my watch while waiting for the bus. It was a little after one. My friend had been alive at that time the day before yesterday; she had eaten lunch and left her house, just as I had done. At that moment she hadn't dreamt of her own death. She had been driving a car without the faintest idea of what would happen in a few minutes. When I thought of this, I felt a chill at the sound of the second hand of my watch. As you said, to have to die suddenly is horrifying. Then I thought: If she had known that it was her fate to die at that time yesterday, there must have been things that she would have wanted to do. If she had had even one day . . . It made me think what I would do if I were to live only till the day after tomorrow.

"During the funeral, and even after coming home, I kept thinking of the things I would like to do. It inevitably made me think of your next marriage. In my imagination it was radically different from ours. For the first time I reflected upon our life. I concluded that we have to make our relationship into that of a real married couple. If we continue our life as lovers, we ought to do so wholeheartedly, even if it means that we fight. In any case, when I finally die, I want to savor my last hours. Even if I had regrets, I would feel that I had lived more fully. I'm not sorry at all that my friend's death made me reflect upon our present life."

When Asari returned from the bath, Noriko said she was going to go.

"I thought you'd been already. You should have come with me," he said.

"I thought it would be too much trouble to lock up the house," she said and left. When she was outside the house she called back, "There's a strange letter in our mailbox."

The moment she put her shoes in the shoe locker and pulled the key out, the outside light of the bathhouse went off. A few people were putting their clothes on. Only one person besides herself was taking her clothes off. "Good night," someone said and left.

In the large, vacant bathroom several women were washing themselves. Wooden basins were scattered on the tile floor. Noriko saw one woman start to wash her hair; she knew she could take her time and stretched her legs and arms out in the bathtub.

Suddenly Noriko heard whistling from the other side of the divider. It was a clear, energetic, straightforward song that children had sung in a popular musical. The whistle sounded lively and loud.

Noriko wondered who was whistling the song. It was probably a diligent young man who works in a factory. He must have worked the late shift. He had finished the day's work and was taking a bath. He had nothing to worry about and nothing to do but go home and sleep; that was why he could whistle so vigorously and cheerfully. When he came to the end of the song, he went on whistling the instrumental part and then went back to the beginning with even more energy. Noriko felt encouraged by the tune.

Boxcar of Chrysanthemums

ENCHI FUMIKO

Translated by Yukiko Tanaka and Elizabeth Hanson

Enchi Fumiko (b. 1905) was the daughter of a literature professor at the University of Tokyo, and from early childhood she was exposed to classical Japanese literature. This and the influence of her grandmother, an avid partisan of Kabuki who often took her to the theater, formed Enchi's literary taste. Later she studied drama with Osanai Kaoru, the originator of modern drama in Japan, and a play she wrote at age 23 was staged at the famous Tsukiji Little Theater. She associated with Leftist writers during her early period but did not participate in their political activities.

After her marriage to a journalist and the birth of a child, Enchi started writing fiction, but it was not until 1952, when she won the Women's Literature Prize, that she finally achieved recognition. She has suffered from many illnesses, including breast cancer, and because of financial difficulties has had to write stories for girls' magazines.

Enchi remains prolific even today and is considered an accomplished writer of both short stories and novels. The persistent theme of her work is the fate of women, whether historical figures or her contemporaries. Though she does not analyze female psychology, she often focuses on dark and repressed passion and the mysterious ways in which women's minds work. She translated *The Tale of Genji* into modern Japanese, a task that took her over ten years and represents one of her major contributions, since it brought this classic masterpiece close to modern readers. Her novel *Onnazaka* (translated into English as *The Waiting Years*), which portrays three women who spend their entire lives in the psychological torment of the paternalistic Meiji family system, shows subtle influences from *The Tale of Genji*.

Though "Boxcar of Chrysanthemums" is about a woman who consciously chooses a tragic fate by marrying a man who is mentally retarded, it reveals some aspects of the narrator's own personality, a woman who is very close to Enchi herself. Enchi is a skilled storyteller with an elegant and graceful style.

It MUST HAVE BEEN seven or eight years ago, since the highway wasn't as good as it is now, and traveling by car wasn't easy.

I was still staying in my summer house in Karuizawa even though it was mid-September. One day a women's group in the nearby town of Ueda asked me to give a talk. I've forgotten what kind of group they were, but I left my house in the late afternoon and spoke to the audience right after dinner, for less than an hour. If my memory is correct, it was a little after nine when I got on a train to go home.

It was too late for the express train that ran during the summer, but I heard there was a local that went as far as Karuizawa, and I decided to take it since I wanted very much to return home that night. There was no second class (in those days seats were divided into second and third class); the third-class cars were old and looked to be of prewar vintage. There were only a few passengers.

Although I said, "How nice, it's not crowded," to the people who came to see me off, I realized after the train started to move how uncomfortable it is to ride on an old train that makes squeaky noises every time it sways, and that has dirty, frayed, green velveteen upholstery.

Well, even if this is a local I'll be in Karuizawa in two hours or so for sure, I said to myself as I turned to look out the window. The moon was nearly full and boldly silhouetted in dark blue the low mountains beyond the fields beside the tracks. The plants in the rice paddies were ripe, so of course I couldn't see the moon reflecting on the water in the fields. Plastic bird rattles here and there glittered strangely as they reflected the moonlight. The clear dark blue of the sky and the coolness of the evening air stealing into the deserted car made me realize keenly that I was in the mountain region of Shinshu, where fall comes early.

I was thinking that I wanted to get home quickly when the train shuddered to a stop at a small station. We had been moving for no more than ten minutes. I couldn't complain about the stop since the train wasn't an express, but it didn't start up for a long time even though no one was getting on or off. It finally moved but then stopped again at the next station, took its time and wouldn't start again, as it had done before.

The four or five passengers in my car were all middle-aged men who looked as though they could be farmers from the area. There was no one sitting near me, and I didn't feel like standing up to go and ask about the delay. I looked out the window and saw several freight cars attached to the rear of the car I was in. It seemed that the cars were being loaded with something.

I realized then that this was a freight train for transporting cargo to Karuizawa that also happened to carry a few passengers. If I had known this earlier, I would have taken the local-express that left an hour before, even if I had had to rush to catch it. But it was too late for regrets; I told myself it would do no good to get off at an unfamiliar station late at night and resigned myself to the situation. The train would get me to Karuizawa sometime that night, no matter what; with that thought in mind, I felt calmer.

I took a paperback book from my bag and tried to read, but the squeaking noise of the car made it difficult to concentrate. I was tired, but I couldn't sleep because of the chilly air that crept up my legs and also because of my exasperation with a train that stopped so often.

When the train stopped for the fourth time at a fairly large station, I got off to ease my irritation. It would probably stop for ten minutes or so, and even if it started suddenly I thought I could easily jump on such a slow-moving train.

A few passengers got off. Some long packages wrapped in straw matting were piled up near one of the back cars, and the station attendants were loading them into the car as if they were in no big hurry. The packages were all about the same size, bulging at the center like fish wrapped in reed mats, but the station attendants were lifting them carefully in both hands, as if they were handling something valuable, and loading them into the soot-covered car.

I was watching the scene and wondering what the packages were when I suddenly noticed a moist, plant-like smell floating in from somewhere. Then I heard a woman's voice ask hesitantly, "Have you already loaded ours?"

I turned toward the voice. A middle-aged woman with her hair pulled into a bun was standing behind me. She wasn't alone; beside her was an old man with white hair and sunken cheeks. The moment I saw the pupils of his eyes with their strangely shifting gaze, and his slightly gaping mouth with its two long buck teeth and fine white froth at the corners, I was so startled that I stepped back a few paces.

"The Ichiges," one of the station attendants said to another, motioning with his eyes, and then he turned to the old man. "Yes, I loaded them. I put them in the best spot. They'll be in Tokyo tomorrow and will be the best flowers at the flower market," he said, speaking to the man as if he were a child.

The old man nodded with a dignified air.

"Oh, that's nice, isn't it? Now you don't have to worry. Well, let's go home and go to bed," the woman said, also as if she were humoring a child, and patted the old man's shoulder, which looked as stiff as a scarecrow's.

The old man stood there and said nothing. Meanwhile the packages were being loaded one after another, and by then I realized that the fragrance in the air was coming from them.

"Oh, that one over there! Those are our mums!" the old man yelled suddenly, extending his arms as if he were swimming toward the package the station attendant was about to load on the train. The old man's little nose was twitching like a dog's. "That smell . . . It's the Shiratama mum."

"Is it? Well, then, we'll ask them to let you smell them. The train's leaving soon, so you only smell once, all right?" the woman said and gave the station attendant a meaningful look. He put down the package the old man was trying to press his nose against and loaded another one first.

"That's enough now. You said good-bye to Shiratama, didn't you?" The woman spoke as if she were talking to a small child and put her arm around the stooping old man. She then took his hand and placed it gently on her lips. The old man let go of the package as if he were under a spell and stood up with his wife.

The door of the freight car finally closed, and the starting signal sounded. I got on the train in a hurry but didn't know quite what to make of the strange scene I had just witnessed. I couldn't believe that what I'd seen wasn't an illusion, like a scene from a movie.

"I feel sorry for them. Living on into old age like that."

I turned around. A middle-aged man in a gray jacket was sitting across the aisle from me. His face was dark and wrinkled from the sun, but he didn't look unpleasant. I realized that he hadn't been on the train before we stopped at the last station.

"That man—is he mentally ill?" I asked, unable to suppress my curiosity.

"Not mentally ill, more like an idiot. I think the term they use nowadays is 'mentally retarded.' " The man spoke without using any dialect. "The old man himself doesn't understand a thing, so he's okay, but I feel sorry for his wife. She's been married to that man for over twenty years now. If he'd been born into a poor family, marriage would have been out of the question, but simply because his family was wealthy, all kinds of cruel things happened."

Not only did the man speak without an accent, but his manner of speaking was smooth and pleasant. The name Ichige that the station attendant had mentioned turned my consciousness to some troublesome, submerged memory, but instead of mentioning this, I said, "Were those chrysanthemums they were loading in that boxcar? That old man was smelling them, wasn't he?"

"Yes, those were the chrysanthemums they grow in their garden. Mums are the only thing the old man cares much about. When they send some off he comes with his wife to watch, whether it's late at night or early in the morning."

"Then all of the packages are chrysanthemums?"

"That's right. Most of the flowers that go to Tokyo at this time of year are. Lots of farmers around here grow flowers, but they're all sold in Tokyo, so it's a big deal. Not only flowers, either. The people who work in the mountains around here collect tree roots, branches and other stuff, put prices on them and send them to Tokyo. Once they get them to market they can sell them, I guess, because money is always sent back. Tokyo's a good customer that lets the landowners around here earn money that way."

"I see. I was wondering why we were stopping so often to load things. It's a mistake for people to take this train," I said, smiling.

"You're right. It takes a good three hours to get to Karuizawa on this train."

"Oh, that's awful! No one told me that at Ueda when I got on."

"I don't think the people around here know that there's a train running at this hour that carries mums. Well, you might as well just get used to it and consider it an elegant way to travel."

My family would worry if I got to Karuizawa after midnight, but as the saying goes, there's nothing you can do once you're on board; even if no one had told me that I'd have to resign myself to the situation, I had no choice but to do so.

And so our conversation returned to the couple who grew chrysanthemums. The man across from me, whose name was Kurokawa, said he used to teach at an agricultural institute in Tokyo, but after he was evacuated to this region during the war he bought an orchard and settled down. He made extra income by collecting alpine plants, something he liked very much. He was taking this train because he had decided on an impulse to go to the town of Komoro and then climb Mt. Asama early the next morning.

It was the year after the end of the war when Kurokawa learned about Ichige Masutoshi and Rie.

Luckily Kurokawa didn't have to leave the country to do his military service, so as soon as the war was over he went to a village where his family had been evacuated. The village wasn't far from where he was born, and since he had never been particularly fond of city life and had also been hit hard by the war, he decided to settle there. At first he taught at a middle school in a nearby town. It was quite a while later that he bought an orchard and began to grow grapes and apples for a livelihood.

Food was scarce for most people in those days. No one grew fruit or flowers; everyone was busy growing potatoes and corn on the plots of land that weren't suitable for rice paddies. Kurokawa's father was still alive and healthy then and worked hard with his wife and daughter-in-law to grow vegetables. After living there for a while, Kurokawa noticed a new Tokyo-style house on a fairly large piece of land not far from his house. On his way back from school he often saw a woman in her thirties busily working in the garden behind the house. She wore a kerchief over her head and work pants, but her fair, unburned complexion and fine features had a calm sadness that reminded him of classic Korean beauties.

"That house is built in a different style from the others around here. Was it built during the war?" Kurokawa asked his father one evening during supper.

"That one? That's the house Ichige from Tokyo built during the war." His father, born and raised in that region, said this as if his son would know who Mr. Ichige was even if he didn't explain.

"Who's Ichige?"

"Ichige? He's the owner of a big paper company in Tokyo. I heard that he went bankrupt after the war. His father was the famous Ichige Tokuichi."

"Oh, I see." Kurokawa finally remembered the name. "But he's been dead for a long time, hasn't he?" Kurokawa had heard of Ichige Tokuichi of the Shinshu region, one of the success stories of the Meiji era.

"Right. Tokuichi was the father of Hanshiro, who was also known as a fine man. Hanshiro built the house, but his only son, Masatoshi, and his wife live there now."

With this as a beginning, Kurokawa's father then continued: Masatoshi was Ichige's legitimate heir, but he had contracted meningitis as a child, and although he was not actually an idiot, he was capable of only a few simple words. When he reached adulthood, however, it was decided that he should have a wife. Rie, who had come from the city of Iida to work as one of the Ichige's servants, was chosen as the human sacrifice.

"That's ridiculous, like a feudal lord and his serf. There's something wrong with any woman who would go along with it, too," Kurokawa snapped, but secretly he couldn't comprehend how the ladylike woman he saw when he passed the back of Ichige's house each morning and evening could be so lacking in expression and yet also give an impression of innocence and purity.

"That's what everyone says at first. When I heard the story, I despised the woman for agreeing to marry a man like that, no matter how much money was involved. But you know, after we came here that house was built nearby, and so I've seen a lot of Rie. She always showed up for volunteer work days and air raid drills, and ever since I was head of the volunteer guards I've known her well. Your dead mother and your wife Matsuko would agree that there's nothing wrong with Rie. She works harder than anyone else and doesn't put on the airs of a rich person. The catty local women used to sit around and drink tea and make fun of the Tokyo women who were evacuated here, but they stopped at Rie. They agreed that she took good care of that idiot husband of hers and only pitied her.

"It was like that for two or three years, and then before the war ended Hanshiro died of a stroke. His mother and son-in-law were careless and used up what money there was. They say only that house is left. In these times when there isn't much food, Rie has a hard time finding enough potatoes and flour to feed that glutton of a husband. She knits things for the farmers and sews clothes for their kids. You can't do that much for others if you're a fake and just trying to make a good impression. Sometimes I even wonder if she's a reincarnation of Kannon* . . ."

Kurokawa's father spoke earnestly. He seemed to believe what he was saying. He was the kind of old-fashioned man who would want

* Kannon is the Buddhist Goddess of Mercy.—Translator.

to believe that a person like Rie was a Kannon, or at least her reincarnation; at the war's end and in the years that followed he had
seen whatever trappings human beings find to wrap themselves up
in cruelly pulled off to reveal their naked, shameful parts.

Kurokawa certainly understood his father's feeling. He realized
that he too wanted to purify his image of Rie and think of her as a
reincarnated Kannon. Rie had lived up to the expectations of Kurokawa's father and had continued to be a devoted wife for more than
ten years. She had converted most of Ichige's land into apple or-
chards and supported her husband and herself with this income.
Growing chrysanthemums was partially for income but partially
because Masatoshi enjoyed looking at flowers. Kurokawa said there
didn't seem to be much money in it.

"It was two years ago, I think. Rie won some kind of prize. Hmm,
what was it called? It was to commend her for having devoted herself to her mentally retarded husband for so many years; you might
say for being the model of the faithful wife. In any case, it's a rare
thing these days, and I think she deserved the praise."

While I listened to Kurokawa's long story, the train kept stopping
at every station, and it looked as though chrysanthemums wrapped
in straw mats were being loaded into the freight cars.

Between Komoro and Oiwake the train picked up speed. The
moon seemed to be high in the middle of the sky; I couldn't see it
from the train window, but the rays of moonlight had become
brighter, and they shone upon the scene along the tracks with the
coppery glow of an old mirror. This copper color changed to the
smoky silver of mica when we reached a plateau and a mist settled
onto the ground. After Kurokawa got off at Komoro, the only passengers left were a pair of men sitting near the far entrance to the
car. Since it was late at night when we reached the high land, a chill
that was enough to shrivel me crept up from the tips of my socks
as I sat there and quickly permeated my lower body.

I didn't actually mind the chill, even though I shrugged my
shoulders now and then and pressed my knees together tightly,
shivering. I was too absorbed in adding some facts from my own
memory to the story that Kurokawa had told me about Ichige Masatoshi and his wife.

When I heard the names Ichige Tokuichi and Hanshiro, I was
reminded of the story I had almost forgotten about the retarded
son of the Ichiges. I had barely stopped myself from saying to Kurokawa, "Yes, of course, I've heard about him too."

I happened to have heard about the marriage between Masatoshi and Rie just about the time it took place. It was a year or so after the outbreak of the China Incident, when the image of the red draft notice calling soldiers to the army burned like fire in young men's minds. I had a friend whose husband was a psychiatrist, and although he practiced primarily in one of the private hospitals, he spent a few days a week at the Brain Research Institute of S Medical School. Interns and volunteer assistants who worked at this Institute often gathered at my friend Nagase's house to talk. I became acquainted with this group in the course of writing a play that dealt with a mental patient; I visited the hospital to ask the doctors questions about their experiences. One day when I met with three or four of these young doctors at Nagase's house, I noticed that Kashimura, who had always been with the group, was missing.

"Where is Dr. Kashimura? Is he on duty tonight?" I asked. The young doctors looked at each other and laughed before saying things like, "I guess you could call it 'duty,' " or "He sure is on duty," or "It's some duty."

I thought he might have gone to see a lover, and so I kept quiet, but then Nagase interrupted and said, "It's all right to tell her. It might be helpful to her."

"It's not a very respectable story, though."

"But a job's a job. Maybe she'll write a story about how we have to do this kind of work to support ourselves."

One of them sat up straight and said, "Kashimura is on night duty tonight at the home of one of the patients."

"I see. Does the patient get violent?" I asked without hesitation, since such cases are common among psychiatric patients.

"Yes, you couldn't say he *doesn't* get violent, but it's a tricky point." The young man who spoke, Tomoda, looked at another and said, "How was it when you were there?"

"Nothing happened, fortunately. You always had bad luck, didn't you?"

Tomoda nodded. "Yeah, my luck is bad. I'll probably die first if I go to war."

"I don't agree. You got a chance to see things you can't usually see. A voyeur would even pay for the chance."

"Idiot! Who said I'm a voyeur?"

"If everybody talked like that, no one would understand. I'll tell the true story in a scientific way without any interpretation," Nagase said, and he then told me the story of Ichige Masatoshi's marriage.

Of course he didn't mention the name, but I learned of it quite a while later.

When Masatoshi reached physical maturity, his father consulted with a professor of psychiatry because he was troubled about how to find a partner to meet his son's sexual needs.

"The best way would be to provide him with one woman who would be kind to him. You should disregard her family background and her appearance and find someone who would take care of him like a mother," the professor told the father.

Masatoshi was particularly pitiful because his mother, Shino, had always disliked her retarded eldest child and had barely tolerated living in the same house with him. When she was young, Shino had been a hostess at Koyo-kan, a famous restaurant of the Meiji period, and had been popular among aristocrats and wealthy merchants because of her beauty.

Ichige Hanshiro had won her and made her his wife. For Shino the marriage meant an elevation in her own status, but her own background made her unyielding and vain, and she was determined not to be outdone by anyone. Her daughter was normal and married a man who was adopted into the family, but Shino was ashamed because she couldn't show off her only son in public. This shame turned into a hatred that she vented on Hanshiro.

Since Hanshiro had a sense of responsibility as a father, Masatoshi was raised at least to give the impression of being a son of the Ichige family. If the matter had been left to Shino's discretion, he probably would have been confined to one room and treated like a true moron.

When Masatoshi reached puberty he would sometimes become excited like a dog in heat and chase the maids and his sister. When Shino saw this happen, far from feeling sad, she would grow so livid that the veins would stand out at her temples.

"It's your responsibility! You let him wander around the house like an animal! Let's hurry and put him in a hospital. If we don't, all of our maids will leave us, I assure you," she shrieked at her husband.

"You don't have to shout for me to understand. I have my own thoughts about this," Hanshiro said calmly. Shino, who had given birth to Masatoshi, had no comprehension of the pain and unseverable strength of the parental bond Hanshiro felt in his very bones.

The next day Hanshiro went to see the psychiatry professor again and asked him to arrange for his son to be sterilized before he was married.

"I know a woman who might become my son's wife, but I can't imagine bringing the subject up to her whenever I think of the possibility of a child being born. Once the operation is finished, though, I think I can hope for a marriage. I feel sorry for the woman who'll be my son's wife, but from a father's viewpoint, I would at least like to give him the experience of living with a woman."

The professor agreed to Hanshiro's request, and the operation for sterilizing Masatoshi was performed in the surgery department of the hospital where he worked. It was a very simple procedure and was guaranteed not to interfere with the performance of the sex act.

It was said that after this Hanshiro talked to Rie about marriage. No one knew how Rie had reacted, or how long it had taken her to accept the proposal, or what sort of conditions Hanshiro had promised. It was clear only that Rie was not promised a bright future. The young couple began their married life in a small house that was fixed up for them in a corner of the grounds. It was originally built as a retreat. Rie took care of Masatoshi by herself, without any help from the household maids.

On formal occasions like weddings and funerals, Hanshiro and his wife attended with their daughter and her husband—their adopted son and an executive at Hanshiro's company—and their second daughter, who was also married. Of course Masatoshi didn't go along and neither did Rie.

"When they were married, he gave Rie a lot of stock in the company," one of Hanshiro's employees said, as if he had been there and seen this happen.

What I had heard at Nagase's house, that several young psychiatrists were hired to oversee the married relations of Masatoshi and Rie, was true; they were dispatched because it was assumed that there would be some times when Rie would be subjected to some violence. Hanshiro had heard from the psychiatrists that retarded men like his son sometimes perform the sexual act interminably, beyond a normal limit, since they are unable to control themselves, and that in some cases women had been killed as a result. To assure Rie's safety, Hanshiro had arranged for young doctors from S Medical School to take turns standing by every night in a room next to the couple's.

In teaching hospitals before the war, many young doctors worked for nearly nothing after receiving their degrees before they found a position somewhere. Of course not all of them had fathers who owned private clinics, so even if they were single it wasn't easy for them to support themselves unless they did some moonlighting.

The job at the Ichiges' was unusual even for psychiatrists, and the pay was much more than the average. There were many applicants. The professor chose several whom he felt could keep a secret; three of them were among the five or six young doctors who came to Nagase's.

"Rich people do such awful things. In fact, that woman was bought, but to have a doctor waiting on them like that . . . It's like some kind of show. Even if the father did want his son to enjoy sex, it's too big a sacrifice. Why didn't he have them castrate his son instead of sterilizing him? I think that father is perverted." I spoke forcefully. I couldn't control my anger while listening to the story. Looking back on it now, I realize that at age thirty or so I knew little of life's unavoidable bitterness. I feel ashamed that I was so naive, but at that time I detested not only Hanshiro—though I didn't know his name then—but also Rie, the woman bought to be Masatoshi's wife, for her cowardice.

"Hey, don't get upset so fast. All of that made life a little easier for these guys," Nagase said, trying to act the mediator.

"That's true," I said, but I still felt revulsion, even toward Tomoda and Kashimura, who had worked for the Ichiges.

They say that when the wind blows, the cooper prospers; applying this logic, I could find no reason to criticize a man like Ichige Masatoshi, who had in fact helped the poor young doctors. Leftist ideology would probably explain this as the contradiction inherent in capitalistic society. Still, I simply could not feel comfortable with a situation where young, single doctors watched a young couple in bed from beginning to end, paying diligent attention until the two fell asleep. If one does not make a fool of himself when doing such things, then he is making a fool of his charges. The doctors were too young and well educated to see themselves as fools, and if they were making fun of someone else, it was of the woman who was the victim of this marriage. Obviously I didn't like their making fun of her or their seeing her as an object of erotic stimulation. At the same time that they were ridiculing her, they were acting like fools who couldn't see the spittle on their own faces. Someone had used the word "voyeur," but I had thought at the time that there was a basic difference between a voyeur and someone who kept such a nightly vigil.

After that I heard nothing more about the Ichiges from the young doctors, but through Nagase I learned there were in fact times when what had once seemed an absurd possibility had come to pass; Rie had fainted once, and there was a big row when Kashimura went to take care of her. It turned out that Masatoshi had forced himself on Rie when she was menstruating, and as a result she had lost a great deal of blood.

The interns from S Hospital must have stood duty at the Ichiges' for about a year when they decided there was no longer any danger and so stopped going there. A few years later, in the spring after the outbreak of the Pacific War, Kashimura was drafted as a military doctor and left to go to the South Seas. At the party to see him off, he came to me with a sake cup in his hand.

"I've been wanting to talk with you, but it seems like time is running out. If I return safely I'll tell you. It's about the family where I did night duty," he said.

"Oh yes, that family," I said, nodding. It was better not to mention the Ichiges' name in a place where there were so many people.

"The wife—Rie, I mean—I fell in love with her. To tell the truth, I wanted to marry her and talked to her about it." Kashimura spoke loudly, without concern for the people around him. Going to the battlefield seemed to have made him free from the petty restraints of normal times.

"Did you really?" I was intrigued and looked into Kashimura's eyes. I remembered that I had once secretly scorned the trio who had done that night duty for the Ichiges, including Kashimura. Now that I heard from Kashimura himself words that seemed to prove he had not been making a fool of either himself or Rie, I couldn't help reacting with a tense curiosity.

"What did she say?"

"She said no. She really loves her husband. But she said she was grateful for my having asked. She said it was more than she could have expected, after I had seen her in such unsightly circumstances. Masatoshi couldn't go on living, and probably wouldn't live for very long if she left, she said, and when she thought of this she felt sorry for him and couldn't possibly leave. Then she cried and cried. I thought there was nothing else I could do, and so I gave up," he said. Kashimura's face was flushed with sake, and tears welled up in his bloodshot eyes.

"I got married after that and have children now, but I haven't forgotten her. For a while I thought I had to rescue her from that

place, but now it seems natural that she stays with that husband,"
he said.

"Why were you attracted to her in the first place?" I asked Kashimura impatiently, trying to make sense of a situation I could not
comprehend in many ways.

"Well . . ." After thinking for a moment, Kashimura said, "I
felt the same as I would if my mother were in an animal cage. It
was like a bad dream."

"Does she look like your mother?"

"No, not at all." Kashimura shook his head vigorously.

"What are you two talking so seriously about?" said a colleague
of Kashimura's, patting his shoulder. Seeing this as a chance to excuse himself, Kashimura stood up to leave. He didn't seem particularly interested in talking with me anymore.

I thought about my brief conversation with Kashimura more than
once after I returned home that night, and I tried to imagine what
this woman Rie, whom I had never met, looked like. His words
about his mother being in a cage excited my imagination, but in
truth I couldn't picture Rie herself.

She was the daughter of a quilt merchant in the city of Iida. Her
father had not been very well off, and although she only finished
grammar school, like many children in those days, she was smart,
wrote neatly, learned to sew and knit after arriving at the Ichiges',
and acquired the knowledge of a high school graduate. Nagase said
he had not heard any rumors about her family receiving a large sum
of money when she married.

I suspected that she might have had something physically wrong
with her as a woman, but when I learned that Kashimura had proposed to her after doing that strange nightwatch, I decided Rie must
be normal.

It was extraordinary that a man who had witnessed a most private part of her life would ask her to divorce Masatoshi and marry
him. Kashimura was a quiet, scholarly type—tall, well-built, and
handsome. He was popular among the nurses and patients at the
hospital, and I wondered how Rie felt when she was proposed to by
a man who was beyond comparison with her husband. It puzzled
me that she could calmly refuse such a proposal, since she was only
twenty-four or twenty-five.

Four or five years after the end of the war, I learned from Tomoda,
an old friend of Kashimura's, that Kashimura had died of malaria
in the South Seas. Since my friends the Nagases had moved to the

Kansai region after the destruction of the war, I heard almost nothing about that group of friends.

I myself went to Karuizawa to live after I lost my house in the bombings. A year after the end of the war when I returned to Tokyo, I became very ill, and for a year or two after having surgery I struggled to keep going during the hard times, even though I was still not completely well. In those days of rapid change after the war, I might have heard about the death of Ichige Hanshiro and the subsequent collapse of his family business, but it was not until I heard the news of Kashimura's death that I remembered Rie and her husband, whom I had forgotten; I thought at the time that I might write a story with Rie as the central character.

By then I had gained firsthand experience with the extreme situations of life, having gone through a war and a serious illness that had been a matter of life and death. I had lost the naiveté that had made me feel indignant about Hanshiro for having married his retarded son to a girl like Rie, as if it were a privilege of the bourgeois class. Nevertheless, Rie still remained a mystery to me.

When I thought about the story I would write about Rie, I imagined Masatoshi as the young kleptomaniac owner of an old established shop. His wife, ashamed of her husband, had an abortion, but unable to get a divorce, she continued to live with him as the lady of the household. She then fell in love with a young employee and in the end poisoned her husband.

This was all my own fabrication, but since it had been Kashimura's death that prompted me to start writing it, the metamorphosis of the main female character into a malicious woman left a bad taste in my mouth, for this would surely have made Kashimura sad.

Later I thought off and on of writing down just what Kashimura had told me that night, a more lucid account that would convince even me, but the limits of my own imagination simply did not include a woman like Rie. I felt that if I forced myself to write, the character of Rie would end up being like a listless, white cat. Meanwhile the months and days passed, and once again I almost forgot the name Ichige.

Only one or two other passengers, shrugging their shoulders as if they were cold, got off the train with me. The chrysanthemums were still shut in the freight cars, so their penetrating fragrance didn't reach the platform.

I didn't see a taxi in front of the station, so after I called home from a public phone and asked someone to meet me with a flash-light at the corner of a dark field, I started walking alone through the town.

The moon was at its zenith, and the night mist was hanging low under the cloudless sky, spreading its thin gauze net over the pine trees and the firs. I could see the swirling motion of the mist under-neath the street lamps, where the light made a circle. As I walked along, treading on the dark shadows that seemed to permeate the street, my footsteps sounded clear and distinct. Between the stores with their faded shutters I could hear the thin, weak chirping of some insects. It felt like autumn in the mountains.

Now I recalled fondly that I had been riding on a freight train full of chrysanthemums. In those dark, soot-covered cars hundreds and thousands of beautiful flowers were sleeping, in different shades of white, yellow, red, and purple, and in different shapes. Their fragrance was sealed in the cars. Tomorrow they would be in the Tokyo flower market and sold to florists who would display them in front of their shops.

"She's a white chrysanthemum, that's what she is," I said, and wondered the next moment to whom I was speaking. I realized im-mediately, however, that I was addressing the dead Kashimura. The words had come out so effortlessly that I felt vaguely moved.

That evening at O Station I had seen Rie with her husband for the first time, though only for a few minutes. Then by chance I had heard from Kurokawa about her recent life. Twenty years had passed since I had heard about Rie at Nagase's house. After that I had heard Kashimura's brief confession at his farewell party, and after the war I learned of his death. Did Rie know that he had died in the war? It didn't really matter now. I felt that Kashimura wouldn't mind if she was uninterested in his life and death.

Seeing Rie that night and hearing Kurokawa's story didn't add anything new to my image of her. Rie was the same as she had been; I was the skeptical one who hadn't believed she was like that.

Rie's devotion to Masatoshi had seemed absurd to me. I had no reason to say she was a fake, but I simply couldn't accept a way of thinking that was so different from my own. What I mean is that I couldn't accept what she did without imagining that some handi-cap was part of her devotion—she must have been jilted or raped or experienced something to make her unhappy. I even wondered if religion had motivated her, an inclination to follow an authority higher than that of human beings. That was why, when I had intended to write about Rie, I had explored the psychology of a woman who would kill her husband, and who was not at all like Rie. Even though Kashimura had said he had had no difficulty accepting Rie's refusal, I couldn't.

But now I was humbly reaching out to Rie. I wanted to accept the Rie who had lived with Masatoshi as she was and to disregard her background, any misfortunes she had had before her marriage, or any religious inclinations. I wanted to take her hand and say "I understand."

Did this mean that I had grown old? Should I be grateful that I had reached an age when I could accept without explanation the fact that human beings have thoughts and behavior that seem beyond rational comprehension? I felt a sense of joy in thinking of the flat features of Rie's melancholy, middle-aged face as being somehow like the short, dense petals of a modest white chrysanthemum.

The Three Crabs

ŌBA MINAKO

Translated by Yukiko Tanaka and Elizabeth Hanson

Ōba Minako (b. 1930) was the eldest daughter of a Navy doctor who was transferred frequently, and she learned at an early age to occupy herself with reading and writing. Her family was living near Hiroshima when the Second World War ended. She was in the compulsory work program that turned her school into a factory, and she often read books in air-raid shelters. On the day that the atomic bomb fell on Hiroshima, she saw a mushroom-shaped cloud in the distance and later witnessed a mass of people passing by with disfigured faces. This experience, she says, has haunted her and comes back as a recurring image when she writes.

She once considered becoming a stage actress and was involved in acting with a dramatic group when she was in college, but a few years after graduating she married and went to Sitka, Alaska, where her husband had been transferred. Ōba said that she married on the condition that she would be allowed to pursue a career as a writer, and during the eleven years that she lived in the United States she spent several years on university campuses as a student. This experience of living abroad among both her contemporaries and younger people was an important factor in establishing the basic themes of her fiction. When she won the Akutagawa Prize in 1968 for "The Three Crabs," she was living in Sitka and was unknown to the literary world in Japan. She and her family returned to Japan in 1970.

Ōba is a craftswoman with words, and although her style has shifted from the allegorical and fantastic to the realistic, her characters have a cosmopolitan background that gives her stories a sense of exoticism, wit, and sophistication.

"The Three Crabs" is the first of a kind of story that has started to appear more and more frequently in recent Japanese fiction. The main character of such stories is a Japanese person who lives in a foreign city. Although this reflects the fact that Japanese have more firsthand contact with foreign countries, the writer uses the foreign setting not necessarily to create an exotic atmosphere but to convey the sense of freedom, loneliness, and homelessness her characters feel. "The Three Crabs" also treats the sexual adventures of a housewife, another new theme for Japanese writers.

THE SEA LAY SLEEPING in the milky fog, breathing peacefully. The birds in the tall rushes were awake, however, flapping their wings and making a shrill cry that sounded like a piece of metal scraping against glass. A seagull the color of dirty snow turned his marble-hard orange eyes in one direction, then abruptly looked in the other direction, scratching at the sand in an arrogant manner.

As Yuri walked along, the fog seemed to be streaming down around her. She felt some gritty sand that had worked its way through a tear in her stocking, and she flexed her feet to push the sand aside.

The sea was dark purple. A young man with a hunting cap and a canvas bag was standing by the yellow bus-stop sign.

"It's going to be a nice day once the fog clears up." He nodded as he spoke. It was not clear whether he was speaking to Yuri or to himself.

Yuri stared at the sea, which gleamed faintly, as if at the bottom of a milk-colored pot that was filling up with the fog. She pushed aside some of the sand under her sole with her little finger. Looking down, she saw two crabs, one following the other, only seven or eight inches away from her foot. For some reason every time she saw a crab's warped shell, she couldn't help but think of a human face.

The crabs, with two long watery eyes that stuck out from their shells, were crawling as if their legs were entangled, their shells the same dark wisteria color as the sea; they had sharp edges.

"Here comes our bus," the man with the hunting cap said. There were only a few passengers on the bus, the first one that went into the city from the suburbs.

"I wonder why the fog is so thick . . ." The fog flowed around Yuri's neck and shoulders as if it were blowing against them.

"L City, please," she said, unzipping her bag.

"Eighty-five cents," the driver said.

Surprised that she had come so far, she looked for some money but couldn't find enough change. She opened her wallet, thinking there was a twenty-dollar bill inside, but she couldn't find it. The man with the hunting cap was waiting behind her.

"Wait just a minute, I have to sit down and look for some money." She sat down in the seat closest to the driver and began searching in her wallet. The twenty-dollar bill was not there. The twenty-dollar bill she had put in her wallet the night before when she had left home was not there. She always put bills in her wallet and change in her coin purse. There was only sixty-five cents in the coin purse. The man with the hunting cap sat down heavily next to her.

"What's the matter? Did you lose some money?"

"I think so." Yuri groped around in the bottom of her purse for any change that might have fallen there. She found a few more coins, gathered them up and paid the driver.

"Do you stop at the amusement park?"

"Which gate?"

"Near the Opera House."

"Is that the North Gate?"

"I think so," Yuri said, feeling for the car keys in her bag.

"We'll stop near there," the driver and the man with the hunting cap said at the same time.

Yuri began searching through her wallet once again. The twenty-dollar bill was not there, but she found a crumpled dollar bill in a compartment of the bag where she kept various small things. The bill was limp and stained with lipstick.

"The fog sure is thick . . . ," said the man with the hunting cap, addressing neither Yuri nor himself.

Yuri gazed in turn at the dark purple sea sunk in the middle of the fog, and at a neon sign that read "The Three Crabs." The sign looked strangely forlorn in the hazy sun that had just begun to shine.

While Yuri was mixing some cake batter, she felt a faint pain somewhere deep in her stomach. She cracked eggs and stirred them into the butter mechanically, then shook salt and baking powder into the bowl, feeling a faint nausea like morning sickness rising in her throat.

Rie was whipping the cream. She wanted to lick the cream off the beaters when she was done.

"Who's coming, Mommy?" Rie asked, licking the cream off her fingers.

"It doesn't matter. And don't tell Susan or anyone else who's coming," Yuri said, enduring the pain in her stomach.

Rie sniffed, disgusted, rolling up the whites of her eyes.

"Mommy can't tell anyone what she really thinks, you know, so that's why I want to tell you the truth now and then. For instance, I don't like Sasha and I hate baking cakes so much I feel like throwing up, but I make them anyway. But you mustn't tell these things to anyone. When Mommy says something strange, you just listen to it and let it go as Mommy's foolishness. Mommy might be stupid, but you should feel sorry for her too, so you be nice to her once in a while." While she was stirring the batter, Yuri decided she was definitely not going to play bridge that evening.

"You shouldn't say things like that to a child. You're an adult but you don't know how to put up with things," Takeshi said, frowning, as he took a bottle out of the cupboard. "Everyone has to do things they don't like sometimes, Rie."

Rie sniffed and rolled her eyes again.

"I'm sorry, but I have terrible cramps so I can't play bridge tonight. Why don't you invite someone else? I have an idea. Since they'd all feel bad if you told them I was ill, why don't you say I suddenly had to go out? After all, I'm no fun anyway, and I'm a terrible bridge player."

"Whoever heard of a bridge party without a hostess?"

"My sister is stopping over on her way to San Francisco tonight and I'm going to go to see her. How's that? I'll tell them myself."

"Do you really want to cause so much trouble?"

"Trouble? I'm saying this very calmly. I think it's so much more polite to disappear than to pretend to be having a good time. I bet I'll say something stupid or break a plate or something."

"Why do you have to 'pretend'? You're arrogant, and you think you're superior. That's why you think you have to force yourself to be nice to other people."

Yuri held back her tears. "I always know what other people are feeling. That naturally makes me confident, so maybe I seem arrogant. Some people simply can't tell how others feel, or else they ignore it even if they can tell. But I happen to be sensitive, and don't like people who won't respond to me when I open myself up. If I'm being sincere, I get mad at them, so I'd better not even try to start with."

"Do as you damn well please, then," Takeshi said, sipping whiskey and giving Yuri a disgusted look.

"I have an idea—I'll call Keiko. She's intelligent, sexy, pretentious, and loves to be invited to people's houses. She's perfect. She particularly likes to visit a house when the hostess is out."

Rie thought her mother was disgusting when she talked like this and felt sorry for her father. She was only ten but was a precocious child, and could understand most adult conversations.

"Hi, Keiko. I know this is sudden, but could you come over to play bridge tonight? My sister's coming into town and I've got to go see her. If you don't think this would interfere with your studies tomorrow . . . Oh, thanks . . . I really appreciate it. A young lady like you will definitely liven up the party. Thank you so much . . . Yes, that's right. I'll call and ask Mr. Yokota to pick you up. Yes, that's right, we'll have two tables . . ."

After she had made this phone call, Yuri felt relieved and thought she might say something to humor Takeshi.

"I really don't feel well at all. Maybe I've got cancer—or else I'm pregnant," she joked.

Takeshi smiled sarcastically and twisted his lips as he raised his glass to his mouth.

"Congratulations. All's well, then. When's the due date?"

"Twelve months from now."

"Shouldn't we make it nine?"

"How mild-mannered you've become. You know I'm always behind so even twelve months wouldn't be enough."

"Whatever you say, but don't tell lies in front of the child. Like saying your sister's coming from San Francisco . . . Rie knows that's not true."

"Rie is a sensitive and intelligent child, so she knows that telling a harmless lie in order not to hurt others' feelings is not a sin." Yuri began humming a tune.

"Don't sing off-key like that. My ears are sensitive."

"One can't tell a lie in front of the child, but not the truth either. La la la . . . Things like Keiko has sex appeal or that Sasha is Father Baranoff's wife and Papa's girlfriend. And that I . . . am baking a cake for all those guests but putting a curse on them at the same time. I wish ten blackbirds would spring out of this cake. La la la . . ."

"Of course you're right. You can't tell your daughter that you've slept with Mr. Stein, so you're eager to be a go-between for him and Rhonda. There is such a thing as courtesy in our society, in case you didn't know. That is, you don't talk openly about things that everyone knows."

"In front of children you have to tell sweet, pleasant stories. About a beautiful princess and a gallant prince who fell in love and lived in a glass castle, eating the cotton candy of their dreams." She hummed again as she spoke.

"Would you please stop that singing? You may think you're Carmen but to me you sound like you're learning to yodel."

"Oh, wonderful! I'm a shepherdess, living in a cabin in the Swiss Alps." Yuri banged the oven door open and said, "Take a look at this cake. It's made from the finest ingredients, from an unusual recipe no one else knows. If I opened a shop in the Ginza, I'd make a fortune in no time. I have one wish in baking this cake, though— to make Keiko and Sasha as fat as pigs so they'll have heart problems."

"If you want to make them so fat they'll have heart problems, you'll have to spend a fortune as well as make one."

"Why do you have to insist on being so practical?"

"Your stocking has a hole a little above the knee."

"Didn't you tell me once that a hole in the stocking was suggestive?"

"That depends on the woman and the circumstances. You can't just follow the formula."

Feeling better since she had decided not to play bridge, Yuri decided to put on some makeup. She was putting on eyeliner in front of the bathroom mirror when Rie came in and said in a tone that sounded like a school principal's, her hands clasped behind her back, "You want to look young, don't you, Mommy?"

"That's right. All women do."

"But since everyone knows that I'm your daughter, they're not going to believe you're under thirty, for sure "

"Some women have a child at sixteen."

"Those kinds of girls aren't nice."

"What do you think? Do I look like twenty-six?"

"I know how old you are, so I can't pretend that I don't."

"Why do you keep standing there like that? It's not nice to go around criticizing people. People don't like it, particularly if you're a girl."

"I want to use the toilet. That's why I'm waiting."

"I'm not a boy. I'll just look the other way."

"That's okay. I'll go later." Rie walked out with a toss of her head.

The way Rie looked at her almost always made Yuri think of her own mother. She then recalled that she herself had once looked at her own mother in the same way.

Yuri put on her favorite blue-green dress with a boat neckline, and a long necklace made of brushed silver. The chain, made by riveting together pieces of silver in abstract shapes, had been a birthday present from a boyfriend three years ago; she still thought fondly of him. The pieces of silver had been rounded off like coral, and the craftsman had molded them into various shapes using a torch. He had oxidized the silver and then polished it in places so that it shone brightly.

Takeshi was lying on the sofa in the living room where the bridge tables were arranged. He was leafing through a magazine a student from Japan had brought him.

"The coffee, tea, and cake are all ready to serve, dear. You'll mix the cocktails yourself, won't you? I've put out three kinds of glasses—for martinis, old-fashioneds, and soft drinks. The napkins are in the usual box."

"Sometimes you look very pretty, you know." Takeshi said, glancing at Yuri as he held the magazine with its picture of a nude woman high above him. "Why don't you stay and chat with the guests for a while since you took the trouble to look so nice? Besides, I'm not as good at lying as you are, so I want you to explain things to the guests yourself."

"There may not be enough olives, but if there aren't, I think it will be all right without them. Use vodka if you run out of gin."

The doorbell rang.

"They're here."

"Will you please put that magazine with nude pictures away? People notice Japanese magazines right away since they're unusual around here, and then they start leafing through them . . ."

"I'm not going to pretend I'm above such things. Every country has magazines like this. Everyone likes to look at them."

"You can look at them at a stag party."

"Women enjoy being looked at, too."

Yuri opened the door. It was Frank Stein, wearing a corduroy jacket and suede boots.

"I came casual like this since you told me to, but you're dressed up, Yuri."

"Well, I have a bit of a problem. My sister just called and said she'd be stopping over for a few hours on her way home this evening, so I'm going out to see her. Will you excuse me?"

"Oh, I see. But don't you want to invite her here?"

"No, she's with someone else and will only be at the airport for a few hours to change planes."

"You don't have to go, do you, Takeshi?"

"I'd rather play bridge. Besides, for some reason I win like mad when my wife isn't around."

"So that's how it is," Yuri said. "Come and sit down, please. I'm not in such a hurry. I'll stay and chat for a while."

Frank looked at Yuri as if he were challenging her and said, "Too bad you have to go since Rhonda is coming."

"Yes, Takeshi feels the same way, since Sasha is coming," Yuri replied curtly.

"But the priest is coming with her, isn't he?" Frank asked.

"They say it's popular among veterans to bring back a part of a Vietcong's body as a souvenir. Is that true?" Takeshi said, pretending he hadn't heard the exchange between Yuri and Frank.

"Is that right?" Frank asked. "I can believe it, though. War is always like that. Men can fulfill their dreams of killing and raping without being sent to the electric chair. But Takeshi, I have to warn you before the other people get here. No one says what they really think about the Vietnam War at a party. So let's not play guessing games with each other. The Japanese will spit on the Americans and look the other way, and the Americans will pull back into their shells like oysters in front of other Americans. Father Baranoff is probably the only one who thinks a party is a good chance to make a big speech. Whatever he might think secretly, he has God on his side . . . God is certainly convenient for a priest. When he insists that killing is against God's will, no one opposes him. It's so easy. No other reasons are allowed. I bet he'll get pompous and give a long, snooty speech, twitching his nose. And Sasha will listen to him, pretending that she agrees, but actually thinking how ridiculous he had acted in bed. 'I hate all wars,' she'll say, taking advantage of the woman's right to be irrational. It's a way of showing courtesy.

"Even the faculty at the university," Frank continued. "Half of them are supporting the war, two-thirds of the other half are ignoring it. Only a small minority actually protest, and they end up sounding like an ugly, bitchy girl who enjoys finding faults in men. The majority just don't care. If you're drafted, all you can do is try to avoid the bullets."

"What puzzles me is why you Americans keep insisting that you have to withdraw from Vietnam with dignity and honor, as if nothing else matters. You laugh at the affectations of silly old Englishmen, but you yourself can't get rid of the dandyism of the characters in a Western movie," Yuri said.

"Americans include stubborn Southern gentlemen, arrogant Western outlaws, jealous Northerners, and egotistical Easterners; I happen to be a cosmopolite. But you are gypsies and don't have roots anywhere, although you claim to be Japanese," Frank said.

"That's why we can sing so beautifully," Yuri said. "Everyone who comes here—Sasha and the Yokotas—can sing, more or less."

"You shouldn't be so sure about the others," Frank said decisively and gave Yuri a piercing look.

"I'm surprised. Someone told me that now we foreigners are going to be drafted. The classification is 4-C," Takeshi said.

"That's news to me. I'm 5-A, myself."

"You wouldn't be satisfied with anything but an A and a 5, would you, Frank?" Yuri said.

"It's because I was already drafted once. During the Korean War."

"What nerve, not being married and having a 5-A."

"I have two children."

"Are you supporting them?" Takeshi sneered.

"Of course, I have a strong sense of fatherly love."

"Well, they say if people start talking about the presidential election or Vietnam, the party will be finished,' Yuri said.

"If you talk in sophisticated obscenities, the party will last until morning," Takeshi said.

"I'll bring up the subject of Vietnam for you if you signal me," Frank said.

"How is Rhonda? She's been getting prettier recently," Takeshi said, remembering his role of host.

"How about me? Don't you think I look sexier?" Frank asked, extending his arms to show off his corduroy jacket.

"I didn't notice, since you've always been sexy," Yuri said curtly.

"Hmmm. Is that so. I don't remember your treating me that way."

"You forget things easily, but I have a relatively good memory."

"My wife has become quite sociable lately," Takeshi said and laughed. Yuri sensed a touch of cynicism in her husband's laughter.

"Yuri, I would be pleased if I thought you had a good memory. Being of a poetic nature, I like romantic stories . . ."

Yuri tried to recall the time she had slept with Frank but could not. In any event, he hadn't seemed like a romance-loving poet then.

"Poetic? You? Don't make me laugh. You are definitely prosaic. You have the objectivity of a historian who serves a prosperous emperor," Takeshi said.

"A man has a right to state his wishes. I've always wanted to be poetic."

"I see. That's a different story. How about you, madam? You used to be quite a poet yourself," Takeshi said as he looked at Yuri, then went to the kitchen to fill the glasses.

"You do love Takeshi after all, and he's in love with you," Frank said.

"If that's the way you see it, it must be true. After all, you do have the objectivity of the emperor's historian."

"Come on, don't be like that. A husband and a wife should have their separate spaces and conversations with themselves. Otherwise life is too empty. I decided to get divorced when I realized that I had been forced constantly into meaningless conversations with my wife, and I felt in danger of losing my own words."

Takeshi came back and handed Frank a martini. "Did I come back too soon for you to make a pass?"

"No, there was enough time," Frank said.

"You came back a bit too soon," Yuri said as if she were disappointed.

"By the way, Takeshi, the conference this year is in A City. I'm going to take several days off to go see one of my kids after the meeting," Frank said, returning to the subject of children.

"Which one?"

"The older one. He is already nine and has started making rather caustic remarks."

"I know what you mean. I tend to be more careful in front of my daughter than I am my wife. My wife makes me listen to her, but she herself listens more carefully to her daughter than she does to me."

"I can see that. Rie is a clever girl, and she's been looking rather pretty lately. You must worry about her."

"Particularly about men like you."

"I've been perfectly respectable lately."

"Yuri has been complaining about stomach trouble lately, and I'm wondering if she's pregnant."

Frank stared at Yuri's lower abdomen. "In the twentieth century, pregnancy is not a symbol of fertility but of sterility and destruction, you know. In American literature this has been so since Faulkner, or maybe since Hawthorne."

"I see. But that seems to be the case in any modern civilization. In our home, however, it's a symbol of peace, I'd say," Takeshi said.

Yuri winked at Frank, who said, "Isn't it a sign of a coming revolution in your case, since your family is living a century ahead of the rest of us?"

"I don't see any sign of such unrest so far," Takeshi said.

Frank turned to Yuri. "By the way, you're not going to see your lover, are you, Yuri?"

"I could have arranged it."

"Don't give her any strange ideas," Takeshi said.

"Don't you worry about her sometimes?" Frank said.

"It all depends on what mood I'm in. We all have moments when we feel strangely light-hearted. Besides, I have to flatter my wife once in a while, particularly at a time like this when she has baked a cake with as much enthusiasm as if she were poisoning the guests."

"Don't you feel like consoling me, Frank? A woman who's being treated like this by her husband?"

"Yes, I do."

"Go right ahead," Takeshi said. "But I can't let both of you go tonight, since we need a certain number of people to play bridge. Try some other time."

"Rhonda said she'll be ten minutes late or so," Frank said, changing the subject.

"How many times did you see her last week?" Takeshi asked.

"Once. She's a possessive woman, and if you don't watch out, you might lose her." Frank said this so that Yuri would hear. She glanced at Takeshi, running her lips over her chain, and said, "I know for a fact that she had dinner with that engineer from Chicago last week. She had him up to her apartment, but unfortunately no one knows what time he left."

"Hmmm. I should have had a date with Sasha or Keiko, then," Frank said, looking at Yuri's chain.

"That's right, you should have. Keiko isn't much fun since she's a self-conscious type, but you'd have a good time with Sasha," Takeshi said and looked at Yuri.

"Don't you two forget that there will be ladies at the party tonight," she said.

Frank grinned. "This is between the two of us. Yuri is Takeshi's wife."

"That seems to be the case," Takeshi said.

The bell rang, and Yuri and Takeshi hurried to the door. It was Mr. and Mrs. Yokota. Beside them was Keiko Matsumura.

"Welcome, please come in. It's finally gotten cool, hasn't it? What a pretty color your dress is, Mrs. Yokota—the color of sunflowers. It's gorgeous. Keiko, you look very chic tonight," Yuri said.

"You ought to let men pay the compliments. Women don't appreciate flattery from other women," Takeshi said.

"Yuri isn't like you, Takeshi," Frank said. "She's polite enough even when she's jealous of her husband. She tries to hide his charm."

"Good evening, everyone. It's been hot, hasn't it?" Yokota said. His thin, wispy hair had been blown by the wind and was plastered on his forehead, revealing a bald spot that you could see even if you looked at him from the front.

"Why don't you comb your hair, dear?" his beaming wife said. She considered herself too attractive for her husband, but she still wanted to keep people from seeing his bald spot.

Keiko went to sit beside Frank. She never sat next to women.

"How is your thesis coming?" Frank asked her.

"The typing is all I have to do now, but since I'm doing it myself, I keep wanting to change sentences here and there."

Mrs. Yokota gave Keiko a hateful look. Although she knew how to dress in bright colors, she didn't know how to talk to men the way Keiko did.

"I've read your article on Faulkner in T Journal. Yuri has told me for some time that you are quite a cynic. I thought your style of writing was very nice," Keiko said. Mrs. Yokota's eyes flashed again. She was proud of her big eyes with their long eyelashes but not of her mouth with its slightly protruding front teeth. She had to constantly make sure that her lips covered her teeth. Keiko, on the other hand, had a pouty lower lip, and her tongue was a bit too long, making her speech somewhat babyish. When she found out that men liked this, however, she became more talkative.

"I heard Mr. Stein's 'American Literature of the Thirties' is very popular among the students," Keiko said.

The bell rang. Takeshi and Yuri went to the door. It was Father Baranoff and Sasha, who was wearing black fish-net stockings and a black satin Chinese dress embroidered with peonies.

"Well, you're all dressed up, Sasha. I feel like I'm in a box in an opera house," Frank, in his corduroy jacket, said.

"Oh, no, this is only my nightgown," Sasha said, taking a deep breath as if she were going to sing an aria.

"Well, well . . . ," Frank grinned.

Mr. Yokota, his hair neatly combed back, cleared his throat as he lifted his head a bit. He was sensitive to erotic suggestions.

"Sasha, would you mind teaching Yuri how to sing the part where Carmen scolds José—the one that goes like this . . ." Takeshi hummed a few notes. "It seems to me my wife's out of tune by a quarter of a note."

"Takeshi, you ought to realize that insulting your wife in public can affect the amount of alimony," Yuri said solemnly.

"What happens when the husband doesn't mean to be insulting? I'd like to know, just in case," Yokota asked.

"Ignorance has always been considered a crime," Frank said.

"What happens if the husband has no intention of divorce?" Takeshi said.

"That'll give the wife grounds to divorce him," Frank said.

"But when we go to divorce court—supposing we do—it won't be in America. The laws still favor men in Japan."

"Men get a better deal here, too," Sasha said.

"But if it's no worse than this, I can stand it," Mrs. Yokota said, acting modestly coquettish. Father Baranoff's eyes shone lustily. Sasha looked at Mrs. Yokota condescendingly. Sasha's coarse skin was oily and bumpy, reminding Yuri of a grapefruit rind.

"Did you take your case to court when you got a divorce?" Keiko asked.

"No. I didn't have the money to hire a lawyer."

"But you had the money to pay your wife alimony, obviously," Yokota said, showing considerable interest.

"No, I was the one who was cuckolded."

"I see. That was lucky," Yokota said politely.

"Your martini's going to spill, dear," Mrs. Yokota graciously warned her husband, smiling so that wrinkles appeared around her nose. Yuri thought the wrinkles made the woman in the bright, sunflower-colored dress look shabby. They also gave a feeling of femininity to this woman, whose laugh was like the cooing of a pigeon. In another forty years that cooing will sound like the screeching of a monkey, Yuri thought. She sensed in Mrs. Yokota the coquetry women often have and that she had herself. It was so transparent and obvious—the same meager plans for the future, the same frivolous longings devoid of passion . . . Yuri felt dizzy with nausea at the thought. Unless her liver or some other organ that produced it was removed, she could not get rid of the poison that caused the nausea, since it was made somewhere inside her body.

"You seem preoccupied, Yuri, as if you were sitting on top of a cloud," Frank said.

"Why yes. I am actually floating above the clouds."

The bell rang. "It's Rhonda," Takeshi said and went to the door.

She was wearing a black dress and carrying a bouquet. She hugged Yuri and pressed a cheek against hers.

"You are beautiful, Rhonda. Like a forest nymph that appears at night," Takeshi said.

"Thank you. You look charming, as usual." She kissed Takeshi's cheek. "And Frank, you have that I-am-the-wisest-man-on-earth look." She blew him a kiss.

"The loneliness of the genius is sort of an incurable illness, don't you think, Father?" Yokota asked.

"You might say that," the priest replied. He was drinking vodka straight. The tip of his nose was as red as a cherry.

"By the way, how would medicine or physics explain a person who cannot be hypnotized?" Frank asked, looking at Takeshi and Yokota in turn.

"Well, since my field is gynecology . . . ," Takeshi said.

"Then you should be all the more interested. How do you treat women who cannot be hypnotized?"

"We physicians are rather careful when our friends seem to be trying to get a free consultation."

"I see. How about physicists? Do you talk only when you read papers at a meeting?" Frank turned to Yokota.

"I try not to tax my brain by thinking about things unrelated to my own field," Yokota said in a gloomy voice. Sasha, sitting next to Father Baranoff, laughed aloud.

"Public toilets can be cleaner than the one at home," Frank thought, looking at Sasha. "Sometimes I feel all my sexual drive is gone," Takeshi thought, looking from Sasha to Rhonda to Mrs. Yokota and Keiko. "Why does she have to stick her stomach out like that?" Yuri thought, looking at Keiko. When her eyes met Takeshi's, Yuri moved her body closer to Yokota and whispered to him in Japanese while giving Mrs. Yokota a sincere, pleasant smile.

"Mr. Yokota, you are a true poet. Frank is a Faulkner scholar but he's not as poetic as you are," Yuri said. She felt something like a yawn bubbling up from the bottom of her stomach along with the meaningless words she had just spoken. "I wonder how much easier my life would be if I weren't so sensitive to gentlemen's charms," she continued nevertheless.

"I heard Sasha is going to be giving a recital next Saturday," Yokota said, ignoring what Yuri had just said.

"My husband will go, I'm sure," Yuri said, looking at Sasha's thick lips and her throat, which was moving grotesquely like a frog's.

"This recital is going to be a casual one. She's going to sing quite a few Russian folk songs," Father Baranoff said, as if he were her manager.

"But you'll sing Carmen too, won't you?" Takeshi asked, moving closer to Sasha.

"Well, that's her best," the priest said in a voice that reminded one of a partially deflated ball being squashed.

Takeshi and Frank had the same peculiar grin on their faces, and they looked at the priest out of the corners of their eyes. Yokota was drinking in silence, staring at the ceiling like a pond snail in the mud, but no doubt he did not miss a thing.

"I heard you play the bamboo flute very well," Takeshi said to Yokota.

"Eh? Did you say something to me?" Yokota said in a high-pitched voice, but it was not possible that he had missed a remark like that.

"I'd like to hear you play sometime," Frank said.

"You must be making a mistake," Yokota said curtly.

"His wife is a good koto player," said Keiko, who rarely paid women compliments.

"Anyway, where did you find this Chinese dress?" Takeshi asked Sasha.

"I lived in China for ten years. In Shanghai and Peking."

"Did you sing on the stage then?"

"Yes. I sang at churches, too."

"Were there attractive priests like Father Baranoff in those churches?"

"All men are attractive to women in their own way," Sasha said, laughing and shaking her broad hips.

"You men are all charming to us. Don't you agree, Keiko? And we women remain a mystery to you. Don't we, Takeshi? Even my feelings about men are so tangled up that I can't control them or make any sense out of them, either."

"A church wouldn't be so bad if I could find a charming woman like you there. The hymns must have been captivating," Takeshi said and whispered something in Sasha's ear, then slowly turned toward Yuri.

"Rhonda, you should stop imitating this pop art stuff that's popular now. You could teach at a university, if you wanted to. You should apply yourself to more serious work," Frank said.

"Oh Frank, are you telling me to be more serious? I must have fallen as far as I can go."

"You are so confident in yourself that you're stubborn."

"You only think so because you're confident yourself," Takeshi said quickly over his shoulder to Frank, still keeping his attention on Sasha.

"When I painted a serene, elegant picture, Frank said it was like an illustration for a girls' book," Rhonda said and sighed.

"Mr. Yokota, why are you so quiet?" Yuri whispered softly in his ear, taking care that her lips wouldn't brush his earlobe. She looked at his wife with the smile of a doting mother. Mrs. Yokota looked back at Yuri with the clear eyes of a fairy, and then leaned toward the priest, laughing with the coos of a pigeon.

Sasha sang the gypsy's song from *Carmen* for Takeshi.

"My goodness, it's time for me to go," Yuri said and gave a lengthy excuse. Mrs. Yokota looked unhappy, Keiko was indifferent, and Frank and Yokota looked sympathetic. Only Rhonda followed her to the door.

"I'm sorry you have to go, Yuri. I'll serve coffee for you. Say hello to your sister," Rhonda said. Following Yuri to the car, she then whispered, "I'm going to Chicago tomorrow. Maybe I'll stay with the engineer . . ."

"You should do what you want to. You are still young and you don't have to try to catch a man. You have your own life, which isn't going to be easily disturbed by others. You ought to do whatever you like and enjoy yourself. But Rhonda, love is treacherous. You won't be satisfied if your man is only gentle and kind, but if he's the clinging type, he'll become a burden to you."

"A relationship between a man and a woman can develop in unexpected ways for the smallest reasons, or it can be over after a single collision. You may see me when I come back next week looking like a naive, brokenhearted girl. Or I may come back in a stylish new dress, looking both fulfilled and melancholy. Isn't that the way it is, Yuri, at our age? But perhaps Frank is just right for me . . . as a lover."

"Is it true, Rhonda, that after you've divorced you're attracted to men who are different from your ex-husband?"

"I don't know about that. That's not all there is to it. Once a man and a woman start hurting each other, the damage only becomes worse as you try to do something about it. Just like trying to pull out a thorn that's stuck in your finger. And in the end, the only thing left is a bitter aftertaste."

"You sound as though you still love your ex-husband."

"That doesn't mean that I'm not attracted to other men as well."

"Rhonda, men are cautious, you know, and calculating. As much as we women are. So when you are certain that you can see through them, they know what you're thinking too."

"I agree, but I'm going to go to Chicago anyway. Besides, there's someone there who'll buy some of my paintings."

"Why are you intentionally telling me this? You have your own life. Even if you did fly from Chicago to Paris and had a good time for a week, your life would still be here, just as it was—your two children, your job as a teacher, and Frank too."

Yuri started the engine.

"I feel lonely, Yuri. Don't you understand? I'm lonely, that's the problem."

"You can't help it, I know. One has to live with it, I guess. Well Rhonda, so long . . . Have fun." Yuri turned the wheel.

She drove the car slowly for a while, but when she realized that she was holding up several cars behind her, she accelerated. Fortunately she had to stop at a red light at the next intersection, so she had time to think about where to go, but she couldn't come up with an idea. She saw the monorail entrance ahead and decided to go to the amusement park. She didn't care where she went. This would be better than going to a movie. After she had made up her mind, she felt better and started to concentrate on finding a place to park. She parked the car in the lot next to the north entrance of the Opera House.

Yuri stood in front of the Opera House and gazed at a poster advertising *Swan Lake*. Next to it was another poster for an exhibit of crafts by Alaskan Indians. Not knowing where to go, she started walking toward the Exhibition Hall. As she walked, she yawned; instead of trying to suppress it, she opened her mouth wide as if breathing in the fresh air.

It was after nine, so there were hardly any children in the amusement park. Lovers, hand in hand and with blissful expressions, were watching the neon-lit rides. Yuri stood by the pond with motorboat races and watched the lovers in the boats as they gazed at the splashing water as if in a daze.

Yuri stopped again by the entrance to the exhibit of Alaskan crafts and stood there for a while, looking up at an airplane ride circling around a tower. Though she had no particular interest in Alaskan Indian crafts, she went into the exhibit anyway.

The Exhibition Hall was deserted, and in the empty, dimly lit room Yuri felt as if the head ornaments were supernatural beings glaring at her. The ornaments were in the shape of animals' faces and heads, but they didn't look like masks or hats. One ornament looked like a crow with large, slanted, human-like eyes. Its long beak extended from the forehead, and a part of the red tongue showed between the slightly opened beak. It looked real, like that of a live bird. At the back of the head there was a lock of human hair—it seemed to be a woman's black hair. The crow's head ornament was made of wood and was carved with simple lines that made abstract patterns. Even though they were painted with strong primary colors of red, yellow, green, and black, these had a certain subdued harmony, created by the natural dyes or the passage of time. Strangely enough, the ornament did not look like a real crow when each part—the beak, the eyes, the front and the back of the head—was seen separately. Even though the eyes were abstract, they looked like those of a human being or perhaps like the wide-open eyes of a man. As a whole, the face represented a certain life force that was a combination of a human being and a crow. The primitive people had a certain sense of affinity with the natural world—grass, mountains, valleys, and animals—and had a reverent belief in their ability to communicate with nature that was close to religion. Among the exhibits were headdresses in the shape of frogs and eagles, an ash-brown mask made of driftwood with grinning mouth and eyes on its flat surface, an object like a baby's rattle that might have been used by sorcerers, an instrument engraved with pictures of a family history that resembled a totem pole, vessels and boats with carvings of animals, and blankets woven from animal fur.

In the dim room Yuri thought she heard someone softly mumbling what sounded like both a prayer and a curse. A bored-looking man in a pink shirt was sitting near the entrance.

"I have to close soon," the man said. He seemed to have been waiting for Yuri to finish looking and leave.

As she turned around suddenly she lost her balance and nearly fell. Pink Shirt rushed over to her and grabbed her to keep her from falling.

"Oh, thank you," Yuri said, blushing. "I have such poor motor coordination I often fall. It irritates my husband. He doesn't like to see his wife fall down in front of other people. Thanks to you, I didn't have to fall and embarrass myself. Thank you very much. Well, good-bye." Yuri started to walk away.

"Wait a minute, there's something sticking to the heel of your shoe. You'd better take it off before you slip again," Pink Shirt said.

Yuri turned her shoe up so that she could see the heel, leaning on the sofa to balance herself.

"Not that side, the left."

The heel of her left shoe was worn out and a strip of leather was dangling from it. The strip was almost two inches long, and when she pulled at it, the leather continued to come off until the wooden base of the heel appeared.

"Nothing's sticking. It's part of the shoe, some worn-out leather," Yuri said indignantly. "Well, that's that. These are old shoes. If I pull any more, all the leather will come off," Yuri said, looking glum.

"I have a knife here," Pink Shirt said, taking a knife out of his pocket and cutting the leather strip off.

"Thank you very much. You're very kind," Yuri said. There was a tinge of irony in her voice.

"That's all right." An ambiguous smile appeared on Pink Shirt's face.

Yuri left the Exhibition Hall, but since she couldn't think of any place else to go, she leaned against the door and stared at the neon-lit fountain. There was a large elm tree by the fountain and underneath it she saw a stone bench. Just as she was thinking she would go and sit down on it, some lovers came and took it.

The lights of the Exhibition Hall went out and Pink Shirt emerged. Having given up the idea of sitting on the occupied bench, Yuri started walking and almost bumped into him since she wasn't watching where she was going.

"Oh, you're still here," Pink Shirt said, grabbing Yuri's arm. "You left your purse on the sofa." He had Yuri's bag. "This is interesting leatherwork. Is it from your country?" Pink Shirt held up the bag, which was decorated with a design of seaweed and fish. "I was going to take this to the Lost and Found office." He handed it to her.

"Sorry," she said, surprised. She realized only then that she wasn't holding anything. When she had tried to pull the leather strip off her shoe, she must have put her bag down on the sofa. "I'm really absentminded."

Near the Exhibition Hall were several game stands; the prizes of clowns, stuffed tomcats, and elephants were jumping up and down on a platform fixed with springs. Next to this was a stand with large glass fountain jars of orange and grape pop. Yuri smelled coffee.

"Let's have a cup of coffee," Pink Shirt invited Yuri, who neither followed him nor turned away. He jingled some coins in his pocket, then started to walk toward the fountain. "You'd better wake your-self up with some coffee. You look like you're up in the clouds," Pink Shirt called to her from the stand, holding out a paper cup of hot coffee.

Pink Shirt put the cup in Yuri's hand. He had coarse black hair that was mixed with some silver-gray, and his eyes were greenish blue.

"I am one quarter Eskimo, one quarter Tlingit, one quarter Swed-ish, and one quarter Polish." Pink Shirt said, introducing himself and his ancestry. His face looked young in spite of the gray hair. This is what they call prematurely gray, Yuri thought.

"Don't you smoke?"

"I have throat cancer," Yuri said, shaking her head.

"That's too bad. They'll discover some cure soon, if you can hold on a bit longer . . ."

"I don't think I have even one-sixteenth non-Japanese blood in me, but long, long ago there might have been a bit of Eskimo blood in my lineage."

"Sure, that's possible. Alaska and Siberia were connected and you could walk from one to the other over the ice. The northern tip of Japan was part of the continent."

"That might have been."

Pink Shirt undid the top button of his shirt and shook his head, as if he were hot.

"Do you like pink shirts?" Yuri asked.

"Not particularly. My wife bought this for me," Pink Shirt said.

"It's a pretty color," Yuri said, glancing at the wedding ring on his finger.

"Is it hard work, being a housewife?"

"Well, it's probably about the same as being a husband."

"There isn't any easy job, then," Pink Shirt said.

"It seems that way," Yuri agreed, then said, looking at her watch, "I have to go now."

"Going back to your husband?"

"I guess so," Yuri said and started to walk away.

As she walked along she sensed that the man was right behind her, but she didn't feel like trying to get rid of him. There were still plenty of people in the amusement park on a Friday night. She ab-sentmindedly watched a teenage couple as they shrieked and hugged each other, spinning around and around in a ride that was called "The Mad Hatter's Tea Party." The girl's miniskirt was blown up and her flax-colored hair was twisted around the boy's wrist. Circus music was playing and the air smelled of hamburgers frying. She went toward the roller coaster. Many years ago, before she was married, she had gone to an amusement park in Tokyo with Takeshi. They had waited in a long line for their turn to ride on the roller coaster; Yuri recalled that they finally had given up and had gone to the garden in the park.

The entrance to the monorail was right next to the roller coaster. Yuri glanced in that direction; the inside of the monorail was lit with a pale purple light. She watched the men and women shrieking on the roller coaster. It was so late there were no children about. She thought she might buy a ticket for the roller coaster.

"Want to take a ride?" Pink Shirt asked. Yuri nodded. She was not used to finding a man right there next to her every time she turned around.

Pink Shirt put his arm around Yuri's shoulder and handed her a ticket for the roller coaster.

"I'm scared. I might not be able to take it," she said.

"Have you tried it before?" Pink Shirt asked. He had put a tweed jacket over his pink shirt.

"No."

"You'll be all right. You hold onto me."

Yuri thought of the long line of people who had been waiting for the roller coaster in Tokyo . . . "Let's give up. It'll take another hour or so." As she had said this to Takeshi, she had seen disappointment cloud his face. "Because I might get sick," she had added, and had seen another change in his expression. "I'm scared," she had said finally, and then his expression had softened. She had felt weary with her own sensitivity and the way she responded to the faintest changes in her lover's mood . . .

Yuri did not feel like looking at Pink Shirt's face. She remained silent while he whispered something in her ear. "It's really fun. It'll make you wonder what's going to happen next and that's the best part," the man said and squeezed her shoulder.

With the sound of a whistle the roller coaster started moving. At first it wasn't bad, but soon they came to a steep slope and plunged down into a valley at full speed; she thought they were going to crash, but the next moment they rounded a sharp turn, making her feel as if she were being thrown out of her seat. Pink Shirt put his arm around her hip and held her tight, pressing with his fingers. She leaned against the man's shoulder. As they went forward and backward she let her body be thrown about like a cat being flung around in the air. The dark night whirled above and around her; it seemed to have become a deeper color of blue. The street lights flowed around her like twinkling stars. Occasionally she gave a small cry in a low voice but she was neither excited nor terrified enough to scream. She felt as alone as a cat being flung around in the air.

Pink Shirt was holding her tight. When the roller coaster stopped, Yuri found her face buried in the man's shirt. He pulled her to her feet, still holding her, and looked into her face.

"Are you all right?"

Yuri nodded and started to walk. The air was cool and clear. The man stopped for a moment to light a cigarette.

"You were huddled there like a dead bird," he said. He was tall and slightly stooped. "Want to try another ride?" he asked, looking down at Yuri. She shook her head.

"Want something to eat?"

Yuri shook her head.

"Something to drink?"

She shook her head.

"A cigarette?"

She shook her head.

"You don't want anything to eat or drink and you don't smoke. So what do you want to do? Want to go dancing?"

"What kind of dancing?"

"Fast dancing."

"I don't know how to fast dance. I'm an old-fashioned woman and too old to do that new kind of dance."

"You can slow dance. I know how to slow dance a little. It's just like walking. Let's go and dance."

"Well . . ." Yuri thought for a moment. While she was thinking, they walked toward the fountain, holding hands. The water was spouting gorgeously like fireworks illuminated with a blue light. Someone had left a white handkerchief, a man's handkerchief, on the stone bench under the elm tree.

"Let's go dancing," Pink Shirt said.

"Well . . ." she said and sat down on the handkerchief. She heard some music—Debussy, perhaps. Apparently there was a speaker installed somewhere near the fountain.

"Is it Beethoven?" Pink Shirt asked.

"I don't know," she said, staring at the water splashing in the fountain. "It probably is . . ."

Ten people or so came out of the Opera House, dressed up. Since it was too early for the performance to be over, it must have been the intermission. Men in dark suits leaned over bare-shouldered women, as if to hide them, whispering.

"There was a concert, I guess."

"Looks like it," Yuri said.

"The only music I can understand is jazz. I hate opera most of all. When I hear it my throat always tickles and I have to yawn."

"It does tire you out," Yuri said.

"Let's go dancing," Pink Shirt said and pulled Yuri up by the hand. She turned toward the parking lot and stepped back.

"You don't want to?"

"That's not it . . . Is the dance hall near here? I have my car parked over there."

"I'll take you back to your car." They began walking.

"I don't mind going if it's within walking distance," Yuri said.

"There's one near here, but we can drive somewhere if you want."

"Let's go to a place here in the park. It's too much trouble to drive somewhere."

"But you don't have to do a thing. You just come with me."

Yuri stopped walking.

"All right. Let's go to a place here in the park," he said.

They started walking toward the rock 'n' roll music.

Pink Shirt ordered beer for them. Yuri brought her glass to her lips and looked at the dancers through the glass. It seemed so easy that anyone could do it. All you have to do is move your body to the rhythm, she thought.

"Let's dance," Pink Shirt said. Yuri put her glass down and stood up. She moved her body any way she wished in the man's arms. After a while they pulled apart and started to move freely. Although the dancing couples looked as if they were moving independently, they were obviously taking their partner's movements into consideration. Still, this kind of dancing seemed to give the dancers more freedom to be creative than the old social dances. By the time the first set of music had ended, Yuri felt much more relaxed.

"Let's dance the next one, too," Pink Shirt said when the music had stopped, making no move to return to their table. They danced the next three numbers. One of the pieces was a jitterbug. Yuri preferred to dance on her own; in fact she did her own dance, enjoying herself, even though she pretended to be following her partner.

"Why don't you wear a miniskirt?" Pink Shirt asked when they returned to their seats.

"Because my legs aren't very good-looking," Yuri said curtly.

"That's not true," the man said, bending over to take a look at her legs.

"Don't do that, silly." Yuri pulled Pink Shirt's ear. He hugged her, laughing, and kissed her beside the ear. They sat there without saying anything and drank beer. Yuri sipped her beer slowly as if she were drinking brandy.

When the music changed to a slow tune, Pink Shirt stood up to indicate that he wanted to dance, and he walked around, holding her close. Yuri was tired and occasionally she would push Pink Shirt away from her. She recalled a time long ago when she had wanted to dance well with Takeshi; she remembered that she had been nervous and had held her body rigid, trying not to make a wrong step.

Pink Shirt was smiling at her gently. Yuri smiled back. They were merely walking, having given themselves to the music as though they were on top of a drifting cloud.

"You are light as a feather. You'd float away if I didn't hold onto you," Pink Shirt said.

They returned to their seats and drank the rest of their beer. Yuri took her time drinking as before, thinking it was the best way to decline when the man offered another beer.

"Let's take a drive somewhere," Pink Shirt said.

"Hmmm . . ." Yuri stared at the man's hand, which he had placed on top of hers.

Pink Shirt stood up. They walked slowly toward the exit of the park. Men and women were shrieking in The Mad Hatter's Tea Party and clutching each other. Yuri glanced at her watch. It was eleven. They wouldn't have finished playing bridge yet. Pink Shirt's car was an old Chevy that made a noise like a cart going up a mountain road. When it came to a stop, it sounded like a steam locomotive.

"Where shall we go?" Pink Shirt asked. As he spoke, he turned the car into the street. Yuri saw a drunken couple stepping out of a neon-lit club called The Flamingo. A black man, leaning against a post with his hands in his pockets, was watching them.

"Why are you so quiet?" Pink Shirt asked.

"Why? . . . I don't have anything to say," Yuri said, leaning her shoulder against the door.

"You can come and sit closer to me. You're strange," Pink Shirt said. "I like a woman who talks a lot."

"Why don't you look for one, then? Let me off here."

"That's not what I meant. Don't get upset."

"I'm not upset. But I really have nothing to talk about."

The street became darker; they had apparently left the town.

"Let's go to the beach," Pink Shirt said. They didn't speak for a long time. "You like the ocean?" Pink Shirt asked.

"Sometimes I like it, sometimes it scares me." When she opened the window, she could smell the sea.

"Can you hear the sound of the waves?" Pink Shirt asked.

Yuri nodded. She could tell that they were near a beach where tall rushes were growing. The sea was as quiet as a misty lake; it shone softly.

"This is an inlet," the man said, resting his chin on the steering wheel.

Suddenly Yuri was reminded of a girlfriend who had lips like ripe strawberries. The friend, whose name was A, had chapped lips that were always cracked in places, with blood oozing from them. Her skin was always broken out.

"I look unclean," A used to say, a discouraged, gloomy look in her eyes. But she had long, slender, beautiful fingers that gave an impression of purity. She would rest her chin on her hands, covering her pimply skin with her beautiful fingers.

"Why don't we drive somewhere far away?" Pink Shirt said, pulling Yuri closer to him. Holding her around her hips, he kissed her, then began to grope between her thighs with his free hand.

Yuri and A had once swum in the dark sea just before daybreak. It had been near the sand dunes of the Japan Sea coast, and the farmers had brought their oxen to the shore on the hottest days of the summer. In those days some farmers still used oxen in the fields. Behind the dunes silverberry bushes spread out, just like in the song that went, "The sea is rough / Yonder is Sado Island / Let's go home through the silverberry bushes . . ." In their bare feet, Yuri and A had walked through red pines and black acacias, then through the silverberries. They had swum in the pitch-black sea. The dark waves had been eerie, with the mysterious depth of some monster's mouth that enfolded their bodies with a great warm tongue. They had been large waves, lukewarm, that had sucked and choked. When the sky had begun to lighten, the two girls had thought that they were as beautiful as mermaids. Indeed, they had been at an age when they were as lovely as mermaids.

The oxen had stood by the water with their small red eyes, letting themselves be washed off and watching the two girls. Yuri and A had been roommates in the university dormitory and there had been a hint of lesbianism in their friendship. That was why Yuri had wanted to visit A at her house by the Japan Sea when she had broken off with her first lover. The girls' relationship in the school dormitory, however, had been more ridiculous and pathetic than gloomy. Eventually they had realized that they were normal, only overly emotional. They had nothing to give each other. Later both of them got married.

Yuri wondered if they were still friends. She did not know. Perhaps they no longer had anything to talk about. Even if I returned to Japan, I would have no friends, Yuri thought. It would be worse with her lovers; each time she thought of them she felt that the gap between them grew wider. Even though she should look forward to returning to Japan because she missed certain people, she could not think of a single person with whom she felt she could have a pleasant conversation. She wondered if her close friends would look at her in the same way they had many years before. Generally speaking, the Japanese disdain those who return from America. Yuri had once felt the same way. She certainly felt that way now. This means I don't like myself, she thought.

A red neon sign that read "The Three Crabs" was flashing on and off beyond the beach grasses. The man was not starved for sex. He simply enjoyed it. The feeling of emptiness and sadness in him was transmitted to Yuri, and within her it became something gentle and calm.

"Why are you so quiet?" he asked.

"Because there's nothing to talk about," Yuri said.

"Let's go in there." With his chin he pointed to "The Three Crabs." The car started to move, making a noise like a freight car. It resembled the weary sigh of an old woman.

"I don't feel like going home," the man said. "Let's stay here for a while, like this."

He seemed relaxed next to Yuri's limber body. She pressed her cheek against the windowpane and looked at the sea. She was remembering Frank Stein's thin, wide nostrils, Sasha's thick lips, the pathetic creases beside Mrs. Yokota's nose and her funny laugh. She then thought of Takeshi's voice, which sounded like a piece of aluminum being flexed, and of Rie's voice, with its brassy ring, saying, "Hmph, nice girls don't do that." Somehow both father and daughter had the same metallic voices.

"The Three Crabs" was a log cabin, appropriate for a lodge by the beach. A green light was switched on in front.

Luminous Watch

TSUMURA SETSUKO

Translated by Elizabeth Hanson and Yukiko Tanaka

Tsumura Setsuko (b. 1928), the second daughter of a silk merchant, lost her mother when she was nine and her father when she was sixteen. Like Kōno and Ōba, she spent her adolescence in a factory rather than in a classroom. Two years after the end of the war, she decided to learn a skill to ensure her future financial independence in case she did not marry, since many eligible men had been killed during the war. She enrolled in a dressmaking school; when she was twenty, she opened her own shop and the next year hired three seamstresses. Although her business was going well, she closed her shop two years later and went to college to study literature.

She started writing and, as with most other would-be writers at the time, joined literary groups that published small magazines. In 1953 she married the editor of one of these magazines. Tsumura wrote stories for girls' magazines to supplement the income of her husband, who was also trying to write and did not have a steady job. When her husband's part-time business failed, she traveled with him to small towns to sell the leftover merchandise.

Literary recognition came very slowly for Tsumura and her husband, and the couple shared frustration and disappointment. Finding time to write, however, was more difficult for her, the mother of two children. She would often write standing up with a small child strapped on her back. She also struggled with the guilt she felt whenever she devoted herself to writing instead of her duties as a wife and a mother. Earning money by filling a paper with letters, she once said, was like being a counterfeiter.

In 1965 Tsumura won the Akutagawa Prize, and since then she has been an energetic writer, traveling to places where she can see and study various types of people, including prostitutes in mining towns. Not only does she dramatize her own experiences in her fiction, she also portrays many kinds of women of different ages and circumstances, which gives a breadth and an objective feel to her writing.

Even if I were to stab this man, he wouldn't react but would probably die in his sleep, Michiyo thought as she stared at his sleeping face.

He was sleeping quite soundly. It seemed strange to Michiyo that he was able to leave himself so defenseless in the room of a woman he had known for only a few days. He didn't seem to be an easy-going type; when he wasn't sleeping, he always had a pained expression, and it was difficult for her to tell what he was thinking. If she addressed him, he would look slightly startled for a second. He was extremely reticent, and Michiyo still knew very little about him.

She herself didn't understand why she and this man had come to have such a relationship.

She had met him about two months earlier. It had been a day when she had gone to meet her daughter, Chikako, at the entrance to the park where the school bus stopped. When the children first began going to kindergarten, all the mothers had gone out regularly to see them off and meet them, but within a month's time the children became used to commuting and could go back and forth by themselves. All but a few mothers stopped showing up at the bus stop.

Chikako was excited when she saw that her mother had come to meet her. It was a bright afternoon. Michiyo had done more laundry than usual that morning, and her back hurt a little. When she thought how well the laundry would dry, though, she felt refreshed.

"It's not raining. Why did you come to get me?" Even Chikako seemed to understand the nature of her mother's work, which was always busier on clear days.

"The weather was so nice, I wanted to get out and get some fresh air." Michiyo felt it would be a waste to go directly home, so she went into the park with Chikako. There were some swings, a sandbox, and a pond with some rowboats. A narrow path followed the edge of the pond, and some benches were set on the grass.

"I want to ride in a boat."

"We can't. Mommy doesn't know how to row."

"It looks easy. It looks like anybody could row."

"It just *looks* easy." Michiyo sat down on a bench. Chikako seemed bored.

"I'm going to go play on the swings," she said and ran off.

Just then a ball flew by, bounced once in front of Michiyo and rolled to the feet of a man who was sitting on a bench next to the pond. The man looked at the ball, then watched it as it rolled from near his feet into the pond. He made no attempt to retrieve it.

The boy who had been chasing the ball yelled when it fell into the pond. He made a tisking sound and looked with disgust at the man, who had watched it even though he could have easily reached out and picked it up.

The man looked up for the first time and saw the boy.

"You could have picked it up," the boy said reproachfully. The man seemed to have suddenly come to his senses and looked again toward the surface of the water where the ball had fallen in. A few minutes before the man had seemed to be watching the rolling ball, but in fact he hadn't seen anything.

He was wearing a suit and seemed to be some sort of office worker. He didn't look very young. Michiyo wondered why he was sitting in such a place at that time of day; yet there was nothing at all strange about someone who works outside an office, like a salesman or an insurance agent, resting for a while in a park when worn out from his job.

The man was still sitting there even after Michiyo had stood up. She had been vaguely disturbed by the man's vacant expression when he had looked up at the boy, and when she turned back to look at him, he sat there gazing blankly at the surface of the water with eyes that seemed to see nothing.

The next time Michiyo saw him, he was also on the park bench.

Michiyo didn't necessarily go to the park consciously thinking of the man. She went because the brief time she had spent sitting on the park bench a few days previously had provided a break from the monotony of her day-to-day life. Her work was far more tiring and required more patience than she had first imagined.

Michiyo lived with her daughter in a small apartment building. They had an ordinary six-mat room with a sink. There were apartments lined up on both sides of the hallway, and Michiyo's place was on the west side with a window. She had chosen a room facing west because the rent was cheap, but even though this was nice in the wintertime, when summer came the sun shining in from the west in the afternoons made the entire room like a steam bath. There was only one window, and since the walls on both sides were shared by the neighboring apartments, there was nothing she could do but leave the door open to make a pathway for the breeze and then endure as best she could. She hung a bamboo screen in the doorway. When Michiyo began working at home, however, this room that faced west proved to be convenient.

The woman who lived next door to Michiyo was named Tamae, and she worked in a bar in one of the nightclub districts. Since she wore kimonos to work, she dirtied a pair of white *tabi* socks each evening. She returned home late and slept during the morning, so she didn't have enough time to wash the tabi every day. She had once complained to Michiyo that it cost 50 to 60 yen to send them to the cleaners.

It had been two years since Michiyo's husband had met another woman and left. Michiyo, who had no income, had sold the small house registered under her name and moved to this apartment. She had been thinking of ways to make a living so that the small amount of money she had would not be exhausted. She couldn't go out to work since she had a small daughter, and when Michiyo heard the neighbor's story, the idea of laundering tabi occurred to her. For this she would need neither capital nor a particular skill.

If she offered to wash one pair for 30 yen, wouldn't she find lots of customers? After all, it was only tabi; it wouldn't be hard work even if she washed 20 pairs a day. Twenty pairs, 600 yen. It would be considerably more profitable than working from morning till night without a break making artificial flowers or embroidering gloves for 350 yen a day, because there would be no middleman to pay. Of course it wasn't pleasant work, but she wasn't expecting much.

Tamae sounded eager when Michiyo told her her idea.

"Why, I'll give you 20 to 30 pairs a month myself. There are two of us working at my bar, and I'll tell the women in the other places in the neighborhood too. They'll be glad to give them to you for 30 yen a pair."

Starting with the place where Tamae worked, Michiyo eventually established about 50 regular customers. Each person gave her a minimum of 20 pairs of tabi a month, so she washed a thousand pairs and made a monthly salary of at least 30,000 yen. Two days a week she went around and collected the tabi and delivered the laundered ones.

At first Michiyo washed the tabi in the small sink in her apartment. She didn't like the idea of washing bargirls' socks in the same sink she used for washing food and doing dishes, but she was too proud to let the gossipy tenants in the building know about her work. Already it seemed that people were wondering among themselves how Michiyo, alone with her daughter, was making a living.

Eventually she decided that it would be better to publicize the fact that she took in tabi to launder than to make people suspect that there was a man who was giving her financial support; and besides, she wouldn't be able to manage with the small sink as her business increased. She began taking the many pairs of tabi out to the communal laundry in the back of the apartment building. It was called a communal laundry, but in fact it was no more than a cold water tap and a concrete slab that was just big enough for two washtubs set down side by side. It was impossible to do laundry on rainy days since there was no roof.

It takes longer to wash tabi than you might think. You have to dissolve detergent in hot water, then soak them for 30 minutes or so, and when the dirt floats to the top, scrub each pair with a brush. The toes won't come clean unless scrubbed with a special brush made of fine wires tied in a bundle. The yellowed tabi have to be bleached; then they all have to be starched and hung out to dry. Tabi never come clean if they are tossed in a washing machine. It took Michiyo all morning to do the washing when she had many pairs to do, and the window with its western sunlight was perfect for hanging up the freshly laundered tabi in the afternoon.

She ironed them after supper while she was talking with Chikako. She sprayed each pair with water and worked with great care. Since this was her business, she couldn't allow herself to do just an adequate job. Besides this, Michiyo was by nature fastidious to the point of compulsion. She couldn't stand not washing underwear every day, even if this had meant stripping off whatever her husband had been wearing. She couldn't bear the cigarette ashes her husband dropped everywhere, and she had to wipe them up right away whenever she saw them. The fact that she had thought of washing tabi for a living must have been because of her diligence and love of cleanliness.

But when laundry work became her business, 30 pairs of tabi meant 60 a day to wash. As might have been expected, the work of washing 60 white objects of the same shape was too much. There were even times when she felt so fed up that she wanted to throw them all away.

She put the clean tabi in bags according to the names stitched on them. She collected and delivered tabi twice a week, but since she went to different areas on different days, she began to pick up and deliver a week's supply at a time. She could have had more customers, but she refused other women who had heard about her business because there were limits to her stamina as well as to her time. At first she went around to each woman's apartment, but then she asked her customers to take the tabi to the bars where they worked and give the payments to the owners. She didn't want to disturb her customers while they were working and besides, Michiyo couldn't leave her apartment in the evening.

Sometimes when Michiyo went over to a woman's apartment, she wouldn't come to the door even though she was obviously at home. At these times Michiyo guessed that a man was inside and so the woman couldn't open the door; but even if a man was in the apartment, if the two were not in bed together the woman wouldn't be bashful with Michiyo. She would come to the door with a gown wrapped around her naked body, squat down without worrying about exposing herself, take the bag, pay the money, and hand over the dirty tabi. When it was a one-room apartment, Michiyo would see the man whether she wanted to or not. Neither the man nor the woman seemed to think twice about this, probably because they simply ignored Michiyo.

"Honey, do you only wash tabi? How about washing some panties for me?" a woman once asked. She said it would be a big help if Michiyo could wash a pair of panties for 30 yen, since cleaners charged 50 to 60.

"You pay 60 yen to send your panties to the cleaners? You could buy a new pair for the cost of three washings."

"I don't have cheap ones like that. They cost 400 yen."

"Then it would be seven washings."

It made sense to send tabi to the cleaners, since it was difficult to do them well, but how much trouble could it be to wash a pair of panties the size of a handkerchief? If Michiyo washed panties for the same price she charged for tabi, she would certainly make a profit.

"Young men at the cleaners are always glad to take them, you know."

"Then go ahead and send them there." Michiyo didn't feel like washing the underwear a woman wears closest to her body, no matter how good the profit might be. The day when the woman's underwear, crumpled in a ball and permeated with body odor and the smell of perfume, had been thrust at her, Michiyo had felt completely drained and had gone to the park to cheer herself up.

Chikako went to a friend's place in the same apartment building to play when she got home from school, since Michiyo was always late on days when she made deliveries. No matter how tired she was, Michiyo always went straight home, since she didn't feel like stopping to rest at a tea shop with a bagful of dirty tabi. That day, however, she didn't feel like going home immediately. She was going to take Chikako out to do the shopping for dinner once she had taken the tabi to her room. Chikako must have been looking forward to this and waiting for her mother to return. But Michiyo was so tired that even the thought of Chikako, who would probably come and cling to her, made her weary.

The days were long and children were still in the park, absorbed in their play. People were rowing boats and lovers were snuggling on benches surrounded by thick grass. It seemed that the type of people who used the park began to change at this time of day.

While she was walking around the pond looking for an empty bench, Michiyo glanced for no special reason at the bench where the man had been sitting, stopped suddenly, and strained to see it. The man was looking at the surface of the water with exactly the same posture and gaze, as if he had been there ever since she had seen him the time before.

She sat down on the only empty bench, the same one she had sat on the time before. The bench the man was sitting on was near the pond, and she could watch him at an angle from behind without his noticing.

This man must work outside of his office, she thought. Even if this were true, it was too much of a coincidence to have met him twice in this way. It was probably his custom to rest in this park during his work day. Just as it was more agonizing for Michiyo to deal with the women than it was to wash tabi, perhaps this man wasn't suited for working outside an office.

She couldn't guess his age. His look of surprise when the boy had yelled, "You could have picked it up!" had made him look as if he were in his thirties, but seeing him from behind, he looked like an old man who was tired of living. He might have looked haggard because the hair at his nape and temples was shaggy.

Didn't the man's wife say anything about that bushy hair? People who work outside of an office should pay more attention to the way they look, Michiyo thought, then smiled faintly at herself for being so curious. She would have nagged her husband to go to the barber.

Her husband's lover was barely twenty years old, and one of the shop people who made deliveries reported to Michiyo that she was an extremely slovenly woman. Michiyo had suspected that her husband was having an affair for a long time, but this boy had seen him go into the woman's apartment and had told Michiyo, with a cheeky expression on his face. Michiyo realized that a woman like herself might be tedious for a man to live with, but her husband seemed unclean when he came home after having physical contact with some strange young woman, and she couldn't forgive him. In the end Michiyo's obstinate attitude sent her husband to the other woman, and one day he left the house, never to return.

More than once Michiyo had reflected on her own attitude after she had been left by her husband. Being asked by her daughter about the father who would never come home was worse than anything else. For a year he didn't send any money for living expenses. Once, when she couldn't stand it anymore, Michiyo went to the apartment building where the woman lived that the shop boy had told her about. She couldn't bring herself to knock on the door, however; she would have felt too wretched, asking her husband's lover, a woman much younger than she, to send her husband home.

Even though she had been treated badly, some nights Michiyo thought she heard her husband's footsteps turning the corner, and she lifted her head from the pillow. She realized she was hearing things and bit her lip at her own sentimentality. Then to stop herself from feeling foolishly disappointed again, she packed her husband's clothing and other things, sent them to the woman's apartment, and sold the house. If she hadn't sold the house, she would have had a hard time making a living.

Even after she had moved, she couldn't completely stop expecting her husband to come looking for them. But almost two years had passed; the way he had cut himself off was impressive. Can a man and woman brought together through an arranged marriage who have spent four years together and even have a daughter be separated so easily? Michiyo was surprised by the fragility of it all. Would they continue to live separately even though they were legally married? The next time they met it would probably be to discuss the divorce.

When the sun began to set, it suddenly became chilly. Michiyo wanted a little time to let her mind go blank, but while she was watching the man she remembered her husband. She didn't even know if he was still living with that girl or not. Perhaps this alone was proof that she had lost some interest in him.

The bell sounded at a nearby grade school. This was the signal meant to urge the children playing in the schoolyard to go home. The man slowly stood up from the bench and looked toward her, and Michiyo, who had been observing the man for quite a while, felt flustered and looked in another direction. But the man walked past her toward the park exit, paying no attention to her.

After this, Michiyo began stopping by the park on her way home from work when she felt tired. She wasn't thinking about the man, of course, but he was always there. When she went at a little past noon, the man was eating his lunch on the bench. At other times he was taking a nap with a newspaper over his face. Michiyo was amazed and thought that no matter how lazy he might be, a salesman or insurance agent must have some work he has to get done. Nonetheless, she felt compassion when she thought that the man might be completely unsuited for such work. His company might have gone bankrupt, and so he had no choice but to do this work that didn't suit him. With that attitude, however, his prospects didn't look good, she thought.

That day when Michiyo went to deliver tabi to one of her long-time customers, the woman wasn't home, and a man whom she had seen several times came to the door instead.

"She's gone to the bathhouse. How much?"

Michiyo crouched down and took a note pad from her pocket, since it seemed that the man was going to pay.

"Hey, shut that door there." Perhaps the man, who had been in the woman's apartment all day, didn't want to be seen by the tenants who passed in the hallway.

"Yes, of course, I'm sorry." She had left the door open a crack since the woman wasn't in. Michiyo shut it.

"You don't have a husband?"

"No."

"You must have been in a bad way to decide to wash tabi."

"I don't know how to do anything else."

"A good-looking woman like you could find an easier job."

"I'm not that young anymore."

"That's not true. Don't you want to get married?"

"I have a child."

The man was so persistent in the way he showed his interest that Michiyo answered bluntly and stood up.

"How much?" he asked.

"Next time is all right. I'll leave these here." She gave the man the clean tabi. "Excuse me, but could you get that bag over there in the corner for me?" She pointed to the bag that the woman had put her dirty tabi in.

As the man took the bag and handed it over to Michiyo, he suddenly grabbed her hand and pulled her toward him. She was startled and unwittingly fell into the man's arms.

"If you felt like it, I could fix things up so you wouldn't have to do that work anymore, starting tomorrow."

Michiyo shoved the man with all her strength, and consequently crashed into the door herself. Her shoes had come off when the man had grabbed her, and she fell into the concrete entryway in her stocking feet. She hurriedly jammed her now dirty feet into her shoes and flew out the door.

"Hey, your stuff!" the man threw the bundle of tabi at her, laughing.

Michiyo picked up the bundle that had been thrown at her feet and left the building. She was furious at the thought of being belittled by such a man. She didn't want to taint herself by working in the nightlife districts, but could it be that washing the tabi of such women was even more disgusting and vulgar?

The man had said that if she felt like it, he could fix things up so she wouldn't have to wash tabi anymore, but had he really thought that she was starved for money and sex too?

Michiyo touched her rumpled hair. As she walked along, she felt as if the man's hot breath were clinging thickly to her. When he had grabbed her, he had quickly poked her breast with his fat, brazen fingers. She despised the man but even so, she felt a strong excitement throughout her body. She felt angry for betraying herself this way, and shook her head, saying "How disgusting!"

Lately she had found herself saying at times, "It can't be helped, it can't be helped," as she washed the tabi. While she walked along carrying a bundle of dirty tabi, she sometimes said "Ah, ah, ah, ah," in a meaningless way, as if she were tearing words into pieces. Even when she was with Chikako, she would mumble to herself, and the girl would ask, "Mother, what did you say?"

That day Michiyo didn't feel like going anywhere, and turned automatically in the direction of the park. This time she was thinking clearly of the man. His listlessness seemed endearing and she thought of him with a feeling that seemed to be a kind of longing.

As she neared the park, the sky suddenly became dark and it began to rain. Michiyo hadn't brought a raincoat or umbrella, and she recalled that there was a little hut on the island in the middle of the boating pond.

The children who had been playing in the park were all running for home. Michiyo was the only one who thought, on the contrary, to go into the park. The man was not on the bench. Had he been rained on too and left? Or perhaps he hadn't come there that day.

A bridge with a red railing spanned the middle of the pond to the island. It was an arched concrete bridge, higher in the middle so that the boats could go underneath. Even though it was called an island, it was only about ten square yards, with just enough space for the hut. When she crossed the bridge, the rain started to beat down.

She ran into the hut and saw that someone else was already there. She knew right away that it was he, even though she could see only his back. He was eating his lunch while he watched the rain falling violently on the surface of the pond, but he turned his head, noticing that someone was behind him. His expression didn't alter the slightest bit at the sight of this intruder who had burst into his private retreat.

"Quite a sudden rain." Michiyo was flustered at being right in front of the man and spoke as if to herself while she hurriedly wiped off her wet hair and shoulders.

The man seemed to be uncertain whether he should reply or not, but in the end he said nothing. Michiyo thought that he probably wasn't pleased that she had come rushing in.

"It should let up soon, since it's such a sudden shower," she said, as if to apologize.

The man, looking at Michiyo's flushed face, said in an unexpectedly kind voice, "Why don't you sit down here?" and moved to the edge of the bench, making an empty place. Michiyo sat down near the other edge.

"I've seen you before—are you from this neighborhood?"

Michiyo stared at the man, surprised. He had noticed her as well.

"My daughter's school bus stops near the park entrance." She wanted to explain that she hadn't come there because she knew about him, even though she usually stopped by when Chikako was not with her. "Do you work outside your office?"

"What? Oh, yes." For some reason the man sounded uncertain.

She thought she had gone too far and felt sorry. The man probably thought he had revealed his lazy work habits to Michiyo.

"Even a park like this is better than nothing. The water and the greenness are a nice change." Why do I keep saying such apologetic things? Michiyo wondered, feeling disgusted with herself.

The man scooped the leftover rice out of his lunch container with his chopsticks and threw it into the pond. There weren't any carp, but there were some other kinds of fish. He then dug a hole in the ground at his feet with the heel of his shoe, threw the rest of his lunch in it and covered it with dirt.

His thin, book-shaped lunch container was completely clean, without a grain of rice left. He wrapped it in a newspaper and put it in the bag at his side. Nowadays people commended a wife who made a lunch for her husband every day; more and more families had easy-to-fix, Western-style breakfasts, and mothers felt it was a nuisance to fix their children's lunches, even for school outings, and so bought sushi from a shop instead. The man probably cleaned out his lunchbox neatly, throwing away the leftovers so that not a grain of rice remained, as if he had eaten it all, out of consideration for the thoughtfulness of a wife who would cook rice every morning and fix her husband's lunch.

Had the man lost his appetite because she had come in? It must have been impossible for him to eat his cold lunch while watching the rain, without even a cup of hot tea to drink. He must have felt chilled to his very stomach.

The rain let up, and the sun shone thinly.

"I'd be happy to fix you some tea if you'd like to come to my place." As soon as she had said this, Michiyo was shocked and wondered what she was talking about. Inviting a strange man to the apartment building, with all those gossipy people around . . .

"Really? You wouldn't mind if I dropped by?" He didn't hesitate. Michiyo, on the other hand, faltered but she couldn't retract her offer at that point.

"The place is a mess, but if you'd like . . ." Even while Michiyo was offering this invitation, she was slightly disappointed that he didn't refuse. Later she understood that the man was not being forward, nor was he particularly interested in Michiyo; he simply had more time than he knew what to do with.

The man took one step into Michiyo's room and looked, amazed, at the tabi hung up to dry so that they filled the space under the western eaves. They were hung not only outside the window, but also from a rope strung across the middle of the room.

"Surprised? This is what I do." Michiyo spoke in a slightly off-hand manner.

"I see."

"My customers are women who work in bars and restaurants. Once I tried it, I found it was harder work than I'd thought."

"I suppose it is." He seemed overwhelmed by the number of tabi.

"Please sit down over here. I'm sorry to put you under the tabi, but the water won't drip." Michiyo gave him a cushion to sit on and put a small aluminum kettle on the stove. "But I never have minded doing laundry, so it's all right. I'm not good at dealing with people—there are so many different types."

"I suppose there are." The man's reticence and Michiyo's talkativeness probably resulted from the fact that they both felt awkward.

The water had begun to boil. "Is green tea all right? Or if you'd like black tea or coffee, say so. It's instant, though."

"I'd like some green tea."

Michiyo took out some tea cups she didn't ordinarily use and offered the man a cup of tea. It was the first time she had used the cups since she had come there. The only people who came to the apartment where the mother and daughter lived alone were her next-door neighbor and Chikako's friend.

"Your husband?"

"We're separated."

"I see." Perhaps he didn't know how else to reply.

"You're happily married."

"Why do you say that?"

"You have a lunch your wife made for you every day."

"She's convinced that's a sign of wifely love."

"My, you are smitten." For some reason Michiyo felt a pain in her heart as if she had been stuck with a pin, and she spoke in a way that sounded coy.

"But you don't know what it's like to be married to someone who thinks she's a perfect wife . . ."

"That's all right. No need to explain yourself."

Chikako returned from kindergarten a while later. She sidled shyly up to her mother, seeing there was a guest.

"Go on outside and play."

The girl glanced at the man now and then from where she sat behind her mother. Even when Michiyo gave her some spending money and told her to go outside and play, she didn't leave readily. She was curious about the guest.

When she finally left, the man watched her go out and said, "She'd rather stay with her mother, wouldn't she?"

"Oh, that's not so. She's used to playing by herself since I have to work and can't play with her."

"What did you tell your daughter about your separation?" When the man said this, his expression indicated that he regretted having asked a prying question.

"My husband left when she was about three years old. He hasn't come back since then. So I've been telling her that he's sick in a hospital that's far away. If my husband never comes back, I wonder if I should tell her that he died?"

The man was silent again. Michiyo wondered why she would go so far as to say such things to a man she had only just met, but even so, she couldn't control herself.

There was a folk tale about someone who longed to tell a secret he was forbidden to share, so he spoke into a jar and sealed the secret inside. Telling something to this reticent man, who had nothing to do with Michiyo's life, would be like telling something to a jar—it was unlikely that it would cause any trouble.

His name was Kadota . . . He worked for a spice company near the Suda District in Kanda, and he had a wife and a college-aged son. He seemed to think it would be rude not to tell Michiyo anything about himself, since he had been invited to her apartment, but this was all he said. He didn't even give the name of his company or where he lived. When the bell at the elementary school rang, he took his bag and stood up.

"Is it that late?" He seemed truly surprised.

If he hadn't been aware of time, did this mean that he had been comfortable in her apartment? The time spent with him had seemed horribly long to Michiyo because she had been constantly dreading when he would leave.

"Do you know the story of Cinderella?" Michiyo asked teasingly. "When the clock struck midnight, she had to hurry home." The man's eyes looked frightened for a second—he didn't smile even when he was compared to a girl in a fairy tale. He seemed to be a serious type who didn't like jokes very much; she remembered that he had tried forthrightly to explain himself when she had teased him about his wife a short time before.

She hoped that Kadota would come by again, but on the other

hand, she thought that he wasn't the kind of man who was easy to get to know. She would miss him if he didn't come, but if he did come back soon, she knew she would be disappointed. It was difficult for Michiyo herself to gauge her feelings.

When she went to the park several days later, Kadota wasn't there. She thought he must make his rounds during the morning, and she timed it so she would be there when he was starting to eat lunch. She sat on the bench he always sat on and waited for him to come. After about an hour, a thought suddenly occurred to her and she went to the hut on the island.

Kadota, who had been looking at the pond, turned around at the sound of Michiyo's footsteps.

"You were here all along, weren't you?" she said. She thought there was some significance to the fact that he was here and not on the usual park bench. "Are you finished with your lunch?"

"No."

"Then I'll fix you some tea."

Michiyo went several more times to see Kadota and brought him back to her place. He started going to visit her. She told him that she wasn't home on Tuesdays and Fridays, the days she went out to make deliveries. After he began coming by, she stopped grumbling to herself. It seemed that the other tenants in the building were gossiping about him, but she decided she wouldn't worry about it.

One day there was a knock on the door, and when she went to answer it, thinking that it was Kadota, she found a middle-aged man she had never seen before standing there.

"What can I do for you?" Michiyo asked through a narrow opening in the door, leaving the door chain attached.

"You're Takabe Michiyo, aren't you? Your husband asked me to come here."

Michiyo undid the chain and opened the door slightly. "My husband?"

"Your husband wants a divorce."

Just as she had thought—her husband had come looking for her only when he wanted a divorce. But he had asked someone else to do it and wouldn't even meet with Michiyo himself.

"The truth of the matter is that they had a child recently, and your husband's in a hurry. He said he would give you the money from the sale of the house for Chikako's support."

He said he would give her the money from the house; Michiyo's father had originally given it to her, so in fact it was her property. Her husband had taken a lover and left home, and he demanded a divorce when he had a child by this woman—it was all so selfish that Michiyo could think of nothing to say. He must be considering his wife's house as his own, and thinking of it as joint ownership, was turning over a large piece of property to her.

"Please tell him that I have no objection to divorce." He wasn't the type who would give either alimony or child support. She had no desire to cause any trouble because of these things since, in the end, nothing would be left from it but unpleasant memories.

"In that case, the formalities will be taken care of at another time."

The divorce was arranged through this conversation in the doorway. Just then Michiyo saw Kadota, who appeared to be turning back on seeing that she had a guest.

"Mr. Kadota!" Michiyo called to him with no concern for the neighbors. "Come on in, Mr. Kadota! It's all right." She spoke his name with intentional sweetness, wondering what the man would tell her husband about him.

When the door was locked, Chikako would assume that her mother was out, so would pass the time playing outside or at a friend's house. Michiyo was in Kadota's arms when Chikako came home. Even though the door was locked, she stood outside and called, "Mommy!"

Michiyo wondered if Chikako knew instinctively that her mother was inside; she tensed her body and held her breath.

After she had called for her mother once, Chikako's small footsteps could be heard walking away. She probably was used to calling her mother's name once even when she knew she wasn't home.

When the sound of Chikako's footsteps had faded, Kadota's arms tightened around Michiyo.

"Is it okay?"

It frustrated Michiyo to be asked such a foolish thing by a man, and she moved her body impatiently.

As soon as he had laid his hand on her shoulder a short time before, she had felt that her body was separate from her will and was flowing along ceaselessly like some thick liquid. Even though she couldn't recall feeling any particular physical desire since her husband had left, and even though she didn't think she loved Kadota, she felt annoyed by the way she was reacting, and yet she had an urge to let herself flow into Kadota with more passion than she had ever known.

The next time he came, Kadota put a white envelope in front of her.

"What's this?"

"You've been so kind to me, but I haven't done anything for you . . ."

"But I haven't done anything . . ."

"Washing tabi must be pretty hard work. I've just been sitting around while you've been doing that."

Michiyo was touched by the kind words, "I haven't done anything for you." Even if he did nothing for her, life had more meaning simply because he came to visit. But she couldn't tell him this.

"That's the reason for this," he said.

"The reason?" Michiyo took the envelope Kadota had given her and peeked at the contents, then gave it right back. "What do you mean by this?" She had glimpsed some bills, but she had been so surprised that she couldn't tell how much money it was. She had never thought of receiving money from him.

Kadota seemed confused when he saw Michiyo's expression. "Did I offend you? While I'm here, you can't work, so even when I want to come it's hard for me . . . It's tedious to spend half the day in the park."

"That means, then, that you come here to kill time?" Michiyo noticed that her resentful tone at seeing through what he had said was mixed with coyness. She was pleased that Kadota had said he wanted to visit.

"I thought coming here might have been a nuisance."

"If it had been, I wouldn't have invited you in the first place."

"But I come so often."

"Don't be so formal." Michiyo felt desolate at his reserve, considering what had happened the time before. She was almost ashamed of how eager she had been then, but he had seemed to be holding back a part of himself, and this made her feel slightly uneasy. "I don't mind if you want to kill time here. Even if I'm gone, you can come inside and rest. Go ahead and have some tea, take a pillow and blanket out of the closet and take a nap." She gave him an extra key.

"But I can't come in while you're not here." He forced a smile.

The next day, however, when she came home carrying the bundle of dirty tabi, Kadota was sleeping below the white tabi that had been hung up to dry all over the room. He had put two cushions down side by side and had covered himself with a dirty raincoat.

Michiyo was supposed to put the bag of tabi down and go immediately to fetch Chikako, but she locked the door and sat down quietly by Kadota's pillow. She wondered when he had arrived; he had locked the door to guard against unexpected guests and was sleeping peacefully in the room as if it were his own.

It felt nice to have a man sleeping there, after coming home to an empty apartment for so long. Perhaps there was nowhere else he could go. She wondered why he didn't go home, but she thought he might want his family to think he was a busy, competent salesman. She felt sorry that he had to keep up appearances.

Even so, why did his sleeping face show such deep exhaustion, if his work was not that tiring? The school bell would be ringing shortly but he probably wouldn't notice, he was sleeping so soundly. She was going to take Chikako out to shop for supper, and he would probably be sleeping when they came back. Wouldn't Chikako think it strange that a man had come into the apartment to sleep while they were gone?

Michiyo took a blanket from the closet and covered Kadota with it; but then, realizing she should waken him, she put a hand on his shoulder. As she did this, her hand was suddenly seized. She had been thinking that he was sound asleep, but he had awakened without her noticing it.

Michiyo expected him to pull her hand hard to bring her toward him, but he just stayed as he was and simply said "Thank you."

The sound of a child's running feet came along the hallway, and Chikako called "Mommy!"

Kadota stood up quickly, and just as Michiyo had wadded the blanket up and thrown it in the closet, the door opened.

"You're back?"

"I just came in." Michiyo sounded apologetic. Chikako didn't respond when Kadota said hello.

He left first, and a little later Michiyo left the building with Chikako, who was dead silent, as if she disapproved. Michiyo didn't know if she was angry because she hadn't opened the door right away, or if she had suspected something when she saw Kadota in the room.

"Tonight let's make that macaroni and cheese you like, okay?" Michiyo said, trying to cheer Chikako up.

"Mommy, is that man my father?" Chikako looked up at Michiyo with an earnest expression, as if to say that she wouldn't be fooled.

"Why do you ask? I've told you he's sick and in a hospital far away."

"Where is far away? Is it so far we can't go see him?" Chikako was old enough now that simply "a faraway hospital" wouldn't satisfy her. Michiyo should have thought of a more complete explanation. When the divorce became final, she thought she would tell Chikako that her father had died in a distant hospital; did the fact that she couldn't think of a better answer mean that she still hoped her husband would return? Eventually Chikako would understand that her father had become infatuated with a younger woman and had left, but now Michiyo, suddenly confronted by her daughter, didn't know how to answer.

"You know, your father is very ill, so we won't be able to see him for a while." She gave this awkward excuse and pulled Chikako's hand hard to urge her along. "Well, let's hurry and finish shopping and go home. Mommy's starved."

The mother's answer hadn't cleared up anything about the father, nor about the man who had recently been coming to the house. Chikako pressed her lips together and said nothing more.

A cold rain had been falling since morning, even though it was April. The newspapers and television reported that the weather was the same as it had been the previous February.

When it rained Michiyo felt depressed. She thought this was because the rain made it difficult for her to do her work, but it was probably also because of the cyclical changes in her body. She felt irritated just looking at the damp tabi, dangling down so that there was hardly any room left in the apartment. She turned on the space heater to dry out the room but the steam from the wet tabi filled the apartment with a muggy odor. She started to iron the tabi while they were still quite damp, hoping to dry them out more quickly. She was talking to herself without realizing it.

A week had passed and Kadota hadn't come by. She had gone to the park, but he wasn't on the bench or in the hut. Michiyo regretted that she hadn't asked his address; she should have at least asked his office phone number, but he didn't seem to want to tell her, so she had been unable to ask. There were so many things she didn't know about him. It wasn't that she didn't want to ask—she didn't want to annoy him.

Even when it rained, she had to deliver the tabi on the day she had promised. The women gave her a week's supply at a time, and only a few owned extra pairs. Dense steam rose as she ironed the damp tabi. Even when the steam stopped and the tabi seemed completely dry, they were still moist when she felt them a while later.

Michiyo felt more and more depressed since she wasn't able to finish them properly.

There was a knock on the door. She thought at once that it must be Kadota, and her mood brightened. To her surprise, however, a young policeman wearing a black raincoat was standing there.

"I have some news that's difficult to tell you," he said solemnly. "Your husband has committed suicide."

"What?" Michiyo stared at the policeman. She hadn't understood what he had said.

"Your husband hung himself in K Cemetery last night. Someone passing by this morning found him and told the police. We'd like you to go to the police station now."

"My husband? Why would my husband . . ."

"It seems there is a will for the wife at the police station." The policeman had come on his bicycle from the police box after the police station had contacted him.

Michiyo was confused, and for a moment she stood up straight in the middle of the room, not knowing what to do. Chikako would soon be home from kindergarten, but she couldn't take her along.

She shut the window, put a raincoat over her housedress, and closed the door. On rainy days she went to meet the school bus, but she told a woman who lived in the same building and had a child who went to Chikako's kindergarten what had happened and asked her to bring Chikako home and watch her. The woman was pleased to be the first to know of this unusual occurrence, and promised, excited, to look after Chikako.

Michiyo went out to the main street, hailed a cab, and told the driver the address the policeman had given her. It wasn't far. While she was staring at the wipers moving busily across the windshield, she wondered why her husband would have committed suicide. The middle-aged man sent by her husband to tell her about the divorce had come by only half a month before. She didn't know if this messenger had told her husband about Kadota, but it was very unlikely that he would be shocked on hearing that she had met a man. The messenger had told her that since the woman her husband was living with had had a child, he was in a hurry to get a divorce. But since she had agreed to the divorce with no conditions attached, why would he have killed himself?

She didn't feel the slightest bit of sadness, but she was pained by the thought that her husband hadn't found happiness even with a younger woman. He wasn't the type of man who would contemplate suicide.

It must have been quite an incident for this police station, which was in an area that had only recently been annexed to the city. Michiyo climbed a splintery wooden staircase to a second-floor room where a plump, honest-looking, middle-aged policeman was sitting.

"Are you Takabe Michiyo? Please accept my sympathy," he said and lowered his head. "Did you have any suspicion that your husband might commit suicide?"

His voice sounded somewhat critical, but since she and her husband hadn't been living together, she couldn't have been part of the cause . . .

"He was a careful person, wasn't he? He fixed everything up so there wouldn't be a chance of failure. He hung a rope on a tree branch and wound it around his neck, then he sat on a tall tombstone in a cemetery and took some sleeping pills. The rope didn't have any slack, so when he went to sleep and fell off the tombstone, the rope tightened around his neck. He was being careful in case the medicine didn't kill him."

When Michiyo heard about the meticulous suicide, she wondered why her husband would have been so depressed that he would have planned such a foolproof death. She couldn't imagine him doing it.

"You're sure it was my husband?"

The officer's eyes seemed to be saying that this was understandable, since she probably didn't want to believe what had happened.

"This is the will." He placed an ordinary envelope and a small package in front of her. The address was not precise, but instead read "Mrs. Takabe Michiyo, Tokuwa Apartments, The Street That Runs Behind X Bathhouse." The ink was blurred, perhaps from rain, but she could tell it wasn't her husband's handwriting.

"May I open it?"

"Go ahead, it's for you."

Michiyo had felt a foreboding when she saw the address, and her fingertip trembled as she opened the letter. The will was neatly written on a single piece of stationery: "I didn't have any place to go. I spent the entire day looking at my watch—each minute was so long. I was able to forget time only when I was in your apartment. I have nothing to leave you. This watch is my only possession. It's an old watch, but please accept it."

The trembling in Michiyo's fingertips spread throughout her

body. Even when she tried to control it, it continued to well up from some deep part of herself.

"I am sorry." The officer seemed relieved that Michiyo had finally realized that her husband was dead. "We have to ask you to identify the body."

"He's not my husband." Michiyo was still trembling when she spoke. "This man is not my husband. Please let his wife know about this."

The officer looked at Michiyo with surprise.

"I hardly knew this man," she said. "Please hurry and tell his wife."

"But this is the only will he left. He didn't have another thing on him to show who he was." The officer spoke as if he were trying to explain his mistake.

"I don't know where he lived, but he said he worked for a spice company in the Suda District in Kanda."

The officer told one of his men to check in the phone book for spice companies in the Suda District to find out if a man named Kadota Nobuo worked for one of them. They found the company immediately. It was true that Kadota had worked there, until four months before . . .

"This man Kadota was sick for a long time, and while he was taking time off, it looks like he was fired," the officer reported. "He quit working four months ago."

Michiyo gasped. For four months he had taken the lunch his wife had made and left the house, then killed time until the school bell rang.

The police got Kadota's home phone number from the company and called at once.

"His wife was shocked. She said she didn't know anything about him being fired. He went to work every day for four months, I guess. Where in the world did he spend his time?" The officer seemed startled and watched Michiyo as if something had flashed in his head. She said nothing and stood up. When she started to leave the room, he handed her the small package that was on the desk.

"Said this was for you." The officer's way of speaking had changed.

Michiyo put the package in her handbag, went down the creaking stairs and outside. She felt tired, as if she had suddenly grown older. Kadota seemed like someone in the distant past. The rain soaked through her clothes to her skin, and her teeth started to chatter.

The neighbor who was taking care of Chikako had been waiting eagerly for Michiyo to return, and started to shower her with questions. When she saw Michiyo's pale, despondent face, however, she stopped and asked nothing more. Michiyo had intended to do her best to speak to the woman and to Chikako as she always did, but her mind was blank; she wasn't thinking of anything.

Once Chikako was asleep, Michiyo opened her handbag and took out the package. Inside was an old watch she remembered seeing before. It began to tick when she wound it. Kadota's heartbeat had stopped forever, but this watch that had been around his wrist until just a moment before he died was still working. Michiyo remembered that several years before they had gotten a puppy, and when it whined all night from loneliness, she had put a small clock in its bed. She had heard that a puppy would think this was the sound of its mother's heart beating and would sleep peacefully.

Michiyo put Kadota's watch beside her pillow, but the sound of the second hand kept her from sleeping. When she picked it up and looked at it, she saw that the hands, which had been painted with a luminous substance, were pointing to two o'clock.

Had Kadota stared at this watch even in the middle of the night? During the daytime he suffered because the hands moved so slowly, but in the middle of the night had he dreaded the morning when he would have to leave for work?

Rain continued to fall for two days. The tabi were left on the line.

Michiyo had no desire to do anything. Even Chikako, as young as she was, noticed her mother's strange mood and didn't run around or make noise.

One evening three days after Michiyo had gone to the police station, a woman came to her apartment. She had high cheekbones and thin eyebrows, and was dressed fastidiously in a dark silk kimono. She seemed to be about Michiyo's age.

The woman looked at her intently. Michiyo knew intuitively that this was Kadota's wife.

"I'm Kadota's wife," the woman said in a high-pitched voice. Even though Michiyo had guessed that she would show up, she was completely unprepared for it.

"Please come in." Michiyo moved out of the narrow, concrete-floored entry and invited her in from the doorway.

The woman stepped into the room and looked startled for a second at the sight of the drying tabi that filled the room. She sat down so that she faced Michiyo and asked with a hard expression, "How long had you known Kadota?"

"Not even a month." Before that she had seen him on a park bench, but she couldn't call that knowing him.

"I suppose he came to this apartment."

"No." Michiyo thought she might ease this unfortunate wife's suffering a bit.

"That's not possible! Are you saying he had somewhere else to go?" the woman said accusingly.

"I only saw Mr. Kadota in a park near here, and sometimes exchanged greetings with him."

"I see, you met him in a park and then brought him here, to this place."

"You are insulting your husband by saying that." She could understand the woman's shock but she couldn't allow her to speak that way.

"Insulting, you say? Are you saying that you two weren't insulting to me? Kadota didn't confide that he had been fired because you were around. Being fired was a stroke of luck because he could go back and forth to this place. He got severance pay but he didn't give any of it to his family. That's because he had you."

Michiyo was shocked and stared at the woman.

"Is the money all gone?" the woman asked. "Tell me, how much did he give you?"

Michiyo thought that any severance pay must have been a small amount. In the mornings Kadota had probably gone to cheap movie houses, or coffee shops with breakfast specials, and in the afternoons to art museums and libraries; no doubt he had gone to places where he could pass long stretches of time cheaply. He had finally become bored with places where he could waste time, and so spent more than half the day in the park. Even so, he had used up the money in four months.

The money he had wanted to give Michiyo must have been the leftover severance pay. He had already been thinking about dying then, she thought. She was tempted to tell the woman that she had refused to accept the money he had offered, but realizing that nothing she said would do any good, she just said, "I don't know anything about his severance pay."

"That's not possible. He gave it all to you, so he couldn't come home. That's why he killed himself."

Someone actually thinks a man would give up everything for me, Michiyo thought, smiling a little. The woman, who seemed to misunderstand this smile, said angrily, "But they told me you took his watch!"

Michiyo pulled up the sleeve of her cardigan and took off Kadota's watch. The woman grabbed it, then stood up. As she was leaving the apartment, Michiyo called after her, "I wonder why Mr. Kadota didn't leave you anything in his will." The woman glared at her with bloodshot eyes, slammed the door, and left the building.

Michiyo thought painfully of these words that she shouldn't have spit out; she could hear the distraught woman's footsteps moving farther and farther away. When she stood up and looked out the window, she saw the woman hurrying along with a stooped back.

I wonder if I've reached the age when I too have started to walk like that, Michiyo thought uncomfortably as she watched the woman walk away.

The clasp on one of the tabi that was hanging from the eaves felt cool as it brushed against her cheek.

Family in Hell

TOMIOKA TAEKO

Translated by Susan Downing Videen

Tomioka Taeko (b. 1935) was born in Osaka, the eldest child of working-class parents. An intelligent child, she was indulged by her father, who made a small fortune with a foundry and then left his family to lead a freer life. Tomioka, too, eventually left home to live with a poor painter, whom she followed to the United States only to be abandoned for another woman.

She began her literary career by publishing several volumes of poetry. A few years after her unhappy love affair, however, she began to write fiction, which she has continued to write prolifically ever since. She switched to prose because she felt that poetry was an "elitist art," an art that could not stand up against mundane reality. In her stories she has consistently written about people who do not know how to express themselves in words but nonetheless have a solid sense of everyday reality. Her desire to understand these nameless people and her willingness to look at herself from their point of view give her fiction a sense of openness and objectivity. With her unique style and critical eye, she has played an increasingly important role in contemporary Japanese literature. She married at the age of 34.

"Family in Hell" is the title story of a set of four stories for which Tomioka was awarded the Women's Literature Prize in 1974. Though based on her own love affair, the story is not strictly autobiographical. Indeed, Tomioka seems to have employed techniques common to traditional Japanese comic tales, in which all the characters, not merely a protagonist, are revealed through each other's eyes.

Tomioka has written several screenplays, and "Family in Hell" often seems to read like one. The characters reveal themselves dramatically through dialogue with little explanation from the narrator. The speech of the characters is crucial to the story. Nahoko's mother speaks in heavy dialect, a hybrid of the dialects spoken in Kyoto and Osaka. Shō's parents, by contrast, though no better educated than Nahoko's mother, speak a plainer form of standard Japanese. At the beginning of the story Nahoko herself speaks standard Japanese, sounding much like Shō and his family, but after staying with her mother she begins to speak her mother's dialect, a telling sign that she is moving emotionally and intellectually further from Shō and his view of life. Nahoko does not, however, accept her mother's world view, and eventually she moves away from both Shō and her mother.

H ER NAME was Nahoko, but on rare occasions his mother would call her Shinako by mistake. Shinako was the name of his previous wife; for his mother, then, it was the name of her previous daughter-in-law. Whenever his mother mistakenly called her Shinako, he would look disconcertedly at Nahoko. But names grow on a person, and within a year his mother's mistakes were heard no more.

He, of course, had never called her by the wrong name, but some time later he confessed that he had not been without his worries. What if when they first began sleeping together he had called her Shinako or even cried out his old wife's name? All along, then, he had been consciously suppressing any recurrence of the old habit.

Though it required a train ride of many hours from her home far out in the country, the mother devotedly came to visit her son in Tokyo. This was mostly because she liked to go on trips, or, perhaps more accurately, because she liked to go on rides. What others took to be devotion on her part actually involved not the least devotion or hardship for the mother herself. Besides, she found herself getting bored out in the country, and what better antidote to boredom could there be than taking one of her beloved rides into Tokyo? She had no other children, only this son living in Tokyo.

The first time the mother came to stay with her son and new daughter-in-law, Nahoko was sick in bed. She had caught the flu that was going around and had been confined to her bed for three days. To make matters worse, the couple lived in a nine-foot-square room in a sort of outbuilding behind a house in the business district. With all of Nahoko's sleeping mats spread out, the tiny room was filled to overflowing; and the mother, who had come all that way looking forward to this first meeting with her daughter-in-law, was forced to sweep aside an edge of the mats just to find a place to sit.

Though it was not without some effort that she had managed the long trip in from the country, the mother was not even to be rewarded with a home-cooked dinner prepared by her new daughter-in-law. Instead she had to settle for a Chinese-style hodgepodge of meat and vegetables that her son fixed in the little communal kitchen

down the hall. Still, since her son was a good cook and had a taste
for the same salty foods of which she herself was so fond, she was
quite likely happier with her son's cooking than with anything her
new daughter-in-law might have prepared.

Anyone looking at the situation with ordinary common sense
would think that in this case the mother would cook dinner for her
son, inconvenienced as he was by having a wife sick in bed and unable to get around. But the mother did no such thing! Come what
may, she had taken this trip to enjoy herself. So what if it was her
own son's house? No one was going to catch her on a trip heading
resignedly out to the kitchen, where she would be a good mother
and fix something to eat. Consequently, it did not bother her in the
least to have her son fix dinner for her instead of his wife. It was
the daughter-in-law who felt both uncomfortable and a little disappointed.

Only one thing amid all the fun of the trip and the fun of talking
to her son after a long separation was marring the pleasure she took
in her visit and causing her some uneasiness. As her inadvertent mistakes over Nahoko's name might reveal, the woman now living with
her son was not really his wife. Under such circumstances, then,
what should she as a mother say by way of formal greeting to her
son's new woman on this, their first meeting? She was content to forget the matter entirely, except that in the end, she knew, she would
have to say something one way or the other. But what really depressed her much more than speaking with the new woman was the
business of making some formal declaration to her son's old wife,
Shinako.

Here she was on a nice trip to visit her son in Tokyo, and there
was all this unpleasant business to attend to, unpleasant business
that she herself had never volunteered to tackle. Her son had asked
her to come and help out, and now there was nothing for it but to
do the best she could.

"You know, Nahoko," she said, "as far as I'm concerned, you're
Shō's wife. Yes indeed, that's the way I think about it." And with
that she settled the problem of what to say to her son's new woman.
Such an approach, however, would never do for the previous one.
There was no getting around the fact that Shinako was her son's
legal wife, married to him four years before and entered in the family
register with the full consent of his parents, and that the marriage
was as valid today as ever. The thought therefore occurred to her
that Shinako would not be as easy to handle.

After finishing the first order of "unpleasant business," that of the formal greeting to Nahoko, the mother chattered gaily with her son. Happy thoughts of the two of them gadding about Tokyo were restored completely, and she was in high good spirits—so much so that the physical suffering of Nahoko, still in bed with a considerable fever and struggling vainly to make conversation, never crossed her mind. Nahoko, watching the cheerful way she talked, felt that here was a strange sort of mother indeed. Her own mama could never have acted that way! The pillowcases and sheets were soiled from having been constantly stepped on in the tiny room, and in the closet there were piles of dirty clothes. Although Nahoko had stayed up as long as she could before finally taking to her bed, she had felt too sick to do as much of the wash as she wanted. If her own mama were here, oh, she might have complained about it, but surely she would have done the wash for her. Surely she would have fixed something for the two of them to eat, since her own daughter was sick in bed. Even if she had taken the trip for pleasure, surely she would have resigned herself to the inevitable and for a day or two at least taken care of the chores piling up around the house. But this mother was really happy-go-lucky. She was discussing with her son the bus tour she would take tomorrow to see the sights in Tokyo.

The only way for the mother and the two young people to sleep in the tiny room was to make two sets of sleeping mats out of one by stripping off one of the two bottom and one of the two top mats and laying them one on top of the other close beside the other pair. But to have Shō's mother lying there right beside them when she had only just met her made Nahoko too nervous to sleep. Besides, every joint in her body seemed to ache from her fever, and the bed seemed all the more cramped when she realized that she must try not to move very much in her sleep. But there was one thing that displeased her more than anything else. Nothing could dispel the embarrassment she felt at lying so close to Shō on the narrow mat with his mother right there beside them. One's actions in bed are as much a matter of habit as are names. What would she ever do, she worried, if by some chance Shō, forgetting his mother's presence, should hold her close and cradle her head on his arm? But Nahoko need not have worried. No sooner had his mother changed into the nightgown she had brought and curled up comfortably under the quilts than she began to snore. And such sonorous snores were they, indeed, that Nahoko could not help thinking it quite hopeless to try to sleep in the same tiny room with her. And yet, despite everything, they managed to sleep as snug as three peas in a pod.

Since Shō's mother was still only forty-eight or forty-nine, one could hardly call her an old lady, although having lived her life in the country she looked older than city women of the same age. She had brought with her a great quantity of some standard remedy for high blood pressure—obtained, she said, from her doctor—and this she would take after meals and before going to bed. It seems that having fainted once from high blood pressure, she had been warned by her doctor to avoid salty foods. But she lived in a cold, snowy region of the country where everybody, perhaps because of the cold, relished salty foods. Their pickles were salty, their bean-paste soup, their boiled foods—everything they ate was salty. Therefore, though she was not particularly unusual by her neighbors' standards, to Nahoko, Shō's mother seemed to consume a prodigious amount of salt.

Nahoko became truly alarmed as, having heard from Shō how his mother had once fainted from high blood pressure and seen for herself the quantity of medicine with which she came provided, she watched Shō's mother take pickle after salty pickle from the gift box she had brought them from the country. Alarmed though she was, however, Nahoko could only watch helplessly while Shō's mother poured soy sauce on every one of the dishes that she prepared for her in the course of the next two or three days. But then Nahoko's cooking may have been too bland to serve as a reliable standard of judgment.

"You know," Shō's mother exclaimed happily as she returned in the evening with her son, "up till yesterday I had a backache, but ever since we rode that 'jet coaster' thing after the bus tour today, would you believe it but the pain's gone away completely!" She was referring to the many rides they had taken at the amusement park after the bus tour was over. "Dad always says he hates to take even tour buses, so if it hadn't been for you, Shō, I'd never have gotten to ride something like the jet coaster!" she added by way of thanks to her son. Then, hungry and tired from all the sightseeing and the excursion to the park, she sat down to the meal Nahoko had prepared, proclaiming her approval as she ate. And dashing soy sauce liberally on all the side dishes . . .

"I thought I'd treat Mom to lunch," Shō was saying. "So we went into a sushi shop. But she said it was too expensive, so out we came again. Then she said noodles would do just as well anyway . . ."

"That's too bad," Nahoko said. "You should have had sushi before you came home."

Though it was true that Nahoko's fever had abated somewhat,

her throat was sore and she still had a temperature, robbing her of
her appetite and making everything she ate seem tasteless. At a time
like this she would sooner have eaten a thin rice gruel or a porridge
of rice and vegetables and stayed in bed as long as she wished. Her
own mama would have fixed her rice gruel if it had been she who
had come visiting. In their house there had been a deep, earthen-
ware pot called Yukihira, and whenever anyone got sick her mother
would make rice gruel in it—white rice gruel made from scratch with
fresh rice, not with cold, leftover rice. The amount of rice in the
gruel depended on how sick the invalid was. In serious cases, when
the person had severe diarrhea or was not allowed to eat, Nahoko's
mother would make a watery gruel in which she took care that not
a particle of soft, cooked rice remained. This gruel, with its delicate
flavor of rice, was delicious in its way, but something even better
awaited the person only suffering from a cold or other minor illness.
Then she would prepare a thicker gruel containing half liquid and
half rice; and with all the good flavor of the rice trapped in Yukihira
as it cooked, the gruel would have a body that Nahoko had not once
known ordinary rice to have. What Nahoko lacked presence of mind
to consider was whether the gruel itself was truly superior, or
whether it only seemed that way to one who had started to regain
her health. Whatever the reason, no matter how dull her appetite,
she could always eat rice gruel from Yukihira . . . Or so she
thought as she listened to Shō's mother chatter gaily about the
events of the day.

Days filled with pleasant excursions were one thing, but the next
day, when Shō's mother realized it was high time that she tackle the
other order of "unpleasant business," settle it one way or the other,
and be on her way, the world seemed a darker place.

"You know," she said when it was all over, "Shinako was different
this time. Not like the time she came screaming out to our place.
She was so meek! Why, I've never seen Shinako so mild-mannered
before. She said she'd just wait patiently for Shō to come to his
senses. She said she wouldn't dream of leaving him over such a little
thing."

Though Shō's mother had visited Shinako to arrange a separation
on her son's behalf, it was she, it would seem, who had ended up
being wrapped inextricably around Shinako's little finger. When
Shō had first run out on her and gone to live with another woman,
Shinako had gone in a frenzy to his mother's house in the country.
"What are you going to do about this, Mother?" she had demanded.

"Look what your son is doing to me! Well, I'm your son's wife, so aren't I your daughter? It's only reasonable to expect you to say something to him for me!" And so she had railed, laying a sort of direct appeal at her mother-in-law's feet. This time, however, when the mother visited her, she had undergone a complete and utter transformation. "It's partly my own fault that this has happened. It's up to the wife to wait until her husband comes to his senses. I'm sorry to have caused you any worry," she had said, taking the punch out of her mother-in-law's appeal as easily as twisting the arm of a baby.

Optimist though Shō's mother was, she was at her wits' end. She had already told Nahoko that she thought of her as her son's wife . . . Now if only she could settle the matter of Shinako so easily. If things didn't go well, she would be left to face a troublesome, complicated problem, and she would hate that—in fact, she was just no good when it came to such situations. Yes, she had hoped that the matter of Shinako could be solved easily, but Shinako's unexpected behavior had spoiled everything.

If only Shinako had clutched at her sleeve when she saw her, cried, shrieked, and uttered all manner of abuse at Nahoko and Shō, how much easier her job would have been. Then she could have said, "See, it's no wonder that Shō left you when you get hysterical like this. Nahoko's a nice girl . . ." Then she could have found a way to broach the subject of a separation.

"What should we do?" Shō's mother said. She looked troubled.

"It's all right," said Shō, coming to the rescue. "Things will work out before long." He seemed loath to distress his mother further.

"You're right," she agreed. "Things like this always work out before long." And the downcast expression that had darkened her face till that moment gave way to the carefree look that she usually wore.

"When you married Shinako," Nahoko said to Shō, "Mother and everybody else thought it was just fine. So what do you expect when Mother comes along afterwards and starts talking about a divorce? No woman is going to say yes right away to that." Secretly disgusted at how easily Shō's mother had given up, Nahoko no longer felt like arguing. "I'm the one you should be talking to now about leaving," she added.

"But I want Shō to do as he likes," the mother replied. "It's all right, Nahoko. Whatever Shinako may say, it's you who's here with Shō. She'll give in before long, you'll see."

"That's right," said Shō. "I haven't the faintest desire to go back to Shinako."

"Things will be all right now, won't they Nahoko," said the mother. "From now on the two of you will live happily together!" And with that she had discharged all of the unpleasant duties, finished all of the unpleasant business attendant on this visit.

Shō and his mother had said that before long things would work out, but in fact nothing worked out at all. Indeed, far from working out, things only got worse as Shinako began to launch her attacks. Needless to say, they were directed at Shō and Nahoko. At first, letters addressed to Shō would arrive every three days or so. They contained rambling accounts of everyday happenings at home. Shinako had hung new curtains in the living room. Or, she had eaten dinner at Mrs. X's, and of course the pièce de résistance had been that Italian-style salad the woman takes such pride in. Or, she wondered whether Goldie, their goldfish, wasn't getting old, for he hadn't seemed very lively of late. The letters were obviously written with the idea that Nahoko would read them.

Through the letters fragments of Shō's past, that daily life that Nahoko had never known, began to unfold before her. The letters became the means by which she learned all sorts of little stories, even how Shō had often gone to buy fresh eggs at a farmhouse some distance away. Nahoko, who had not yet lived with Shō for even two months, was just no match for Shinako, who had lived with him for four years and possessed the ingredients for endless stories. Nor had Shō's life with Shinako been any penny-pinching affair. There had been a cat and goldfish, and it seemed they had even had a patch of garden where flowers had blossomed in season. But Nahoko had nothing. Not even a neighbor she could call a friend. Nothing.

Whenever one of these letters came Nahoko would feel dejected and ill-humored, and she would always vent her temper on Shō. For an entire day they would hardly speak to each other. After half a year or so the letters gradually began to come less frequently, and their contents also changed. Now there were open challenges to Nahoko and scathing criticisms of Shō. "Once a woman marries she will not leave her man," Shinako would write. Or, "I can never approve of two such dissolute human beings as you." Or, "It is a husband's duty to support his wife." And so on.

"Why don't you bring her to reason for yourself instead of expecting your mother to take care of things for you," Nahoko would badger Shō whenever one of Shinako's venomous letters arrived.

"No matter how many times I talk to her the answer will always be no, so what do you expect me to do," Shō would answer with a long-suffering look. His expression and manner were exactly like those of his mother when she returned in a quandary from Shinako's at the time of her visit; and the way he quickly forgot his troubles and regained the good spirits of living for the moment was exactly like his mother, too.

"What if you gave her some money?" Nahoko had become thoroughly exhausted from the epistolary attacks.

"What money? Besides, if I had any money I wouldn't give a penny of it to Shinako," Shō replied. "Besides, what difference does it make if we get married or not? I'm living with you, aren't I? Shinako doesn't mean a thing to me anymore." The logic and the words of the son echoed those of the mother, spanning two generations.

Shō's living with her did prove that for him, as they say, actions speak louder than words. Yet Nahoko still felt uneasy, and more than that perhaps, she could never shake the fear of how Shinako would next attack them. Nahoko was just no match for Shinako's line of argument and action. Nor could she stand up against Shō's mother. Before the line of argument and action of either she felt helpless.

Nevertheless, a sudden visit from Shinako was to turn Nahoko's fear to panic and eventually to awaken her fighting spirit. It happened one morning around nine or ten o'clock, when Shō and Nahoko were still lying in bed. The instant they heard Shinako's voice at the front entrance, asking the landlady for Shō's room, they leaped out of bed in alarm, threw their clothes on in confusion, and tossed the sleeping mats into the closet. At that moment Shinako arrived, calling for Shō in a loud voice. And before they could ask her to come in, she had opened the door and stood there before them.

"So this is the sort of cubbyhole you live in," she remarked, seating herself before a desk in a corner of the room.

"How did you find the way?" asked Shō in agitation. "It's not easy."

"That Taiwanese restaurant by the bus stop is famous, you know. I was there once before. Mrs. X asked me to pick up some Chinese rice dumplings there for her today," Shinako replied.

Nahoko fixed black tea, as was her custom every morning, and set a cup before Shinako, too.

"It was terrible the last time your mother came to see me, Shō,"
Shinako continued, not even glancing at the cup of tea Nahoko had
poured for her. "She didn't stop crying the whole time she was
there, and I tell you, I had some time trying to cheer her up. I
wonder if she hasn't lost a little of her nerve these days. That was
the first time I'd ever seen her cry like that, and was I ever surprised! Come to think of it, doesn't it seem sort of funny that I
should have been the one trying to cheer *her* up?"

"Was there something you wanted to see me about?" Shō asked.
Before Nahoko, he spoke to his former wife as though to a perfect
stranger.

"Do I want something? I *am* your wife, Shō. Surely it's all right
for me to stay with you as long as I like."

"But," Shō stammered, "I've left you."

"Always the same old Shō, aren't you? Smelling something before
you eat it, like that. I have to laugh!" Her eyes following his every
movement, for all the world like some fond mother watching the
antics of her child, Shinako gave him a loving pat and paid no
attention to his query.

"Anyway, I can't believe you're living in this dirty little place.
Halfway here my throat got sore, the air is so bad!" Shinako continued to speak as she gave the room a minute inspection and leaned
over toward Shō, sitting in the other chair, to straighten the twisted
collar of his jacket. Even in Shinako's most trifling gestures toward
Shō, Nahoko sensed a shocking familiarity. No, it was more than
familiarity. It was more a licentiousness that she sensed.

"Mrs. X's sister gave me this a while back for helping her out
when she moved. Not a bad pattern, don't you think?" Shinako took
a man's summer kimono from her shopping bag and held it up to
Shō's chest.

"Say, dear," Nahoko finally said, "didn't you have that appoint-
ment today?"

"Oh, of course! I've got to be going," Shō answered.

"Shall we leave together, then?" said Shinako.

"But wasn't there something you wanted?" asked Nahoko.

"Not with you, there wasn't," said Shinako, addressing Nahoko
for the first time.

"Then what did you come for?" Nahoko asked. "Wasn't there
something you came to see me about? If there wasn't, then go back
where you came from. You know it's rude just to barge in on people
in the morning. Besides, you look a sight! What you ought to do is

go home and take a long look at yourself in the mirror. Why, a woman of your age! Just to look at you makes others ashamed. Don't you feel any shame for yourself?" Nahoko could not say a tenth of what she wanted. "Yes, that's what you ought to do," she repeated. "Take a good long look at yourself in the mirror. Why, a woman of your age!" Nahoko was surprised to find herself shouting. And the instant she heard her own voice she was sorry. She felt it was not right to shout, and getting angry never got a person anywhere either. She told herself to act normally—no, even more politely than usual. Well, maybe that was going too far, but at least she must be courteous. And yet somehow she seemed to lack strength of character, for the more she thought about what she should do, the more curtly she spoke, until she found herself shouting what could only be the worst possible insults at Shinako.

Twice Nahoko had said "a woman of your age," and now she would have given anything to take back those words. It was not fair to finish off her opponent with a blow that had nothing to do with her essential value as a human being. For a long time afterward Nahoko looked back on the incident with distaste, but at the time it seemed that the only way to bring the scene to a satisfactory conclusion was to say what she really felt. Something more was at work than her desire to preserve a spirit of fair play. She was oppressed with an indescribable shame. That was it. The licentiousness that Shinako exuded seemed somehow pitiful to Nahoko, and what made it so, the culprit that betrayed Shinako, must certainly have been that "woman of your age" that Nahoko detected in her. It was this culprit that Nahoko hated.

Shinako did not seem to be any born villain, either. Reeling under Nahoko's one blow, she beat a hasty retreat, unable to counterattack. After Shinako had left with a stony look on her face and her own excitement had abated, Nahoko wondered why it was that she felt something akin to affection for the other woman. Shinako had played the role of Shō's wife grandly and, as Nahoko believed, with all her heart. If only they had met under different circumstances, Nahoko felt that Shinako was the sort of person with whom she could perhaps have become surprisingly close friends.

After this incident, however, Shinako's epistolary offensive continued—though the actual volume of letters decreased—bringing accounts of her daily activities but no mention at all of her visit. Once in a great while she would send things to Shō, a sweater that she had knitted from raveled yarn, or a shapeless pair of pajamas that she had made from a summer kimono, and so on, but there were no violent attacks.

Some two months after Shinako's visit Nahoko discovered that she was pregnant. Since Shō was only an assistant in the lithography studio of a friend, it was all they could do to make ends meet with their single tiny room. Nahoko had been reduced to soliciting students with handmade posters stuck on telephone poles in the neighborhood, and she earned a mere pittance tutoring two grade school children who came to her twice a week. It was thus no small problem should their family increase.

"What a mess we're in," Nahoko said, confessing her worries to Shō. And in that "mess" she had in mind not only the day-to-day problems of living but also, of course, the matter of Shinako. For undoubtedly Shinako would now find material for a fresh attack. "Look at you—a baby on the way and you aren't even married!" she would say. Shō had said that Shinako had always wanted a child, though she had never been able to have one. Shocked by the news of Nahoko's baby, she would surely respond by renewing her attacks with even greater vigor.

"What shall we do?" Nahoko asked Shō over and over again.

"Oh, it doesn't matter," he would always reply. "Whatever you want is fine." Whether it was because he was no good at making important decisions or simply because he disliked making decisions that carried any responsibility, Shō was the kind of person who set great store by other people's thoughts and ideas.

"I'll go ask your mother," Nahoko decided.

Nahoko had said she was going to go ask Shō's mother, but what she really intended was to launch an attack against her. In other words, now that she had material for a decisive attack on Shō's optimistic mother, she planned to spy out her reaction and then harass her. This was the mother who had always gotten by with saying "Things will work out" and "Nahoko, you're our daughter-in-law," laughing and having fun on the jet coaster. Now she would see that things were not going to work out by themselves.

After a train ride of some five hours from Tokyo, Nahoko finally found herself, for only the second time in her life, at Shō's childhood home. It was in a country town, a boardinghouse run by his parents. Since meals were served to the boarders, the kitchen was fitted out as a small dining hall.

Shō's father and mother were naturally surprised at Nahoko's sudden arrival. Some of the boarders eating dinner in the kitchen were not yet acquainted with Nahoko, and they watched Shō's father and mother with evident curiosity. To these Shō's mother explained everything by saying, "This is Shō's wife."

Nahoko waited to break the news of her pregnancy to Shō's parents until all of the boarders had just about finished dinner.

"Well! Well! Congratulations, Nahoko!" said his mother.

"Is it true? Is it true?" said his father. "That's wonderful news, Nahoko! Congratulations!"

"Well, Papa, we're finally going to have a little grandchild to look at!" said Shō's mother. Overjoyed at the unexpected news, the two took turns clamoring their approval.

"They say your grandchildren are always nicer than your own children, and you know, I bet it's true, Papa!" Shō's mother was saying.

"But what shall we do?" Nahoko began her attack. "So what if I do have a baby? I'm not married to Shō, so even if I do have a baby, he won't be your grandchild!"

"What are you saying?" Shō's mother demanded, looking at Nahoko in wonder. "If he's Shō's child, isn't he our grandchild?"

"But the child will have my name," Nahoko pressed on.

"If you have a baby," the father said, "you're sure to come out the winner. Even Shinako will give up then. You have to have the baby. You'll see, in the end whoever has the baby will have the advantage."

"That's right. Even Shinako will give up now. Everything's fine now. Really! With a baby on the way you don't have a thing to worry about." Shō's mother looked thoroughly relieved.

"But what if she only gets more stubborn now that there's going to be a baby? Then what will I do?" Nahoko's attack was unrelenting.

"That's true," said Shō's mother. "This time Papa will go, and he'll tell Shinako that you're going to have a baby. Then everything will be all right. This time if Papa goes and talks to her, Shinako will give up, you'll see!"

"Yes, I'll go," agreed Shō's father. "Shinako or not, even she'll give up when I tell her you're going to have a baby."

The next day Nahoko returned to Tokyo, and two days later Shō's father came. His purpose was to negotiate with Shinako and convince her to give up Shō. Unlike Shō's mother he seemed to enjoy neither rides nor trips, for he had planned a busy day, coming up on the early morning train and returning home to the country that night.

After visiting Shinako he stopped by Shō's place to report on the outcome of the battle.

"How did it go, Father?" Shō, as if he had long been awaiting his father, pressed him eagerly for his report.

"Well, if I wasn't in for a surprise! That Shinako! She came right out and spoke her mind, I'll tell you. And you know what she said? That it's just fine if Shō's going to have a child. But I said wouldn't it be better if you gave him up now that there's going to be a child? I got down on my knees to her, I don't know how many times." Shō's father gave a thorough account of his many attempts to oblige his son and the humiliations he had borne in the process. Since Shō's mother actually seemed to run the boardinghouse by herself, the father believed that his son always thought him an out-and-out good-for-nothing.

"Shinako took it all in stride and wasn't the least bit surprised when I told her about the baby. And no matter how many times I told her to give you up, she said that the child and the divorce were two different things, and there was nothing that would ever change her mind." Shō's father talked on exuberantly, giving the impression that in the end what concerned him most was being absolved as soon as possible from his duties.

To Nahoko, however, there had first to be delivered a parental expostulation. "Nahoko," he began, "Mama is so happy, you'll just have to have the baby anyway. Why, that's what women are for, after all—having babies. Besides, Shō is our only son. What will we do if he doesn't have a child? Why, they always say a child's what makes a marriage stick. Look at Shinako. She didn't have a baby, and now she has to live all by herself."

"Anyway," he continued, "we can forget about Shinako now, don't you think? She'll give up before long. When all is said and done, whoever has the child will come out the winner. Things will work out before long, you'll see." And with these words he left for home.

Nahoko's attack had ended in dismal failure. What strategy or tactics could ever vanquish the doctrine of "things will work out"? An advocate of "do something now" is just no match for a believer in "things will work out." From the beginning Nahoko had never had a chance. She had been defeated *ideologically*!

On a sudden inspiration Nahoko wrote a letter to her mother, informing her of her pregnancy. Nahoko knew that though her letter contained a veiled attack on her own mother, at the same time it was also a part of her strategy in the battle against Shō's family.

By drawing her mother into the fray, Nahoko was not without hope of gaining a protective crossfire.

Three days later a long letter arrived by special delivery. It had been written by some relative on behalf of Nahoko's mother. Though her mother was not completely incapable of writing for herself, she could never have managed a letter of this length and importance. She had, after all, never even made it through one of the old-style elementary schools, and it was consequently quite beyond her powers to compose a letter in any sort of logical fashion. And yet, interestingly enough, the person who wrote the letter must have duplicated her speech quite faithfully, for the letter ran on at great length just as if Nahoko's mother were speaking.

"First you run off with a man who's already got himself a wife and now you mean to tell me you're going to have his baby!" was the note on which the letter began. "And what's this about Shō's parents being happy? If they're wanting to be happy 'cause there's a baby on the way, then they'd best do what's right and proper first! Let me tell you, I didn't raise any girl of mine to be having the grandchild of a bunch of country bumpkins. I thought I knew you better! What can be going through your head, girl, anyway? Saying you're happy to be having a baby who's got no daddy just because the man's parents say they're happy about it? If Shō's parents want to be so happy about this new grandchild, then they sure better get rid of that old wife of his and come here and introduce themselves proper, and if they can't do that much, well then, don't be expecting me to be telling you congratulations or such, 'cause I'd sooner my mouth rotted off first. If his parents want to talk about how happy they are about all this, doesn't it make sense they go sell their lands and fields, even put everything in hock if need be, to make enough money to settle accounts with his old wife? It's not as if I had you marry the fellow. You're the one who had to have your way, running away from home and chasing after a man who's already got himself a wife. You're no daughter of mine anymore, so it's pretty selfish your thinking that now you're pregnant you'd like your mama to say it's just fine. If you're determined to have that child, no matter what, then have your way, go right ahead and have it. You're nobody to me anymore, so why should I be caring?" And so the letter ran on.

Though the content of the letter was much as Nahoko had expected, in a way it did not entirely live up to her expectations. Nahoko was used to her mother's line of argument and was even largely in agreement, and yet she had written her mother hoping for something she could not quite foresee. No, her mother would certainly not extend her congratulations with the unrestrained joy of Shō's parents, but Nahoko had thought that, the situation being what it was, her mother might order her to have the baby. Instead, at the end of that long letter, her mother had written only too clearly that if Nahoko insisted on having her baby, regardless of the consequences, then she was acting out of sheer willfulness—and against such soft-headed behavior as that, her mother declared herself firmly opposed. And yet, might her mother not have written so violently on purpose, consciously setting up a crossfire to protect her daughter in the battle against Shō's parents? Somewhere inside Nahoko there still lurked a yearning to be babied.

No doubt this letter would prove quite useful in Nahoko's second attack on Shō's family. This violent anger of her mother's would surely cause some discomfiture to Shō's parents, optimistic advocates of the "things will work out" doctrine that they were, and set them to thinking. And yet Nahoko felt this to be a cruel and merciless mother, an obstinate mother indeed. That common saying that goes "Gentle as a mother, strict as a father" did not fit her mother at all. What child in time of need does not turn to his mother as a last resort, hoping to bury his head in her bosom and receive her tender caresses? But was this obstinate mother of hers not casting her child away? Her words showed what sort of person she really was. "Have your way, go right ahead," she had said, ending with "I'm against any such soft-headedness as having that child!" It was true that Nahoko did not like the doctrine and methods of the "things will work out" school of thought, but this kind of strict logic was no better. She found it just as unappealing to be *too* sensible. Since when was it soft-headed to be having a child? What kind of thing was that to say?

As she read her mother's letter Nahoko was invaded by a feeling vaguely like sadness, but she could not stop now to dally with her emotions. She was much too troubled. What should she do? What would be best for her to do? Shō's parents, her own mother—they were angry or glad depending on their own point of view, but none of them was looking at the problem from *her* point of view. Maybe that was only to be expected. And yet I'm what's most important for me, Nahoko thought. The old people are certainly looking out for what's good for them, and if I don't do the same, if I don't look out for what's good for me, I'll be the one to suffer. Because Shō, all-important Shō, just runs away.

Armed with her mother's letter, Nahoko paid another visit to Shō's home in the country.

"For some reason my mother is mad about what's been happening," Nahoko told Shō's parents, showing them her mother's letter.

They read the letter by turns and then, not surprisingly, fell silent.

Finally Shō's mother sighed, "Looking at it from your mother's point of view, I suppose it's only natural for her to say such things."

"But, Mama, I just can't understand how any mother could talk to her daughter that way," Shō's father said. "And you know what she's telling Nahoko. That she has to have an abortion."

"But, Papa, that means she's telling her to kill a baby that's already on the way," said the mother.

"Nahoko's baby is our grandchild," declared the father. "What's more, to send a letter like this at such a critical time! Why, Nahoko must have gotten a terrible shock."

Nahoko continued her attack. "Won't one of you talk to my mother for me?" she asked.

"It's such a long way to your house, you know," said Shō's mother in distress.

"Oh, everything's going to be all right. Your mother will take one look at her little grandchild's face and give in. Things will work out, Nahoko, you'll see!" And with these words Shō's father settled the matter of the letter.

No, the "things will work out" doctrine doesn't suit me any better, thought Nahoko. And yet the anger she sensed in Shō's parents was in one way akin to the anger of her mother. It's true they're like parents to me, she thought. And since they're like parents they resemble my mother . . . Nahoko found the thought depressing. She had taken these few preliminary measures, and in both cases her strategies were exhausted. Now it was up to her to make a decision for herself. On the train back to Tokyo she felt terribly alone.

"Shō, listen to me, what are we going to do?"

"Oh, whatever you want is fine."

For a time this conversation was repeated over and over again, leaving Nahoko without a straw to cling to. In the meantime Shinako's letters continued to come, and Shō gave no sign of going to negotiate with her in person.

To rebel against the "things will work out" school of thought, she must not give birth to the baby. And to rebel against the "do something now" school of thought, it would be better to have the

baby. But both of these schools were outside the private world of
Nahoko and Shō's relationship. The best thing for them to do
would be to make a decision within that private world of their own.
In the end such a decision would prove the best way, Nahoko believed, not only to defeat those two schools of thought so alien to
their own private world but to defeat Shinako as well. Yet for one
of Nahoko's ability, it was no easy matter to map out such a complicated plan of action. One must say that in seeking a physiological
solution to her dilemma, Nahoko was extremely calculating. If calculating seems too harsh a term for her particular case, then it can
only be said that because the situation she faced was so very complicated she became calculating in self-defense.

"Shō, what do you think? Do you want a child or not?" she
would ask. And Shō would answer, "It doesn't matter to me one
way or the other."

Since Shō was used to a life of poverty he did not worry over
what further hardships an addition to their family would bring. He
would not feel demeaned by taking in other people's cast-away
sheets and old, hand-me-down cotton kimonos to make diapers for
the baby. Shō had lived his whole life that way. The sweater that
Shinako had sent him was a patched-up affair knitted from bits of
old yarn. Shō was not one to care about that. Being the kind of
person who could calmly wear an old, patched sweater from a wife
he had as good as cast off himself, he would never have felt his
existence threatened by the birth of one small baby.

Even so, Nahoko wanted to have Shō decide. She wanted to have
her man make the decision. Whether it was "Let's wait until all
these problems are straightened out" or "Let's have the baby no
matter what," she wanted him to make a clear statement one way
or the other. Was that not what living with Shō was all about? If
she was to be all by herself, deciding everything for herself, she
would never have come to live with him in the first place. Had she
not come to live with Shō, in full knowledge that he was married,
just because she wanted him to make some clear statement one
way or the other? Besides, it wasn't as if this was some everyday,
trifling sort of problem. The birth of a child was a major event, and
Nahoko was not happy with the way Shō managed to sidestep the
whole issue as if it were no concern of his. She could not get a good
grip on this man.

"Shō, why did you marry Shinako?" Overcome by nausea, Nahoko had spread out the sleeping mats and was lying down.

"Oh, I was boarding in her house. It was a whole lot cheaper than any of the others. But then I only had one small room. Well, there I was, straight from the country and flat broke. So I had to start working the day I got there. There were other boarders, too, but she was always nicest to me. She'd give me my noodles or whatever for supper, and she'd give me rice dumplings. She was about thirty then. That's right, because I was around twenty. One time . . . that's it, I remember now. It was the day her mother died. Well, actually the night of the wake. She came to my room to talk. Well, that was the first time we slept together. She kept talking about getting married, and I'd say nothing doing, but she went off to my parents in the country and had a talk with them. And besides, you know, I wouldn't have had any place to live if I left the boardinghouse. She'd told me to get out if I wouldn't marry her." Shō told his story as if he were talking about someone else.

"Well, then, why did you leave her?"

"What do you think? Because I met you!" replied Shō, smiling, as he gave Nahoko a kiss.

"Oh, I see, you couldn't help it." Still lying in bed, Nahoko continued to talk. "But how could you ever have married a woman just because you didn't want to have to find another boardinghouse? If you really couldn't stand her you could have run away and slept under a bridge or something. But see, you didn't run away, so you couldn't have found her totally repulsive. No, I bet you loved her back then. After all, you were all by yourself in the world, and she was kind to you. She was your only ally."

"From the start she always said she'd let me go whenever I got sick of her. But when I told her I was living with you, she said nothing would make her give me up." Shō looked bewildered as he spoke.

"Well, of course not! You're a fool if you can't see that!"

"Any other woman was okay, she said, but you she couldn't take."

"But she hadn't even met me then."

"Oh, she could tell, she said. Intuition. She said she didn't hate me. You were the one she hated."

"Well, I'm bound to live to a ripe old age . . . if someone hates me that much."

Nahoko was tired. There was Shō's evasiveness, which she had only gradually come to realize. And that drifting aimlessness she sensed in Shō's parents. And Shinako's attacks. Nor was that all. This was the first time in her whole life that she was living beneath the roof of a stranger, staying in a house where strangers came and went, and she was tired of not being able to speak in her normal tone of voice and of being exposed to the outside world of other families the minute she opened her one sliding door and stepped out into the hallway. Coming back from outside and stepping through the front door, she would find that long hallway stretching back into the house, disappearing part way in the gloom. Whenever she looked at the doors on each side, closing off the small rooms of the lodgers, she felt that this cellarlike place in the depths of the gloom was the only place in the world where she could lay her body down, and she would feel the loneliness of one who has nowhere else to turn.

Why had she come to such a place? Why was she here? In the half a year before coming here and in the half a year since, Nahoko had been too busy to wonder about such things. Nahoko had come impetuously, Nahoko had come recklessly here. And the time since coming had passed before she had had a chance to settle what was what in her mind. Days would go by as she lay in bed, drugged with fumes from the briquette brazier; others would go by as she sank in defeat before one of Shinako's attacks; and still others would go by in the warmth of her love as she sat opposite Shō having a meal.

Nahoko did not know what had made her come so impetuously to this place. At only her second meeting with Shō she had already decided to come here. But she could never have imagined that "here" would be such a place. "Here" was not the end of a gloomy hallway; it was a little bit brighter than this. She had never pictured herself seated in a deck chair, occupied with her knitting, on the veranda of a house surrounded by lawns, but she could never have foreseen the darkness she would encounter here.

Why had the two of them sought refuge in this dark place? Why had Shō ever chosen to come here from a place where fish swam, a dog and cat frolicked, and flowers bloomed? Here they were, before they knew it, like two children who suddenly hit upon a new game. Bringing nothing, not even the essentials for setting up house. Just like two children who play house with but a straw mat, she and Shō had come bearing but a single set of sleeping mats.

The words of love they exchanged had been the key unlocking the door to this dark place. Had those endearments not been like a diving board? How the two of them had hurried to make the plunge into this place! The cries of anger and sadness welling up around them had never reached their ears. They had taken a short-cut on the romantic road to love so that they could but eat and sleep together in this dark cellar.

And yet, not once had Nahoko felt the urge to leave this dark place for what she had left behind. Nor did the desire to return to her mother seethe within her. Winter, cold with just the single brazier, or summer, a breezeless inferno with the stucco apartment house behind them so close that when she opened the back window she thought she could almost touch it—and yet she had never thought of leaving. Two lovebirds with only the clothes on their backs, they were more like two bedraggled sparrows. There were no friendly neighbors here to give them old cotton kimonos. Once a week Nahoko cleaned the dirty bathroom used by so many people. Crawling along the floor, she had to scrub the dark hallway with water. The oppressive dampness. Once the young wife next door had put out all her dresser drawers. The dampness made the bugs come out, she had said. Gay sounds of people laughing seldom came from any of the rooms. Was it because people's voices did not carry in the damp air? The old landlady, a paraplegic, would sit holed up in her tiny room with an earthen brazier, always cooking something. When Nahoko brought the rent, "You bet!" were the only words she could get out of her. And something was always broken. Several tiles had come loose in the bathroom. All the faucets were leaky, and water collected in the sinks. The communal washstand would always back up and dirty water flow into the hallway. The front door was so stiff that it took several tries to close it. In the entryway the doors to the lockers for shoes had all come off their hinges.

"Shō! I think there's something the matter!" Nahoko kept saying. And two or three days later she had a miscarriage.

"When you strain your head and nerves too much, all your blood goes up to your head and none of it gets down to your stomach." This was, true or false, the doctor's explanation.

Shō sent a letter to his parents, telling them of Nahoko's miscarriage, but there was no reply. Nahoko also informed her own mother by letter. From her mother there came a heavy packet of Chinese herbal medicine labeled "medicine for female disorders," but again there was no letter. Even Shinako's letters came but rarely now. With the miscarriage Nahoko breathed a sigh of relief.

Shō blamed the miscarriage on Nahoko's trips to the country. "Things went wrong because of those two train rides you took out to the country," he said.

Nahoko felt that she hadn't really wanted to have a baby after all. As she lay in bed, alone in the gloomy room, this was all she could think about . . . Really, I was just as selfish about the child as Shō's parents and my mother were. I was too busy thinking about myself ever to think about the baby, down in my stomach, suffocating from lack of oxygen. And Shō's parents never thought about their son's wife—nor my own mother about her daughter—as she suffocated her baby. And yet why is it, in spite of everything, I feel so refreshed?

"Since your father and mother were so happy about the baby, the least they could have done was send a letter saying they were sorry," Nahoko said to Shō. "Angry as my mother was, she at least sent me some medicine." And yet Nahoko had never bothered to take any of the herbal medicine her mother had sent: it had seemed such a nuisance to brew. That may have been the reason why soon afterward Nahoko, already weakened by a cold, developed inflammation of the bladder, her condition worsening until she ended up contracting pyelitis. She was ordered to have complete rest and quiet, but with Shō gone to work she was not able to do as the doctor said. Besides, her medicine was so expensive that it seemed she was swallowing solid gold every time she took a pill, and it did nothing to abate a low but persistent fever. It may also have been a side effect of this medicine that Nahoko felt a mossy growth on her tongue and that eventually even the soles of her feet seemed to be covered with green-colored moss.

"My mother always said to be sure to find a man who'll take care of you when you're sick. The rest of the time doesn't matter. Now I see what she means," Nahoko grumbled to Shō. The problem was that Shō, having never been sick himself, did not know how to nurse sick people, and did not understand how forlorn they can feel. He never made any effort to come home extra early just because Nahoko was sick in bed. Certainly he would do whatever she asked him, whatever she ordered him to do, but he never did any more than she asked, and there were some things that, well, "a man just isn't good at." Nahoko could not help feeling that he was just insensible to the needs of the ailing.

As for Shō, he had once said, "I've never seen anyone as self-centered as you!" To his way of thinking all a sick person had to do was to stay quietly in bed and everything would be just fine. But no sooner would Nahoko feel a little better than she would be outside at the sink washing clothes as usual. Soon the fever would return, and there she would be, howling with worry because her fever was back again. No wonder that Shō was disgusted!

"No one ever died from a little dirt or dust," he told her. And then finally he had shouted, "I can't be constantly looking after you like your mama! I have to work all day, you know!"

"You just hate to see your hard-earned money go down the drain for a lot of expensive medicine when I can't work!" said Nahoko. "Aren't you ashamed of yourself? You don't like to be the only one who has to work." As a matter of fact, Nahoko had for some time now been turning away the two students who had come to her for tutoring because her fees were so much less than the going rate. Shō had no head for schemes to get them through the present crisis, and whether or not this too was because he stemmed from a long line of believers in "things will work out," absolutely nothing ever changed. This only exasperated Nahoko further and aggravated her sense of uneasiness.

After more than a month of having her fever go away only to come back again, Nahoko resolved to go home to her mama and get over her illness once and for all. Nahoko had left her home feeling besieged on all sides by enemies. To return now in defeat, even under the exceptional circumstance of her illness and no matter how temporarily, could afford her no pleasant prospects. Still, as they say, while there's life there's hope, and she was only giving herself up to be babied, fully expecting to recuperate under her mother's roof and then to kick sand in her face as she left. Besides, an illness like this, which, unlike some that send the patient moaning to his bed, left Nahoko able to be up and about the room, made her chafe even more and feel increasingly cranky toward anyone who happened to be well. Might not Shō be thinking she was really all better and only staying in bed out of laziness?

Shō accompanied Nahoko when she returned to her mother's home. Riding a second-class steam train on the Tōkaidō line, they took seven and a half hours to reach the city where her mother lived. From there it was another hour on a private electric line before they arrived at the little station Nahoko remembered so well. By that time it was already around ten o'clock at night.

In the darkness outside the ticket gate stood Nahoko's mother. As soon as she caught sight of Nahoko, who looked utterly exhausted, she ran up and stood before her.

"Are you all right, looking like this?" she cried. "Eh? Are you all right, girl? Such a fool! What do you mean getting sick like this? So now as you're sick, and heaven only knows the reason, what do you plan to do?" Her words, all rough and pointy, seemed to clatter uneasily on the air before bouncing back to her.

Nahoko was surprised to find her mother there to meet her. "You knew just when I'd get here, didn't you," she said.

"I figured as how it'd be about now," her mother replied. "And I've been waiting since eight or so." The vigil seemed not to have tired her at all. On the contrary, the uneasiness she felt as she worried over this daughter, returning home to her gravely ill, had inspired her with an extraordinary degree of excitement. This was clear from the feverish way she talked. Nahoko, having many times witnessed this half-mad excitement with which her mother met every crisis, was not particularly surprised. All anyone could do was to wait until it subsided without trying to interfere.

Nahoko's mother walked close by her daughter's side through the darkened streets from the station. Since catching sight of Nahoko outside the station, she had had eyes for no one else, her gaze never straying to Shō, who was standing right next to Nahoko and carrying her suitcase. Shō could not even get her to say hello to him. Though standing right next to her, he was ignored completely. He was treated as though he were not even there. Her daughter, wasted with illness, occupied the whole of the mother's field of vision, and the man who had brought that daughter home to her went unnoticed. Such was the force of her excitement that, anxious for the welfare of her ailing daughter, she wished only to run home with her clasped in her arms. Walking along the road to her house, she addressed not a single word to Shō. In silence Shō trudged along behind mother and daughter, carrying the suitcase.

Waiting inside the house for the invalid were light, warm-looking sleeping mats and quilts spread with sparkling white sheets. Such a change it was from that gloomy cellar! Why, it was dazzling! The nightgown warming on the heater. Her mother's speedy preparations. In the twinkling of an eye Nahoko had been put to bed like a proper invalid. Shō, meanwhile, squatted in a corner of the room, merely watching the mother and daughter.

With Nahoko tucked warmly into bed, her mother seemed finally to relax, for drawing over the tobacco tray, she began to fill her pipe. For the first time she noticed Shō.

"What're you doing away over there?" she addressed him. "Come on over!" Nahoko had been furious with her mother all the way from the station. What way was this to treat someone? But she knew that if she made some inadvertent remark or in any way tried to interfere when her mother was excited like this, things were sure to backfire. There was just nothing for it but to wait until her mother's excitement subsided.

"This here's no child of mine, you hear," she said to Shō. "I'm not taking care of her because she's my daughter. It's like some stranger's child took sick and collapsed on my step. A person can't very well send her away, so in she comes and I put her to bed. You got that straight, now, don't you?" Shō was unaccustomed to such a line of reasoning and consequently did not know how to answer. Brought up in the school of "things will work out," he was none too sure how best to deal with such an outspoken greeting.

"Shō took good care of me," said Nahoko, coming to his rescue.

"Took good care of you, you say! You're in pretty bad shape to be saying that!" replied her mother. "Besides, any man'd give his all so that the woman he loves'd get better."

Shō was more at a loss for words than ever. But no matter how much at a loss for words, he showed no sign of wanting to shrink from her sight. He was still smiling his usual smile. And, picking up the pipe Nahoko's mother had set down, he even took a puff in imitation of her and said, "Mmm. Tastes good!"

"It just takes lots of rest and quiet to get over something like this," he said. "She'll be okay."

"She may not look it, but this girl's the nervous sort. She doesn't get over things the way other people do." Since the bonds of parental duty and affection seemed not to hold in her relations with Shō, Nahoko's mother began to lose the hostility toward him that had come with her initial excitement.

"Is it okay to watch TV?" Shō said at last.

"Of course not! Nahoko's going to sleep!" replied her mother in astonishment.

"Well, is it okay if I stay tonight too, then?" he said.

"I can't be telling you to go home now, can I! I've fixed a bed in the next room, so you can sleep there. After all, I can't be letting you sleep with the invalid, now, can I!" Her spirits considerably restored, Nahoko's mother could indulge in her own special variety of humor. Unfortunately, however, it was lost on Shō.

Nahoko received amazingly good care for one who was to have been treated like any passerby who happened to collapse on her mother's doorstep. Indeed, she was treated like a princess, waited on hand and foot. Three times each and every day she was fed the nourishing meals her mother believed essential for the ailing, and even her underclothes were laundered for her. Nahoko could not bear the excitement generated by her mother's uneasiness whenever one of her children was sick, and yet she could not but be impressed each time with the meticulous way in which her mother cared for the ailing. Nahoko recalled that it was only during times of sickness that one could enjoy this kind of uncomplaining kindness from her mother. She had heard, and had no reason to discount, the story of how her mother had gone to some shrine early each morning, braving the cold of dead winter for one hundred days in a row, so that she might pray for the health of Nahoko's little brother, who had been sickly as a child. Several years ago, when Nahoko had suddenly groaned with a pain between her ribs, her mother had applied boiling hot compresses until the skin of both the palms of her hands peeled off from the heat of the water.

However, once Nahoko had recovered her health, a matter of a month or so, she could not stay forever with her mother. She must return to the end of that gloomy hallway. Nahoko realized that the place where a sick person, or rather a sick child, can find rest, at ease in both body and soul, no longer seems that way to the child grown well. It was because she knew this only too well that she left, regardless of the consequences.

Nahoko's mother was not one to use honeyed words or cajolery when one was sick, but this was particularly true when all was normal. Nahoko knew of course that her mother had her own special variety of kindness. But it served only to block off her own, and presumably any child's, avenue of escape. It took more than average strength to loosen the grip with which her mother embraced her children. Nahoko had been forced to set dynamite. And then once she had escaped, having demolished her mother's embrace with her one little stick of dynamite, Nahoko felt somehow forlorn. It was a sorry state of affairs when a cold was enough to make her think back on Mama's rice gruel!

"That Shō, he hangs on to his chopsticks like a kid, now, doesn't he," said Nahoko's mother after Shō had left. "If somebody can't even use his chopsticks properly, it's because his parents didn't train him just so when he was little. Not only that, he's got such a low-class way of eating, shoveling everything out of his bowl and into his mouth like he was in some hurry. Let me tell you, it's no good a man looking so shabby when he eats! He's not going to get himself anywhere in this world with such a shabby way of eating as that!"

"So what's getting anywhere mean?" Nahoko asked. The very fact that this conversation had taken place was proof to Nahoko that dynamite would soon be required.

"Well, go ahead and give yourself to such a good-for-nothing then! I did my best to stop you, but, no, you wouldn't listen . . . Even so, like I told you before, no matter how badly you've fallen for a fellow, if there's something wrong with him, then end the thing there! Yes, indeed, when you left home I felt just like a mama bear. I felt like I was watching my little cub fall into a ravine. It's not like you married the fellow. No, of course not! If there's something wrong you can still come home. If you were married I couldn't be telling you such things, but as things are . . ." The mother watched her daughter, now healthy and growing restless.

"You're wearing the self-same clothes you had on when you left here, aren't you, now?" she went on. "Couldn't you make yourself something new to wear? Well, I suppose your being sick, there was nothing for it, but still. Well, you be understanding one thing—I didn't take care of you because you were my daughter. I wouldn't have given you a cup of rice, even, if you'd come asking. If you'd sold all your things and had nothing left to sell and come asking me for help, I wouldn't have helped you. You're a person who's fallen into a ravine. Anyway, girls, they've always got something left to sell. They've got their bodies."

Nahoko did not talk to her mother about any of the things that had gone on at the end of that gloomy hallway. How Shō's parents had come, how Shinako had come—she told her none of these things. She never offered of her own accord any material that could but buy her mother's scorn.

"There's a place where they sell really good millet cakes. We got some from somebody once," Nahoko said. "When I was sick there wasn't anything tasted good to me, and I felt like eating something sweet, and when I told Shō I just had to be having one of those millet cakes, off he went looking in the middle of the night and walked a long ways to buy some for me." Nahoko prattled on about her lover, an attack on her mother at least partly her aim.

"You're a fool, that's what you are!" said her mother, refusing to take her on. "What's a man doing such sappy things as that for? The thing is, you like that mushy kind of guy."

"Mama, what in the world can I do that will please you and set your mind at rest?" Nahoko asked. Oh, how many times had she repeated those lines before?

"Well, one thing's for sure," her mother continued, "you've got the blood of your dead father in your veins. Liking anyone who'll flatter you and flirt, even if it's all just for show. You like men who'll treat you that way. Well, enough said. Who am I to know? You're wanting to get back to Shō. It's written all over your face. Besides, what a flurry there's been! With you getting one of those special delivery letters every other day, why, it's enough to give a person the fidgets. It's beyond me how he can find so much to write about."

"Now, don't be showing your jealousy so much!" Nahoko replied. "The trouble is, Mama, you haven't got a man who'll send *you* special delivery letters every day."

"Now, what are you saying? I hate mushy guys like that," her mother said, finally laughing.

After a little more than a month, Nahoko returned to her cellar. Shō met her at Tokyo Station, looking as bashful as on the day they first met.

"I feel sort of self-conscious," he said.

"Now, why should you be feeling self-conscious?" Nahoko said, her words revealing traces of exposure to the contagion of her mother's speech. Nevertheless, Shō's boyish manner pleased her.

Shortly after Nahoko's return, her health now fully recovered, the couple moved to an apartment only a little way from their cellar. Even Shō seemed finally to have realized that Nahoko, the sort of person least able to cope with the mental and physical strains of adversity, had found it difficult to bear her surroundings in the cellar. Move though they did, of course, they still had one room, only slightly larger than the one before. But what was ever so much nicer about the new place was that each room had its own individual entrance, and they had their own bathroom and little kitchen. There was even a place for drying clothes. For the first time Nahoko felt like a newly-wed, cramped to be sure, but unconstrained by strangers passing in the hallway outside. Still, the content of their lives was not without its changes, for the rent they now paid was higher, leaving them no money even to go out and see a double feature. If they went out together and had something to eat, they could afford no more than a bowl of cheap noodles.

It may have been because their room was slightly larger than before that Shō began to bring home friends. Shō liked to have friends come to visit. Maybe he did have only his cheap, pawnshop suit to wear and meat patties from the market to eat, but he liked having friends over to liven things up with a drink, though cheap whiskey was all he had to offer. Sho had the talent for making a casual acquaintance into an instant bosom friend. In no time he and his new acquaintance would be back-slapping buddies, best friends from ten years back. Nahoko could never quite understand this.

She believed that no matter how well suited two people might be to one another, they could only get to know each other gradually and could not establish things on a first-name basis so quickly.

"If it were a matter of life and death I wonder who, among all your friends, would come to your rescue," Nahoko said after the departure of one of his friends, unashamedly drunk on cheap liquor and singing at the top of his voice. "You'd be having it that all your friends are good fellows, but I wonder. Isn't it true that nobody's a hundred-percent good like that? You start off with a hundred percent, but for most of the people you know the percentage goes gradually down the more you have to do with them. I start off believing in fifty percent, and sure a few people disappear along the way, but at least there's the possibility of making real friends." To hear Nahoko now was to realize how much her reasoning resembled her mother's. "When I see you with your friends you seem all chummy," she continued, "but you never care about what's deep down inside. It's all on the surface. You give each other a friendly handshake, and that's as far as it goes. If one of your friends was in a bad way, you wouldn't even ask him for a single detail, now, would you?"

Nahoko said this because Shō's friends were always saying, "Missus! I don't drink like this because I like to. The boss at home just doesn't understand me. That's how it is, isn't it, Shō. Let's drink a toast together, Shō. Let's drink to something or other. Shō's a good fellow! Aren't you, Shō!" And whenever this happened, Shō would say, "Drink! Drink!" as he passed pleasantly through that *particular* moment.

Shinako, as soon as she knew they had moved, reopened her attacks. One after another, letters came by certified mail, a form that Nahoko had never in her life known existed. Shinako told Shō that she was going to rent out the house, where she had been living all alone, and move to a room in his apartment house. Maybe this was only a sort of threat or intimidation, but try as she might to think of it that way, Nahoko still felt uneasy. When a letter came, Nahoko would thrust it under Shō's nose, only to be met by that same long-suffering, anguished expression. But by the next day Shō would give every sign of having forgotten the letter completely. A friend would come by with cheap liquor, and they would shake hands and drink to each other's health just as always.

It was at about this time that a message came from Shō's mother saying that she would come for a visit. Apparently she wanted to see the new room to which they had only just moved. The letter said that she would like the three of them, Nahoko included, to go off on an outing somewhere.

"I knew the son in the family was happy-go-lucky," said Nahoko with a sigh, "but I thought your parents might do better!"

"In any case," she said to Shō, extremely upset by Shinako's continued attacks, "you should get together the little money you've saved and give it to Shinako. Talk as much as you like about how young you were when it happened, but you're still the one who did it. If Shinako says she doesn't want the money, then there's nothing we can do about that. And it's even possible she'll take the money and then still refuse to leave you. But I still think we have to do whatever we can now, and then it will be time to think of what to do next. It seems funny for me to have to say this. Your parents should be the ones. But then your parents are different." The instant she finished speaking Shō's hand flew out and slapped her cheek.

"Don't you dare say anything bad about my mother!" he said, his eyes flashing. "My father and mother both went to Shinako's and got down on their knees to beg for us!" Man though Shō was, he had become temporarily hysterical. "Besides, you didn't hear my parents telling you not to have a baby that was already on the way like your mother! They were only too happy for us!" Without another word, Shō left.

Though Nahoko had heard what Shō said, she could still not understand why he had suddenly slapped her like that. And because she could not understand, tears welled up in her eyes. This time Shō returned after two or three hours, but when he left abruptly over a year later he never came back again. Perhaps when he had left Shinako's to join Nahoko in that cellar he had gone out just like this and never come back. And Nahoko, left to take care of Shō's notification of change of address and all the other little formalities that are minimally required for civic life, was probably doing no more than Shinako had done before her.

About a week after Shō had left, his mother came without warning to see Nahoko.

"I told Shō to go back to you," she said. "You got along so nicely together, it's a shame. You're at fault too, though, you know. Shō isn't a fickle boy at all. He's so kind the way he acts. The whole reason he's gone off with a woman so much younger is that you were too obstinate. You and Shinako must have both been born in the year of the wild boar. Women born under the sign of the wild boar are always obstinate. Shō says the woman this time is not a wild boar. His dad says wild boars are no good, too, and it seems to be true after all, doesn't it? Well, things ended like this, but take care of yourself, Nahoko, and don't let it get you down!" And then she asked, "Will you be going back to your mother's?"

"I'm not going back," Nahoko answered.

"Oh? Well, Shō is coming for his baggage tomorrow, so I'll be on my way now." Her message delivered, Shō's mother went home.

Nahoko thought how she would probably never meet Shō's mother again. How many times had she met her during the three years or more she had lived with Shō? She had met Shinako only that once, but Shō's mother she had met on some ten occasions. Despite the number of times they had met, she had no recollection of ever having talked to her about anything. No, she had not a single recollection of the two of them settling down to one of those rambling, inconsequential talks that women will have together. In the beginning she had worried about her high blood pressure and had taken special care with their meals, but when this only seemed to bring scoldings from Shō and the displeasure of the mother herself, she had stopped. Shō seemed to take his mother's happiness at the particular moment and her pleasure at the particular moment more seriously than the progress of her illness. Illness, pooh! Things always work out before long.

Shō's mother had told her that he was living with another woman. To be as young as she had said, the woman would have to be nineteen or twenty, since Nahoko herself was only twenty-seven. That did not bother her. What did bother her was that Shō had not told her about it himself. Nahoko had asked him whether something was going on two or three times before. Every time Shō had said no. He had seemed his old self. He had often bought some of those millet cakes for her on his way home. Until the day before he left he had slept with her in his arms. If only she had not broached the subject of Shinako, he could have gone on without those troubled looks; he could have drunk happily with the friends he brought home and the friends who came to see him; and he would never have complained about Nahoko's culinary disasters. If she had not brought up things that upset Shō, he would have been as kind as on the day she first met him. If she had hidden away those imposing letters that Shinako sent by certified mail, every day would have been as tranquil as the next. But Shinako's moans came enclosed in those certified letters. Oh, in theory she could have left well enough alone. What if Shinako had not been the first to meet Shō and marry him? What if *she* had been second? Then her argument would have made no sense. Nahoko could tell herself that Shinako could say what she did only because she had happened by chance to marry Shō first.

Shinako was making good use of the advantages inherent in her position, but the truth of her attacks may in fact have lain somewhere else. May she not have been pitting herself against something in Shō himself? In attributing her attacks simply to the irritability, crankiness, and sorrow of an older woman, had Shō not miscalculated? And that was why he had fled. Flight had been his only alternative.

The day Shō came to pick up his baggage unfortunately coincided with the day Nahoko's mother, informed by her daughter of recent events, came to Tokyo for the first time in some twenty-odd years, filled with that extraordinary excitement her worry always produced. Shō, who had been hurriedly cramming his belongings into a wicker trunk and a suitcase, was naturally astounded at the apparition of Nahoko's mother. At a loss for words, though only because the present circumstances seemed to call for some special greeting quite beyond his powers, he smiled pleasantly at her. Instead, it was Nahoko who was clutched by panic at her mother's arrival. Since that extraordinary excitement her mother revealed during times of crisis was unquestionably all that could have brought her so far, Nahoko worried about what would happen, the more so because she thought it unlikely that her mother would take to Shō's presence with much relish.

"Shō, it's been a great long time you've looked after Nahoko," her mother said, contrary to Nahoko's fears and Shō's worries. "Well, once you loosen the frame of the barrel, there's no getting it back together again. You two took a liking to each other and set up housekeeping with two bowls and two pairs of chopsticks, and gradually things eased up a bit until you could even afford to buy yourself a suit and Nahoko here a kimono, and, well, here you are today. From the time she was a child this girl has never known what it was to be wanting. Always having her own way, she was. Living a life of poverty may just have been the medicine she needed. I'm much obliged, I'm sure. You're a man, and you've got a bright future before you, and don't ever be saying my daughter here, she ever laid the foundation. My daughter didn't do the least little thing for you. Now, I'm telling you, don't you be worrying about settling up here. You can count on my daughter for seeing that everything here's taken care of."

The presence of her mother saved Shō from having to face Nahoko with apologies. And before her mother, Nahoko did not like to press Shō for the answers that, unresigned, she still wanted. She could only think, it's over now, this is it. Never again would there be a chance for her to share her inmost thoughts with Shō. He left the room, half dragging, half carrying his heavy luggage.

"What about getting a cab out front?" Nahoko said. "I'll go with you as far as the cabstand. You can't carry all that luggage by yourself." She wanted to be alone with him. She wanted to be alone with him and find out what he really felt.

"Don't you dare! For shame!" her mother said to her. "A man is perfectly able to carry that much by himself. Watch out, now, Shō! Take care of yourself!" She walked out with him as far as the entrance to the building.

Nahoko regretted having told her mother so soon that Shō had left her. Instead of screaming in a frenzy when Shō's mother told her that he was living with a younger woman, she had sent a special delivery letter to her mother. She had felt as though the ceiling were shaking, dancing round and round, and the only person to whom she could appeal was her mother. She could almost hear her mother's voice ringing in her ears. See! I told you so, she was saying. But if she did not tell someone—*anyone*—what had really happened, Nahoko had felt she would be sucked up into the whirling ceiling and spin round and round herself. Too overwhelmed to appreciate the passage of time as from spring to summer and summer to autumn the seasons deliberately take their course, she could not help feeling that winter had followed unexpectedly on a spring but barely over. Now she understood what people meant by a surprise attack.

"You haven't resigned yourself to things yet, have you?" her mother said. "There's still something you'd like to say to a person whose heart lies elsewhere. Your mama was mean, you're thinking. Seeing you want to chase after that man. Well, don't be such a crybaby, now!" She continued to talk as she fixed something to eat in the kitchen, barely big enough to hold one person. "Well, I told you this would happen. If you'd gone happily off and had that baby back then, what a fine pickle you'd be in now with a child to look after. It would have been the same with that kind of man whether you'd had the baby or not. Just see things straight, now! By yourself you can always manage to eat somehow. Besides, you can't tell me there's anything sadder than a child who doesn't have both his parents. Look at the bright side of things. This was a blessing in disguise."

"You're wrong, Mama," Nahoko said.

"Why am I wrong? Don't you see how lucky you are? Your wounds are still light. There are people, you know, who have the same thing happen to them, only it's after they've had two or three children!"

"You're wrong, Mama, you're wrong! You're all wrong!" said Nahoko.

She was wrong! It bothered Nahoko to have her mother find such a simple, clear-cut solution to her problem. Maybe she couldn't explain just what she meant, but it bothered her to have her mother see it all as a matter of loss or gain. You're wrong, Mama! Oh, Mama, you're wrong!

Her mother continued with some lessons on life. "You say you'll not be coming home, that you'd like to be staying on here. Well, that's fine with me. You're not a little girl anymore. You should be doing what you see fit. But one thing! You're sweet on the men, and you've got to be stronger-minded. Up till now you weren't single, and I didn't worry what folks were saying. But things will be different now you're single. Mark my words, tongues'll soon start to wag! And there'll be men coming at you from every which way. Even after a plain Jane like you. Now listen, Nahoko, get this one thing straight, won't you. There won't be many men as'll offer you true love. And if you don't mind my saying so, the man as does offer you true love isn't going to be any trifler like that Shō. Keep a sharp lookout for the man as can offer you true love. It's a sight better for the woman if she's chased by the man than if she chases the man for herself."

"You're wrong, Mama, you're wrong! He was never that sneaky. Shō was never so sneaky as that. But yes, he *is* sneaky. Shō is sneaky. But what of that? Shō's sneaky, it's true. He always beats around the bush. But listen, Mama, he's not as sneaky as you!" Nahoko sat alone before the dinner table, weeping. She had watered down some of the cheap whiskey that Shō had left behind and was drinking it all by herself.

"Go ahead, cry your eyes out! Left by a man, how stupid! I'm amazed at you, drinking liquor like that just because you've been left by that good-for-nothing. Cry your eyes out, go ahead! But remember this! The way you look, no one'll give you a second glance. You must have a little saved up. Go to the department store or somewhere tomorrow and buy yourself something nice to wear. If you had on a nice dress and looked a little gayer, even you could almost pass for pretty. After all, what is it they say? When a man's left a widower the maggots start to crawl, but when a woman's left a widow the flowers come out in bloom! Now, then, stop being such a crybaby so you can eat something good and get hold of yourself again!" Her mother seemed in excessively high spirits. Nahoko even thought that, if anything, she seemed happy that her daughter was single again.

Nevertheless, since Nahoko thought that mothers were intended above all else to pat their children's heads pityingly during times of distress, she felt it odd that her mother should so scorn and make a fool of her, indeed take delight in what had happened. Was her own mother not refusing to let her bury her head in her bosom as a mama should? Not only that, was she not laughing at her, saying "I told you so" and calling her a fool? Looking at her mother, Nahoko thought it was because she hated this very practical person that she had fled to Shō. She doesn't like coming off the loser, Nahoko thought. That's it. She's the kind of person who just hates coming off the loser.

"Anyway," Nahoko's mother seemed almost to spit out the words, "you're nothing but a gullible baby!"

Her words made Nahoko feel again that she would like to question Shō. Why did you do what you did so suddenly, so unexpectedly? Why didn't you talk to me about it? What Nahoko wanted was to penetrate to the real Shō. And she wanted to accept what she found. Abandoned as if by some fox in disguise,* she would never be able to settle down.

Her mother gone home, Nahoko could set out to locate Shō. How would it be if she asked his whereabouts of the friends who had always come to see him? If that didn't work she could send a special delivery letter to Shō's parents and ask them. Nahoko thought over the various alternatives like a detective. What concerned her for the present was to ascertain Shō's whereabouts, but in the end what she really wanted was to ascertain Shō's true colors. What exactly was it that made Shō so difficult to get a good grip on? What was it that made him say, "Oh, do as you like" whenever something came up? What was it that made him flee and say he knew nothing about a matter whenever it was something he did

* Foxes are notorious in Japanese folklore for their ability to transform themselves into beautiful women so that they can seduce unsuspecting men. The reference here reverses the usual pattern in that the woman is complaining of having been deceived and abandoned.—Translator.

not want to answer or else opposed? He had told how in Shinako's case he had taken off without warning, saying nothing up to the very end for fear of hurting her, and had he now not done the same to her? There are times when saying what is true will hurt a person, but if you *do* what is true without saying anything about it, does it not come to the same thing?

Detective Nahoko thought about the matter from various angles and elaborated a plan of action, but before she could put it into effect, a call came from Shō to the room of the apartment manager. It was for Nahoko. Since the manager was standing near the telephone, Nahoko could talk of nothing very involved. She could only reply to what Shō said, but he was asking her to forward his mail to him, and he rattled off the address. Borrowing pencil and paper from the manager, Nahoko hurriedly wrote down the address that he gave her.

Shō's voice was difficult to catch, and Nahoko asked him to repeat what he said several times. This was because loud voices, laughing and talking in the background, blended with Shō's voice as he talked to her. The laughing voice sounded familiar to Nahoko. It was the voice of Shō's mother. That free and easy voice just had to be hers.

"Is your mother there?" she asked.

"Why, yes. How did you know?" said Shō in wonder.

Free this time of the unpleasant duty that she had had in the case of Shinako, Shō's mother was paying a pleasant visit to her son's new home and was enjoying a friendly talk. Was it only her fancy? Nahoko thought the other voice sounded like the unaffected, melodious tones of a young woman. Afterward Nahoko realized that though Shō had taken the trouble to tell her his new address, she had forgotten to ask the number of the telephone from which he was calling.

Her mother had gone home. Shō and the others were laughing merrily together. Nahoko sat alone in her room, but she was thinking that from now on things would work out.

The Man Who Cut the Grass

YAMAMOTO MICHIKO

Translated by Yukiko Tanaka and Elizabeth Hanson

Yamamoto Michiko (b. 1936) was born in an upper-middle-class family in Tokyo. She became interested in writing at a young age, and was encouraged by her family. Her father gave her money to publish her first collection of poetry. Having received favorable responses to a piece of fiction she wrote for a student writing competition, she joined the prestigious poetry group that published the magazine *Rekitei*. Soon she established herself as a poet and was able to earn some income while living in her parents' house. She continued to write after she married, but gradually her writing became more and more prose-like. In 1967 her husband was transferred to Australia, and she went with him and lived there for four years. The total change in the environment, including the different natural landscape, made it difficult for her to write. Indeed, she stopped writing altogether for a time, though at the very end of her stay she wrote a short story that won the Shinchō New Writers' Prize.

Since her return to Japan, Yamamoto has continued to write. Her stories give a glimpse of the hidden frustration, guilt, and boredom of housewives, and deal with women living in foreign countries. She focuses on the loneliness and longing of women whose lives seem to maintain a precarious balance between sanity and insanity. Yamamoto is the mother of two children and is currently living in Seattle because of her husband's work. After an initial adjustment period, she was able this time to go back to writing. Her latest novel, *Tenshi yo Umi ni Mae (Dance, Angels, High upon the Sea)*, treats the theme of disjointed lives as it follows the search of the heroine, the young wife of a Japanese businessman transferred to Seattle, for a more meaningful relationship with a man.

A STRONG WIND was blowing. Ten days before, someone had cut the grass that had been growing wild in the empty lot, and the view from Mayo's window had become quite different. Even though the wind was coming as usual from the ocean, Mayo felt that without the tall grass, she couldn't tell which direction it was blowing. There were two similar houses built on both sides of the lot, and next to the right one there was a field where the grass was still growing lushly. The left one was a corner house; she could see a wide street across from it.

Mayo put her forehead on the windowpane and stared at the field where the dense grass was still growing. The tall pampas grass waved as if it were having a fit. The white flowers in full bloom looked like whitecaps on the ocean.

A man with a sickle came to cut the grass in the field. These days one rarely saw someone cutting grass with a sickle. Instead, at the end of the summer one often saw electric mowing machines in their neighborhood . . . a man with a machine on his back would cut the grass, making lots of noise.

Is he going to cut all of that grass by himself? Mayo thought, and kept her eyes on the glinting of the sickle blade. The wind was blowing hard that day as usual. Among the wildly moving grass, the sickle in the man's hand seemed particularly fragile.

It took two days for the man to cut the grass. On both the first and second day Mayo saw him arrive early in the morning in a small truck. Around noon of the first day Mayo went out into the street in front of her house. The field was about two meters higher than the road and built up with a bank of round stones. Mayo stood in the road facing the sunshine and wind and called to the man. He did not hear her right away because of the noise the wind made against the grass.

Mayo went to where the man was climbing up from the lowest part of the bank. The pampas grass was as high as the man's shoulders. He was moving his arms as if he were drowning in it. Approaching him from behind, Mayo stepped on the cut grass. As if he had sensed something, he suddenly turned around.

"May I have some of the grass?" Mayo asked, feeling flustered. "If I could have some of that over there . . ."

The man squinted and looked in the direction Mayo was pointing. The grass that he had already cut was piled near the road. Mayo wanted some of the flowers whose tips were hanging over the bank.

"Sure, go ahead," the man said brusquely. Mayo went back to the lowest spot of the bank and jumped down, keeping both feet together. She then tried to pull off some of the flowers, but they were attached to the sharp leaves and roots, since the grass had been cut skillfully in a bunch.

"I wonder if I could use your sickle for a minute?" Mayo asked the man, returning to the field.

The man stopped cutting and looked at Mayo, then at the sickle he was holding tightly in his hand.

"Which ones? I'll get them for you." The man followed Mayo, glanced at the pampas grass that she wanted, then said in a peculiarly decisive tone, "There are better ones than these." Stretching, he focused on something in the distance. When Mayo saw the man do this, she felt as if she were standing in the middle of a virgin field. In fact there were endless numbers of flowers. The wind was tossing the white flowers so they waved in the same direction. The man extended his arm in front of him and deftly cut a few flowers.

"Those are all in full bloom. I'd like the ones that are still in bud over there."

The man did not understand what Mayo meant and frowned.

" 'Bud' sounds funny but what I mean are those glittery ones over there, and not the fluffy ones," Mayo said quickly and studied the man's expression. She felt an inexplicable fear. "I am sorry, but I like those better." The man seemed finally to understand what Mayo meant, crossed the field and went directly to the pile near the road.

Mayo arranged the pampas grass flowers in a vase, which she put in the living room. She liked the way the hard tips of the silver-colored flowers shone. She never hesitated to throw them away as soon as they became loose and turned white. She could not stand to see them at the stage when they started to scatter like fluffy cotton and seemed to float endlessly, just as they pleased, like small silent flying insects.

When Mayo lifted her face, through the window she saw the man standing by the gate. He still had the sickle in his hand and his long arms were hanging down at his sides. He seemed to be studying her house. Mayo went to the front door and peeked out.

"Is there anything . . . ?" Without answering her question, the man walked slowly toward her.

"Would you give me some water?" he said bluntly. Mayo ran to the kitchen and came back with a pitcher and a glass.

"Here you are. Please drink as much as you want." He looked at the glass pitcher that she extended from the partly opened door and smiled faintly.

"Well, no . . . I want the water over there, to sharpen my sickle." He pointed to a faucet by a small round flower bed that was surrounded by bricks.

Mayo returned to the living room and watched the man through the window. He went back to his truck and returned with a dirty plastic bucket, probably with a whetstone inside. The man squatted with his back toward Mayo and slowly started to move his shoulders. Gazing at the back of his gray-green work shirt, she thought she could tell the rough texture of the fabric of his shirt even without touching it.

The man took his time and kept sharpening the sickle. Occasionally he lifted the sickle high in front of him, checking the results. From where Mayo stood she could tell how sharp the sickle had become.

After a while the man left with the bucket and the sickle. When he stood up he turned around and glanced at the door for a moment. Mayo watched this without a word. When he reached the road he lifted the bucket and suddenly emptied it, the splashes of water looking like a curtain of silk gauze.

The strong wind had not subsided. The wind makes the splashes of water look like gauze, Mayo thought. At that moment the curtain seemed to swell. When the man had disappeared into the grass, Mayo went out into the yard through the veranda. She had a feeling that the man might have left the whetstone there. She continued to look around the spot where he had been squatting, since she thought he might have left something—a lighter, matches, a pen, or something similar. She didn't find anything.

Some broom bushes were waving in the same way as the tall grass. Looking at the way the dark green of the bushes spread in all directions, she felt as if she were seeing them for the first time. The man standing beyond them looked like a pole; he had become a pole that simply stood in the waving grass.

Before the day was over, about half of the grass had been cut. By the time Mayo started preparing dinner, the small truck was no longer there. There were a few piles of cut grass. He'll have to come again tomorrow, Mayo thought.

Mayo said to her husband when he came home, "Someone's going to build a house. A man came and cut the grass. With a sickle. Not an electric one, but a hand sickle. He left a lot of grass. He came into our yard and sharpened his sickle by the water faucet." As she spoke, she looked at the pampas grass flowers in the vase; they hung over like woven bronze-colored cord and glowed dully under the light.

Her husband lifted his face from the newspaper and looked at his wife for a moment. Then he returned to the paper and said, "You'll be careful not to get cut by the sickle, won't you?"

Mayo did not understand what he meant.

"Cut what?"

"Your neck."

Mayo did not respond. Her husband folded the paper without a word. She was thinking of the small sickle that had sparkled amid the green. The man had come into her yard; he had whetted the sickle with water and sharpened it very carefully. He had to smooth the nicked edge. When he finished the job and stood up with the sharpened sickle in his hand, he had seemed to be studying her house.

He must have been looking for me—did he really come to cut the grass? Mayo thought. She tried to remember the man's face, but she couldn't since he had always been squinting when she had seen him. He was taller than the pampas grass; he had no hat, wore a work shirt the color of dried leaves, and had on white tennis shoes.

Mayo suddenly remembered a certain man's face. In no time that face came to resemble to an unnatural degree that of the man who came to cut the grass. It was because of the white tennis shoes. It had been fifteen years before . . .

Two police detectives were talking to her mother in low voices. Mayo had watched them from behind her mother as they stood with their backs to the door. One was in late middle age and the other was a little younger. Neither was particularly well dressed. Their faces were dull like their clothing, their voices were gloomy and difficult to hear.

After a while they went upstairs, led by her mother. Mayo's six-mat room was chosen as their hideout. From this window they could see the house across the street and its garage, five or six meters away from the stone gate, with a hinged double door made of metal. The former owner had used part of the garden to build this garage that the two police investigators were interested in. It seemed that there was a small printing machine inside. Even without actually seeing it, one could tell it was there by the factory-like noise that vibrated through the neighborhood. It was indeed an odd place for a factory to suddenly appear.

Mayo and her mother were told by the investigators that the machine was no doubt a printing press.

"It stinks. It's suspicious," the older investigator said. At that time, there had been newspaper reports for several days in a row of a counterfeiting operation. The counterfeit thousand-yen bills were skillfully printed, and just looking at a picture of the two bills, without reading the article, one could not tell which one was real.

"We are checking on every single printing operation in the city that seems suspicious," one of the investigators said.

The day when they had come to Mayo's house, there hadn't been any machine sounds since early morning. It was dead silent on the other side of the green garage door, and from Mayo's window no one was visible in the one-storied house surrounded by trees.

"That's really a strange house," Mayo had thought. The person who had lived there before the printer had also been wanted by the police. She had seen a short article about him in the paper the day after he had disappeared. She recalled that at that time as well, two investigators had come to question them. She found out that the man across the street, who was short and stout and in his sixties, was in the real estate business. He had a problem with one of his legs and always walked slowly with a cane. He lived with his wife, a gloomy-looking woman in her forties, a maid, and a spitz dog. Even though their houses were right across the street from each other, Mayo's mother had never spoken with the wife. When the police detective came one day to their house to ask questions about their neighbor, both Mayo and her mother felt agitated.

The real estate man was arrested without much surveillance. At that time as well, the house had been deathly silent. Mayo had watched from her window while the detectives left her house and stepped into the other house; one went to the front door while the other went to the back door facing the alley. Right before they went into the house, she had thought of the wife, with her gloomy expression and her dull-colored everyday kimono, waiting with held breath and hugging the yelping spitz. Under the black slate roof the entire house had seemed to be in pain, like the wife with her suppressed breathing.

A few moments later the real estate man had come out of the gate. He wore a neat tie and a brown suit and held his cane. She couldn't see his face with its dark glasses because it was hidden behind the detective's shoulder. She did not see the wife, or hear the spitz's yelping. The plump, red-faced maid had come out and locked the gate. In the next morning's paper Mayo had seen a short article about the man.

I wonder if things will end in the same way this time, Mayo thought. The printer seemed to be in his late thirties. He always wore white tennis shoes and work clothes. No one in the neighborhood knew when he had installed the printing machine in the garage, so when people suddenly heard the factory-like sounds, they turned around as they passed and looked at the garage door.

The two detectives left Mayo's house in the evening. Mayo put away the tea, which they had not touched. "They're strict with themselves, just as I thought they would be," her mother said, taking the tray. The men ignored her mother's hospitality while they kept their lookout all day. Her mother admired this stoicism, but Mayo was not quite convinced. She thought that they did not feel like drinking tea because the house had been so quiet and wasn't providing them the evidence that they wanted.

Mayo had taken a chair to the window that day and watched the house until almost midnight. Nothing happened to the dark house no matter how long she watched. The man was probably not home. How had it been the previous night? Had the light been on? Mayo couldn't remember. She always pulled the curtain when she went to her room to study after dinner. She should have seen the light in that house at that time, and since she didn't remember having seen it, she thought it must have been dark.

Mayo gazed at the night spread over the neighborhood, as if she were seeing it for the first time. There was a light in the old Western-style house next to the house in question. Mayo was a bit surprised that she could see a light in the small arched window. It was a wooden Western-style house with a dark green slate roof, and white paint was peeling off the exterior walls in places. She was curious about two small windows. They had shutters that seemed half broken; they were always closed. Someone is in that room at night,

Mayo thought. At night those lighted windows looked smaller, strangely small for the size of the house.

Mayo stayed up until late that night watching the house, as if she were taking over the detective's job, but she did not notice anything other than the windows of the Western-style house. The next day Mayo came home from school to find some detectives at the door showing her mother a picture.

"Is this him?" her mother asked, pointing at a man in the picture. Surprised, Mayo looked at her mother rather than at the picture. It was next to impossible to tell whether it was him or not. Her mother was pointing to the last row of people in the picture, which seemed to be of a tour group. Every face looked similarly obscure, as if seen through a veil; one could tell only that they were human faces.

"This is him, I think," her mother said again. "The detective thinks so. What do you say? You've seen his face, haven't you?" Mayo's mother lowered her anxious voice.

"Well . . . it does seem a bit like him, now that you say so. I'm not sure, though, since the face is so small," Mayo said and gave the photo back to the detective.

Around nine o'clock that night Mayo saw a dim light behind the garage. It was not an electric light; it seemed to be oozing out of the bottom of the darkness from somewhere behind the garage, illuminating the backyard. He is doing something there, Mayo thought. In that faint light he might be taking out the hidden counterfeit bills and examining them, or maybe he is counting them. Mayo became slightly excited. Perhaps there was a small candle on the machine, and he was gazing at his work in the candlelight. They might be the same thousand-yen bills that she had seen in the paper. How many had he printed?

The mere word "counterfeit" filled Mayo with a strange dreamy feeling. In fact, while she pushed her forehead against the windowpane she fell into an unfocused state as if she were in a strange dream. Beyond the darkness in the lonely light was the fascinating counterfeit money. For Mayo counterfeit money definitely was different from soiled, crumpled bills of real money.

The light remained the same even until two o'clock in the morning. It must be a flashlight, she suddenly thought. Why hadn't she realized this sooner? That's right, he had hung a flashlight up and was doing something in its light.

Mayo saw in her mind's eye three things together: the printing machine, freshly printed counterfeit bills, and a flashlight. Then she thought she could see the man clearly in the center. His face resembled the one she had seen in that obscure picture, that picture of faces that looked like faces only because you *knew* that they were faces.

"Yes, I think so. This is the man," Mayo told the detectives the next afternoon when they came back with a large magnifying glass. Mayo examined the picture through the glass.

"Are you sure? Is this him?" Mayo's mother mumbled a few times. "This is terribly blurred . . ." But Mayo felt that the obscurity itself was a clue. She was certain that the counterfeiter would never show himself to them with a clear outline.

The detectives nodded to each other unenthusiastically, pushed both the photo and the magnifying glass hurriedly into their coat pockets and left. Mayo went to her room and looked at the garage, holding her breath, just as she had done when the real estate man had been arrested.

But things didn't happen as she had expected. The detectives seemed to have gone back that day with no more than Mayo's testimony. She did not see them at the gate. After that the garage door remained shut, and no sound of a machine came from inside. At that time the man had already been dead for some time, having hung himself with a vinyl rope. The detectives discovered the hanging body the next morning. He had killed himself the night that Mayo had seen the dim light.

One of the two detectives came and reported to Mayo and her mother how the man had killed himself.

"The man was clean. It was our mistake," the detective said. When she heard about this from her mother, Mayo had an aching sensation, as if her entire body were being tightly squeezed. It was the sensation one might have if one's body were being compressed into a rock-like shape by some enormous magnetic power.

He had killed himself, leaving many debts and a wife and children. "A few days before he killed himself, he had obviously arranged to have the electricity disconnected. No wonder we didn't hear any noise," Mayo's mother said.

It was not easy for Mayo to accept that he had been preparing for his own death under that dim light rather than examining the counterfeit money. But in truth there was no doubt that he had killed himself. Why hadn't he been printing counterfeit money? He must have died without even knowing that he had been a suspect. If he had known, the suspicion might have inspired him to attempt counterfeitry.

For several months the house was left empty. The door of the garage where the man had hung himself was closed as tightly as before. For Mayo it made no difference whether there was a door or not—a house with no one in it had no secrets.

Whenever Mayo looked down at the green door, she felt as if she were a patient who was tired of being sick. The metal door, with its pale surface, seemed to be blaming her.

Perhaps I was the one who turned that man into a counterfeiting suspect, she thought. She could not easily forget the obscure photo and the magnifying glass. The simple fact that the police had carried the man's picture in their pockets and showed it to people, speaking in low voices, had turned the man into a counterfeiter; I hadn't needed any more evidence than that, she thought. In fact he had not made a single counterfeit bill, but went ahead and killed himself without warning, leaving his wife and children.

One day Mayo was suddenly struck with an idea—perhaps the man had printed some counterfeit money after all. He may have sent the bills to his wife and children in the country and thus eventually eliminated all evidence, including himself. This idea comforted Mayo. He had been a counterfeiter after all. He was in fact a genuine criminal, not just a suspect.

The man who's been cutting the grass will come again tomorrow, Mayo thought. If I see his face, I might be able to tell what the man who killed himself looked like. Such vague thoughts kept coming back to her and didn't seem completely absurd.

The next day too a strong wind was blowing. Around nine o'clock the man came in the same small truck. Until then Mayo had been sitting in a chair near the window and looking outside instead of cleaning up after breakfast. The open field, with half its grass cut, looked odd and unbalanced. The tall grass that was left was swaying in the wind, so that the bare part looked strange, as if some defect had been exposed. Mayo finally got up to do her morning chores when she saw the man, dressed in the same clothes he had worn the day before, get out of the truck and step into the grass.

There was no traffic on the road in front of her house, as usual. While she moved about in the house, Mayo thought constantly about the man who cut the grass. Had he in fact come to cut the grass? That's what he was doing, but his real purpose might have been something else.

The man continued to work without stopping to rest. By noon there was another heap of cut grass. He must have planned to cut all the grass by the end of the day, load it in the little truck, and take it somewhere. Mayo kept watching while the man skillfully cut the swaying grass and piled it up on the ground.

Around noon he sat down, leaned on the pile of grass, and started to eat his lunch. He ate exactly the same way he had the day before. Mayo sat down to eat a light lunch after she had locked the front door and pulled the living-room curtains. She felt a sense of satisfaction at having taken precautions. There's no way of telling what that man is thinking while he eats lunch, Mayo thought. It's impossible to tell what he has on his mind. He may be wishing he could have a cup of hot tea. He'll naturally begin to think about me. "A cup of tea . . . maybe the house where I sharpened my sickle . . ." It's not unlikely. He'll see this window with its curtains drawn. He'll see through them and think, "That woman I met yesterday is doing something in the house, even though she's pretending no one is home."

Mayo looked outside through a crack in the curtains. The man seemed to have finished his lunch and was stretched out on a pile of cut grass. He was lying on his back, and had a handkerchief or something over his face to protect his eyes from the sun. Mayo could see his extended legs. From where she was standing she could see the soles of his tennis shoes. Is he going to take a nap, she wondered. Does he feel like taking a long rest since the work is moving along faster than he had expected? No one would work as desperately as a starving person seeking something to satisfy himself if he thought someone was watching him.

He had almost buried himself in the cut grass. As Mayo watched the man from the window, he seemed peaceful, lying in the midst of the bright sunshine from the autumn sky and the wind dancing in from the ocean. His dull sickle was probably lying somewhere on the ground near him. He would get up, notice his sickle beside him, and begin to examine her house, she thought.

Finished with her lunch, Mayo carried the dirty dishes to the kitchen and washed them, then got an apple and returned to the same place in the living room. While she peeled the apple, Mayo watched the man, who had just sat up. For a while he sat still, looking at the grass he had to cut. Finally he stood up, with a lazy manner that was completely different from the way he worked. Mayo almost dropped the apple she was peeling. The man was staring at the sickle in his hand. He simply stood with the sun at his back and with his head bowed. He's thinking about his sickle, whether to sharpen it or not, she thought. He seemed to be considering this question seriously. Mayo sliced the apple and took out the core. The man slowly started to move. The wind twisted his hair. It looks like a small cyclone, Mayo thought, and kept watching the swirling hair. Feeling vaguely disappointed, Mayo took a bite of apple. The man started to cut the grass. He was moving his right arm swiftly, stooping in the tall swaying grass and holding the bunches in his left hand while he cut.

Mayo bit the apple slowly. If he comes here now to sharpen his sickle, will he eat some of this apple? she wondered. The pale green, hard apples in the fruit bowl in front of her suddenly seemed to be a complex, closely drawn picture. At the moment the apple's tart juice filled her mouth, she had a sudden image of the white tennis shoes that the counterfeiter had worn. For almost twenty years Mayo had thought of the man as a "counterfeiter," but actually she had never spoken about him in this way. When she thought about it, she realized she hadn't even told her husband about him. At some time or other the man had become stuck in her mind as a real counterfeiter.

If I don't remember his face at all, why do I feel that I know his white tennis shoes so well? she wondered. She tried to remember the few times she had seen him in front of that green garage door. Was I looking at his feet rather than his face? she thought. The only time she had been able to study his face was when she saw him in the poorly focused photo that the detectives had brought.

During the six years since she had married, Mayo had developed a habit of falling asleep for half an hour or so after lunch if she was at home. Her body seemed to be sucked into the soft back of the couch and her mind became vacant. It's because I don't have a child, she always told herself when in this drowsy state. It's only this drowsiness that tricks me. If I had a small child, I'd be preoccupied with trying to make him take a nap, she thought.

In the afternoon, children passed Mayo's house on their way home from school. In her sleep she thought she heard their high voices. When she looked up she saw that the man was cutting grass in the same spot as before. What was he doing while I was sleeping? she wondered. When she realized that his work had not progressed at all, she looked around, feeling confused. She saw that the apple slices in the bowl had yellowed; she jumped up to close the curtain.

Did he come here to sharpen his sickle while I was dozing? she wondered. She thought she couldn't trust him because of the way he worked. He was simply acting like a laborer—what was he really? She stood in the kitchen and drank some water. If I don't look at that man again, he'll probably go back with the job half finished, she thought.

The counterfeiter who had killed himself in the garage might have known that I was watching, Mayo thought. She imagined the pitch-dark house and herself, sitting by the window in her room with the light off. He had probably hung himself knowing that she would be surprised; because he had known I would be surprised, he had decided to go ahead and die, she thought.

Six months or so after the man had killed himself, his house was demolished. The lot where the house had been was unexpectedly spacious when the debris was taken away. Bricks mixed with soil were piled all around. An old well stood in the corner where the backyard had been. It was obvious that it had dried up long ago. There had been a similar well in Mayo's garden, which they had closed with a thick lid made of concrete, and then covered with soil, leaving a tiny air hole. The area was on high ground, and it had been necessary to motorize the water main.

Mayo had not been able to look at the empty lot without feeling guilty, but when she looked out her window it came into view whether she wanted to see it or not. She realized that the garage had occupied a very small space, close to the street. In that small space he had hung himself with a rope, Mayo thought.

The empty lot was left there for a while like a dilapidated cemetery; no one went near it. Then one day construction began. A three-storied apartment building went up, rather unusual for the neighborhood. "With apartment buildings going up around here the area's going to get run down," Mayo's mother had said.

The apartment building was of concrete, which was becoming popular then. The exterior was gray and looked dismal, as if it were wet with rain. The windows in the gray walls were divided evenly among the three stories.

This apartment building is like a cemetery, Mayo thought—it's a tomb for the house that the real estate man and the counterfeiter both lived in. It looked like a gigantic gray gravestone.

In fact several families came to live in that gravestone. One day all of a sudden they had begun to live there. Faces appeared in every window on every floor of the building, which Mayo could see from her room. Some windows had flowerpots, and some had a small round device with clothespins used for hanging up laundry. Even though the windows faced north, some had quilts hung out to air that looked like the innards of the building.

At night all the windows were covered with curtains or shutters. Mayo couldn't help but think that the closed windows were flatly rejecting her stare. In summer the voices coming from the open windows were like the breathing of the entire building. One could feel this particularly well on summer Sundays.

Mayo was often reminded of the sound the printing press had made when confined in the garage with the green door. That had definitely not been the sound of human breathing, but instead the dreamy sound of moving iron.

Eventually Mayo began to feel a sense of closeness to the apartment building. She didn't feel the same concern about it that her mother had.

She wondered if they were going to build a house on the lot where the man had cut the grass. In that neighborhood the landowners were afraid that the dry grass would cause fires, so they went ahead and cut it. She would find out sooner or later if something would be built or not. She didn't have to ask the man, but she wanted to find out from him.

Once she went outside, Mayo could tell right away that the sun was not as strong as it had been the day before. Two children passed her, hand in hand, on their way back from school. Mayo stood in front of the gate and looked at the sea in the distance, which she could see between the roof of the neighbor's house and the embankment. It looked like a sheet of aluminum. From the glow of the light Mayo could tell that the sun was about to set.

The man finished cutting the last bunch of grass; as he stretched, he threw his sickle down. Mayo looked up at him from the street and asked, "Is a house going to be built here?" The man could not hear her and so came toward her. He looked at her directly, and she avoided his eyes, then repeated her question.

"Hmmm, I don't know," he said curtly.

Mayo went back into the house. He won't sharpen the sickle today; he'll put the grass on the truck and that will be it, she thought. When she looked outside the man was already in the truck behind the wheel. She looked at the truck, almost in a daze. It didn't move. Soon the man leaned on the steering wheel and began to smoke a cigarette. She remembered that he had not smoked after his lunch. Perhaps he didn't want to smoke amid the tall grass, moving wildly in the wind.

Mayo went out to the backyard to bring in the laundry. She went in through the back door and put the laundry basket by the ironing board in the bathroom, then heard the front doorbell. For a moment she held her breath, both hands on the ironing board.

Finally that man has come, she thought. He's there outside the front door, with his sickle. Mayo plugged in the iron, set it on steam, and poured a cup of water into the hole at the top. The door is locked, so it's impossible for him to come in here, she thought.

The doorbell rang again. Mayo stared at the small lights on the side of the iron, then suddenly decided to go into the living room to look outside. She saw the truck, but as she had expected, the man wasn't inside. She couldn't see him in the field, but from the window she could see him standing at the door with the bucket. His profile looked serious as he faced the door and pushed the bell with a finger of his right hand.

Mayo opened the window slightly, as an answer to the bell.

"Can I have some water again?" Seeing her nod, he immediately went over and squatted by the spigot near the flower bed. The few geraniums that were still blooming touched his arm as if they wanted to bite him.

While she was ironing, Mayo kept wondering how he intended to enter the house after he whetted the sickle. He had finished his work early, she thought, for that reason. He wants to sharpen his sickle because he is up to something, and I am going to be his target; he'll use his sickle for his purpose. It was probably a mistake to go outside to ask him a question. Right after that he must have thought about various things while enjoying his cigarette; he didn't have to think much, though, since he had already made his plans. Anyway, today is the last day; he won't come here again.

Mayo stopped ironing and pulled out the cord. She was as scared of the hot iron as she was of the sickle the man was whetting. Through the window Mayo saw the man's back. He moved his arms with large, steady motions, and in his lack of self-consciousness she sensed something similar to what she had sensed in the obscure face of the man who had hung himself in the garage. She felt anxious, not expecting him to move his arms in such a way.

The cut grass was in two piles. Both dark green grass and white tops were left. If left there like that for a few days, they would dry out and turn yellow, but now they looked fresh and heavy.

As the man was standing up, he turned around and glanced at the front door, just as he had done the day before, not seeming to know what he was going to do. Then he went out of the gate and threw the water out of the bucket with a swinging motion. Mayo felt perplexed as she watched him drive the truck away. He had left the cut grass behind. Was he going to come back?

She went outside and looked around the faucet, which was surrounded by blood-colored geraniums. It was exactly the same as it had been the day before. She saw no trace of the man who had squatted there.

It was about time for the sun to set. Mayo looked at the glowing sky. Whenever the weather was nice, she watched the evening glow. She could hear the cheerful voices of children who were playing on a trampoline. A girl with long hair was jumping, her hair flying in the wind. From where Mayo stood she could not see their cheeks clearly, but she thought they must be as red as the evening sky.

That night Mayo's husband came back with several stalks of pampas grass. They looked wilted, but the tops were as tight as if they were knit together, and they glittered under the electric light. He said he had found them by the gate.

"Put them over there," Mayo said instead of taking them from him. They lay quietly on the dining room table like a sharpened sickle. "Not there, put them in the bathroom," she said.

While Mayo was setting the dinner table, words suddenly came out of her mouth like water gushing through an open door.

"I saw several children playing on a trampoline. That pile of cut grass needs to dry up some more, and then it will be much softer, and the children can jump on it like grasshoppers. Are you listening, dear? I'm surprised that the geraniums are still in bloom. Lots of them. Do you know the hill near the station, the one covered with pampas grass? Have they started to die? I've been wondering every day. It is really something, that hill covered with tall dried-up pampas grass. I'm thinking of going to see them when they are all dead. How did they look today? I wonder if he will come tomorrow to take those away. I mean that cut grass. If children use it for a trampoline, it's all right, but they'll make a mess of it. Are you listening? He came into our garden again today. He went ahead and sharpened the sickle, and then he was looking for me . . . Will you be late tomorrow? . . . No, no particular reason, nothing in particular. It'll be the same tomorrow. I have a feeling the weather will turn bad. My head feels heavy . . . and it'll probably start raining soon. Oh, it feels like bugs making noise in my ears . . . That's right, just like always . . ."

Doll Love

TAKAHASHI TAKAKO

Translated by Mona Nagai and Yukiko Tanaka

Takahashi Takako (b. 1932) majored in French literature at Kyoto University, one of the most prestigious universities in Japan. In 1954, the year she completed her undergraduate work, she married Takahashi Kazumi. For the next eight years, until her husband established himself as a writer, Takahashi did tutoring, translating, and interpreting to earn income. At the same time, she did her graduate work and started to publish stories, book reviews, and translations of French literature. Her husband, who was a prolific writer of novels of highly philosophical content, died of cancer in 1971, the year Takahashi published her first collection of short stories. Since then she has been extremely active in writing fiction, essays, and reviews. In 1974 alone she wrote one novel, nine stories, and about two dozen book reviews and essays. She often travels to Europe, most of the time alone. She has consistently shown a strong interest in French literature, particularly in François Mauriac. In 1975 she became a Catholic.

Takahashi frequently writes about writing, about being a woman, and about her religion. Writing for her is the equivalent of dreaming—that is, entering a realm where the formless and the relative in everyday life are transformed somehow into the definite. The heroines of her fiction quite often live with fantasies and illusions; they are almost always lonely, living in their own enclosed world away from reality. Takahashi states in one of her essays that it is inevitable for a woman who has awakened to her true self to feel dissatisfied with reality, and in "Doll Love" a dream invades reality and finally takes over. Yet despite the possibilities for irony in such a theme, the narrator's point of view and the style convey an intensity and even a certain urgency. Words that are freely used to refer to abstract notions, such as "happiness," seem to be intended to impart a sense of ambiguity. The conclusion of the story is also ambiguous and leaves us with a sense of unresolved suspense.

I

I WAS WAITING for Tamao. Tamao is eighteen.

I was guided by a peculiar sensation to come to T City and stay for a while. I had come to the area several times as a girl, but this was my first visit to T City.

As the train approached N City the sunlight appeared stronger than I had ever experienced it elsewhere, as if the entire field of vision glistened with heat waves. Rather than the shimmer of heat waves, it might be closer to say it was a color more like a mineral. White rays glinted upward and the air overflowed with light, not from the sky but from the ground.

Last month, January, I had boarded an H-line train without having a definite destination. I had a habit of getting on trains without having any particular purpose. When you have a destination everything is defined accordingly, but when you have none the land itself takes on an air of ambiguity. I enjoy the feeling of wandering unaware into that indefinite realm. But my boarding an H-line train last month with no goal in mind was due to special circumstances: my husband had committed suicide. I was still in a daze even though it had been months since his death, and that day I felt like riding a train, any train. It was when the train windows began to glow whiter and more brilliantly, nearing N City, that I realized I was on an H-line train.

My husband's suicide left me in a confused state in which my head had become perfectly clear. On such occasions most people are able to find relief for a while by crying or screaming or some other display, but I was not like them. Instead, confusion sank in deeper and deeper, changing into countless fragments of ice that spread throughout my interior. For me, everything that formed the world thinned out like vapor. In this condition, no matter how I might be jolted or shaken, I could not be roused.

Noticing a white light flickering strangely outside the window, I raised my head. The light was not just flickering, it was floating backward in a wide stream as the train moved. And then I remembered that years ago when I had passed this area several times I had been struck by that same strange white light and had felt a similar sensation stirred within me by the scenery. Although I had not thought about it since, now I recalled that every time I passed the area I remembered experiencing the same feeling as before.

I was thinking about the theory I had formed to explain why such a phenomenon occurs in this area. The R mountain range, which starts near N City, extends as far as port town K, and flat land stretches between the two cities, surrounded by the mountain range and the Inland Sea. The white light starts near N City; it suddenly catches your attention as the train comes into the city, but by the time the train nears K City your eyes have become so accustomed to the light you hardly think about it. I attributed the whiteness of the light to the granite that is mined in great quantity in the R mountains. Perhaps over hundreds and thousands of years the powdered granite has washed down from the mountains, or the soil itself in this area contains some granite.

Since I had no destination, I thought I might as well get off at N Station before the effect of the white light faded away. There was another line that branched out from N Station toward the mountains as far as T City. That's right, I thought, I'll try going to T City. If my speculation is correct, the closer I go to the mountains, the closer I'll be to the core of what puzzles me.

I was standing on the platform at the station. A cold north wind was blowing, and it seemed that the air itself was glittering with powdered granite. Conscious of unexpectedly placing myself inside something like a vast halation, I had a queer feeling as I thought about the contrast between myself at that moment and myself before I had taken the H-line train.

Perhaps my husband's death had been slowly, steadily prepared over our ten years of marriage. Like black ink seeping into his blood drop by drop, his death had accumulated day by day. That truth made me feel particularly uneasy because it seemed linked with the suicide of my lover long before I had married. In both cases there was no immediate reason for suicide. Just as my husband went on accumulating death over the course of ten years, so my lover had been accumulating death during the three years we knew each other. Their weakening was a strange process I can describe only as "storing death." Instead of their life ripening over time, at a certain point it suddenly graphed a downward curve. And that certain point was when they met me. I had begun to think this way because of a fortune-teller's words.

"This means you were born under a lucky star—but too lucky, in fact," the old fortune-teller told me. "When you love a man, he'll enter the circle of death."

It had never occurred to me that I was extremely fortunate. In the first place, I was not very healthy mentally or physically.

"What do you mean, 'enter the circle of death'?" I asked.

A candle was burning on the desk in the fortune-teller's room. There was nothing that looked like paraphernalia for divination other than an old leather-bound book. Around the circle of light made by the candle flame, the brightness quickly dissolved into the dark.

"In this world there are life circles and death circles. Whereas some people can't escape the circle of death no matter how much they try to live, others can't get out of the circle of life no matter how much they try to die. In either case, it's hell. But the majority of us are free from these fixed circles and lead unconcerned and mediocre lives," the fortune-teller explained. "When you look around this world, you can see a transparent circle around certain people. They are trapped inside that circle like prisoners. Some were born inside the circle, but in other cases it shows up some time later, appearing around their feet."

He stopped talking and abruptly lifted the candle high, pointing with his free hand to the darkness in front of him. I saw in the direction that he pointed something like a vast, dark stage where countless people were moving around. About one out of every thousand had a circle around his feet. I could not tell which was the life circle and which was the death circle, but I could see all too clearly that both those in whom life collected despite their wish to die and those in whom death was stored despite persistent efforts to live were existing in hell.

"How is it that death is stored?" I asked the fortune-teller.

"You might think of it as arm wrestling. Without knowing it, you and a partner have been arm wrestling all this time. Let's say your individual fates were groaning and straining with all their strength in their struggle against each other. The strangest thing is that the parties involved are completely unaware of what's going on. But I was able to see that moment by moment a circle of death was forming around your lover's feet . . ."

After my encounter with the fortune-teller I became obsessed with death. I was haunted by the fear that if I focused with sufficient intensity on an insect, for instance, it would drop dead like a dried scale. Even if I did not aim at anything in particular, my fate would exert its influence without my realizing it, pushing an object toward death. When I thought this way, the world in which I had been placed was transformed into a scene filled with skeletons and corpses that fell from the sky day and night. I must not go near anyone or anything. It would be all right if I detached myself from everything. In order not to cause anyone to die, I should act as if I were dead and hide myself somewhere.

Thinking more and more about why my husband and my lover committed suicide, although there was nothing one could remotely identify as the reason, I could clearly see the signs that their lives really had been sucked into the circle of death. Like losing yourself, spinning round and round in a whirlpool that swirls unnoticed in the middle of a dark night ocean: irresistible, all too easy, yet final.

I possess neither the dark power of a person who belongs to death while living in this world nor the superabundant life force that feeds on others' lives. Even so, according to the fortune-teller, when I love a man he will enter the death circle as a result of my excessively strong fate. How does the fortune-teller measure the degree of fate? He says that although I am not aware of trying at all, somehow I have won a game of arm wrestling.

While I was on the platform waiting for a train to T City, gazing at those people on the dark stage surrounded by death circles, a cold wind foreign to that idea blew through me. Wind in January is as dry as ice. Coming from a direction where there were no factories, it was transparent and bright. The brightness of the wind was due to the white light oozing from the ground and radiating toward the sky.

It was then that something like a presentiment struck me.

The train that ran from T City to N City and back had few passengers. By the time it started on the return trip the nature of my presentiment was little by little becoming clear. The ancient rust-colored train with only two cars went slowly, screeching and scraping the rails. As it crept along the air outside filled increasingly with white light. Just as I thought. If the granite contained in the R mountains were its cause as I suspected, the light would become more conspicuous the closer I went to the mountains.

If I could express my premonition in words, I would have to call it happiness. How unexpected to suddenly encounter this feeling while wandering through thoughts of death. To be more accurate, though, rather than "encounter" I could say that happiness was there at a distance, transformed into a substance. Minerals were evaporating from the ground itself, white and bright, in a color that could only be called "happiness."

No, it was more than that. I had a feeling, increasingly strong, that concealed somewhere within the landscape was something more profound. The train went along slowly, stopping at every station, and I could no longer ignore the feeling that with each movement of the train the scenery outside was disclosing something meaningful.

I had passed N City several times when I was a girl, but this was the first time I had taken a branch line from N Station. I had not had an opportunity to go to T City, which was the last stop. Though I had boarded the train without a goal, now I clearly saw my objective. Not that I felt I had conceived of the purpose; rather the purpose itself, animated, stood up in front of me, as it were.

That purpose was to go to T City. There was no particular reason to go, but an absolute order descended from somewhere.

Outside the train I saw the passing trees, large old-fashioned houses, and shrines; each tree and each roof tile was tailored with clean beauty. As the train moved along, scene after scene was momentarily enveloped by bursts of white light as if flashbulbs were exploding.

This entire region maintained a broad sparkling that covered it completely like a thin, thin tent. The glittering substance transmitted something like a signal to me inside the train. I fell into a mood similar to what I feel at the moment of waking. Then I noticed that another sensation was intervening, besides that earlier one of happiness materializing in this region at a certain distance from me. I felt that at some deep level I was connected to that happiness.

Finally I was able to verbalize what my premonition was. I became convinced that somewhere in this residential area I, who had been destined to be blessed, actually did live happily with my family. For whatever reason, that fact came to me from the whole landscape like an obsession. Because it was unreasonable, it seemed all the more real. For that matter, is there anything rational that contains the truth? More likely the truth is tucked safely somewhere in the ambiguous folds of irrationality.

In one of the houses of this residential district that is peculiarly overflowing with white light, I am living: not I who followed a negative route from marriage on, but I who took a positive direction.

A few stations before the train reached T City, I felt like getting off.

I walked among the houses. This land itself filled my body with a sense of familiarity and yearning. And there was a reason. Although I had completely forgotten it until now, this was the ground on which I lived day and night. I knew very well the touch of the dry pavement through the soles of my shoes. On the pavement white shining sand spread out as if swept by a brush. It seemed that the white light reflected off the ground was dyeing me from below with a bright shine. Now that I actually stood on the ground instead of looking from the train window, an even stronger illusion brought the entire land to life.

After walking around for about an hour, I stopped in front of a house that caught my attention. An old Western-style house, perhaps built in prewar times, it gave the impression of being slightly tilted. Possibly it actually did tilt, being so old. Originally it must have been surrounded by a hedge; toward one end a section of shrubbery remained, now withered. In place of the hedge was a gray wire fence, which was the only thing that looked new. Because of the wire fence the garden was now exposed. There were many rose-bushes, in the midst of which I noticed the back of a middle-aged woman who was watering plants. I stood in the center of the side-walk and stared at her, feeling the smooth touch of the copper water-ing can handle in my grasp, and the splashes of water wetting the tips of my sandals. This copper watering can, which has been passed down through our family for many generations, feels full and heavy. I have been growing roses for over eight years now. I always come to the garden at this time in the late afternoon, and when I stand here holding the watering can and a bucket filled with water, the setting sun sends all of its yellow rays toward me. In this area the sun does not set over the mountains but goes down slowly far be-yond the horizon that opens to the sea, which cannot be seen from here. The twilight glow lasts longer than in the mountainous region, stretching forever like golden syrup. Every evening I water my roses————.

"Pardon me," I said, approaching the wire fence.

The woman watering roses turned around.

I was in a fog, the way I feel just at the moment of waking. But being in a fog does not necessarily exclude being lucid. Rather, clarity of mind was steadily taking over inside me. On the brink of waking, when you still want to sleep, it seems as though if you actually voice that desire, with that wish you will tumble into a paralyzing sort of dead sleep and, once there, infinity will open up and everything will appear distinctly familiar and well loved. But you are tugging yourself along toward waking, trying not to fall into that deep sleep.

"This is my first time in this area, and I was wondering whether there's a hotel where I could stay," I said.

"Well, T Hotel might be nice, if you go to T City," the woman replied.

"T City," I murmured.

I had taken a train without knowing my destination, yet along the way for no particular reason I had somehow decided that my destination was T City. And now this woman told me to go there, to T Hotel. I was floating in the pleasant sensation this coincidence brought me, when something occurred so that nothing but white light could be seen, like a scene in a photograph altered by halation.

"Mother . . ." A boy's voice was approaching. The woman walked away toward the voice and disappeared.

I arrived at T Hotel as fatigued as when I am forced to awaken from the middle of a deep sleep.

I had never had such an experience before. And, judging from it, the presentiment that had come to me as the train approached N City did not seem to have reached completion. It appeared to be still growing, more and more.

The clerk at the hotel asked if I preferred the new building or the old one. I naturally chose the old one. The clerk recommended the new; I continued to ask for the old. He happened to have one room available in the old building, but the rooms there were for long-term guests. Wondering what he meant by a long stay, I asked again for the room in the old building. It was a double room for only 3,000 yen; the rate was that low because it was in the old building.

After one night's stay in the hotel I was very pleased with it and, remembering that the clerk had mentioned long-term guests, I thought of staying on several weeks. I caught an H-line train home to pick up some clothes and other necessities. Once again from the train I could see white light streaming captivatingly, lavishly.

It took longer than I expected to get ready, so it was on the 8th of February, about a month after my first visit, that I returned to T Hotel. During that time the white light covered my head like a hat.

On the first night after I finally arrived at the hotel I had a curious dream. In that dream I saw a beautiful life-size male doll made of wax standing in my room. Before I knew it, I had called the wax doll Tamao; he was seventeen or eighteen, definitely not yet twenty years old. It seemed that I had been living in this room with the young man, and in this same room I would go on living with him in the future. His entire body was pure white; only the fullness of either cheek blushed pink. I put my hand on his cheek and, strangely, there was a pulse as if his heart were beating. Feeling like solving this baffling mystery, I tried musing about the secret of life that must be hidden somewhere in the wax doll. Then for some reason the garment covering the doll slipped, revealing the nude body, and my hand stroked the slender shoulders. Next my hand naturally moved downward; when it came to the chest the idea occurred to me to search for the nipples. Men have nipples, too, I told myself, and although they weren't necessarily a strong characteristic of a male, finding them brought a delightful pleasure to my fingertips. Each nipple was a tiny protrusion, like the tip of a needle, on the smooth, cool skin. As I was touching them, thinking how charming they were, before I noticed they became slightly fuller. The dream space was endlessly enchanting, as if a mist lay over it. At what seemed to be the center of the space, someone's heart was beating; I couldn't tell whose heart it was.

It was a simple dream. But despite its simplicity the dream seemed to have lasted throughout the night, and its ambience hung over me through most of my waking hours the next day. Around noon at the elevator door on the sixth floor I happened to meet a young man dressed in a blue denim jacket and jeans who resembled the wax doll, if not identically, then very nearly so. He appeared to be an extremely delicate type.

"Oh, you must be Tamao," I said without thinking.

He did not disagree. And so from our first encounter I have insisted on calling him Tamao. He may have felt he had no choice except to go along with my forcefulness. Because I called this young man Tamao, the bond between us seemed to be, at least for me, something compelling.

A single human being in itself is no one; but once named, a distinctive identity arises that can be nothing other than the name itself. A name creates content. Naming, then, it seems to me, is a kind of magic. By my naming him Tamao, that young man became decisively influenced by the wax doll of the same name in my dream. Without knowing it at all, he had become a person nourished day by day, through me, by the dream I had at night.

It finally became clear what the clerk had meant by saying that the old building was for long-term guests. Tamao's family had left four or five days earlier to go abroad because of his father's transfer to a foreign office. Tamao was going to stay at the hotel for a month or so until early March, preparing for the entrance examination for national universities that was held then. Other long-term guests included university professors and company trainees who stayed a week or two. Since the old building was not attractive to ordinary guests, the management lowered the rates and used it for those who wanted to stay longer. It had an elegance of past ages that was veiled by time; the musty air and faint odor of mildew were a transparent whiteness through which the colors of ceiling, walls, carpet, and furniture were visible. This, rather than a new building that appealed to everyone, was undoubtedly the most suitable place for me. There was no better place for me to take a rest than in this old building constructed according to the aesthetic sense of long ago, where the people who had appreciated that beauty had all died out and only the aesthetic sense itself, like a ghost, continued to float about.

Come to think of it, the morning I awoke from my dream of the wax doll, when I was still drowsily lying in bed, I noticed a slight draft leaking into the overheated room. When I shifted my gaze toward the windows, I saw the lower edge of the curtain moving. The curtain was a shabby sort, fit for a servant's room, probably intended as a temporary furnishing after the building was no longer in regular use. It helped to create an impression of a rich family's extravagance and decline.

To me, ruin was aesthetically pleasing. When I saw the curtain fluttering I suspected something and tried pulling it aside. One of the glass windowpanes was missing. But, viewed from a distance, the space where the glass was missing and the remaining windowpanes were of exactly the same transparency. It must have gone unnoticed that way for days, probably weeks. This seemed to add to the value of the old building even more. I found it beautiful that this window, built with such refined taste, was now left abandoned and dilapidated in this way.

It was about this window that I first spoke to Tamao when I met him by the elevator. I was on my way down to the hotel manager to call his attention to the window again because it still had not been repaired; it was not simply a matter of aesthetics, the cold wind blowing into the room was becoming too much for me.

"Since the room has a steam heater, it's not so bad, but still . . ." I said, calling to mind the lost past to which the radiator as well as the old building belonged.

"Thanks to that, the roses are doing well," Tamao remarked.

The longer I looked at him, the more pure white he seemed. If I

touch his skin, I thought, a trace of cool wax may stick to my fingertips. I could not detect anything raw or fresh about him that indicated life; only a spot on the curve of either cheek was faintly tinged
with red.

"What was that about roses?" I asked, suddenly feeling my mind
go blank.

"I brought along all the roses I was growing in a greenhouse,"
replied Tamao. His voice was high-pitched for a man, the even,
smooth sound unbroken by breathing.

For some reason I was taken aback and asked hastily, "Are you
growing roses?" but Tamao only assumed an ambiguous expression.

No one else entered the elevator until we reached the ground floor.
I kept quiet and observed Tamao. After he stopped talking the sign
of life that had been there during conversation vanished smoothly
within him; his face and limbs became totally expressionless. The
ancient elevator took a long time going down. Unlike modern ele-
vators that descend in no time at all without creating an impression
of movement, this elevator gave one a concrete feeling of actually
being carried down somewhere in a creaking box. Tamao was not
deliberately unexpressive, I knew intuitively; rather, the mode of
his existence was naturally devoid of expression. He seemed to have
forgotten completely that he had been talking with me a moment
ago, becoming just like an inanimate object, and he left me at the
elevator door. As he turned his face toward me upon leaving, a
smile flickered. It was as if his smile, held captive in flesh that suggested an inanimate object, radiated from deep within the innermost
part of his body.

That night again I saw the wax doll standing in the darkness of
my room. Although the skin was wax, the hair had the soft texture
of a living person's. While I was trying to capture that sensation,
my hand touched the ear. It was round and small enough to fit in
my palm. Struck by the idea of how intriguing it would be to feel
the shapes of various organs without seeing them, I moved from
ears to wide forehead, from wide forehead to slender nose, touching and examining them one by one. Under such a scrutinizing hand
the organs each in turn began to awaken, just as the nipples had
done the first night. At the same time I myself turned into a being
which, caressing an object, had only the sense of touch. Each part
that was grasped only through touch, without sight, seemed to be a
distinctive animate being. Then I tried to pursue this further. It was
a continuation of what I had thought in my dream the previous

night. I tried to contemplate a proposition that might be described as "Concerning the Secret of Life Hidden Within the Wax Doll." Ah, within a second I knew the solution.

At that, I awoke.

The next afternoon when I was drinking tea with Tamao in the mezzanine tearoom, I noticed something rather subtle. That something had actually been fermenting little by little ever since I had met Tamao the day before and decided to call him by that name after the wax doll. Tamao was beginning to assume an existence that was permeated by the dreams I had at night. The relationship between the wax doll and me was being simulated in the relationship between Tamao and me. That is, the sensuality between the wax doll and me at night had recurred between Tamao and me during the day. It was a sensation somewhat difficult to express. At the time I sat deep in an old-fashioned armchair in the tearoom, continuing to think about this strange phenomenon. There is a prototype something like the nucleus of a dream concealed somewhere deep beyond consciousness, and it seemed that actually I had always been living intensely, in the depths beyond consciousness, as this prototype. Thus, the existence lived previously is reflected in the mirror of reality—isn't this the mystery, so-called reincarnation?

"And what field have you chosen to take exams in?" I asked Tamao, who sat across a round marble-top table from me.

"Science," he said, "I'm thinking of studying mathematics." In contrast to the way I sat, he sat erect with his back completely straight.

"Math?" I repeated, thinking of something else. The phenomenon of a *previous life* being reflected in the mirror of reality cannot occur just any time or place. Reality that serves as a mirror exists very rarely.

"Yes, I like it," Tamao said.

Yes, that's right, I thought, I like it too. I was reminded that I had liked mathematics when I was younger. As it had occurred to me the other day when I was on the train passing N City, I who at a certain point might have taken the opposite direction of the negative path I had actually taken—I must have been like this.

"Must be hard, studying every day for exams . . ." The dream of the wax doll seemed to be reviving with each word I addressed to Tamao.

"I'm managing somehow," he answered in an easygoing manner. He spoke without changing his expression.

"Are you at your desk from morning till night?" Since my words were charged with the substance of that dream, Tamao, who received the words unknowingly, was as a result defenseless, completely passive, in being affected by *that*.

"Exam day is coming up soon." On his pale, slender fingers, Tamao counted the weeks—one, two, three, four.

"You'll exhaust yourself if you do nothing but study. You don't seem to be very healthy."

The more I talked, the more *that* came out along with the words, making me feel suffocated. Yet, because *that* could not be seen or touched, Tamao was unaware of what was happening.

"Yes, I'm always catching a cold."

"Always catch cold, you said?"

"If I push myself a little too hard, I get abdominal pains right away."

" 'Pain'?"

"What? What did you say?" Tamao asked, perhaps because I had shown my feelings openly. My aesthetic sense is especially responsive to anything related to ill health. For instance, the old building of this T Hotel. Anything that shows the flourishing of life holds no beauty at all for me.

"Isn't this place nice, the carpets and chairs . . . ," I gestured around the large vacant tearoom. The chairs were upholstered in dark crimson velveteen, the same color as the carpet. The tables, chairs, cabinets, chandeliers, and other furnishings seemed to have lost their functional purpose. But things that showed a practical necessity were not beautiful to me.

"Every afternoon I come here alone and have tea," Tamao said. "It's the only way for me to relax."

I had joined him, in fact, after seeing him drinking tea alone when I came downstairs.

"Even though you're young, you still seem to like things I'm fond of, too. Well, what do you think about while you're sipping tea?"

As soon as I spoke, the thought suddenly came to me that during those moments when Tamao sat idle he was reminiscing. And as for what he was recollecting, it was very strange indeed, but Tamao was remembering the dream I had at night. People do not recollect merely what they have experienced firsthand.

"What do I think about?" responded Tamao, with a faint smile.

Ah, at that moment it appeared that we mutually understood everything. Even so, just as before, Tamao knew nothing. Without being conscious of it, he had been caught in the dream space that flowed outward from me.

"Do you know the artist Albert Martin? There's a painting by him titled 'Love.'" Thus I took up our topic without further introduction.

The painting is like this: one large flower like a poppy was drawn filling the entire picture plane. That it is a single flower is evident in the fact that it grows on the top of one stem supported by a large calyx, yet it appears to be a double blossom. These two flowers are opposite each other like faces, and the lower part of each looks somewhat like human lips—one male's, the other female's, pressed tightly together. As a whole, however, it is still one large blossom, and inside that flower a man and a woman, through their lips, are copulating. Conversely, the man and woman coupling through their lips are being imprisoned inside the flower—no, they are contained by the flower. It is not that the man and woman and the flower are two phenomena, nor that the blooming of the flower and the sexual intercourse of the couple have a symbolic relationship to each other, but that the flower is permeated by the essence of the man and woman, and the man and woman are permeated by the essence of the flower. The blooming of the flower is humanized by the copulation of the man and woman; the copulation of the man and woman is transformed into a plant by the blooming of the flower; and that kind of love, sexual love, has been materialized in the picture.

II

I was waiting for Tamao. Tamao is eighteen.

In my dream I had pondered the secret of life hidden within the wax doll and in my dream as well I had received the answer. Needless to say, the secret of life was sex. Sexual love would reveal the secret of life.

Every night I met the wax doll named Tamao in my dream, and then during the daytime I enjoyed talking with Tamao over afternoon tea in the tearoom of the old building almost never used by the other guests. This went on day after day. By identification through the same name, that is, by my forcibly calling the two by the same name, a composite that could not be dismembered by any means—something one might call fascinating—came into existence.

With examination day just around the corner, Tamao had entered the last stage of preparing for exams. I was worried that he would think about the night during the day and thus disturb his studying. About the night? The night! The more I dreamed, the more Tamao would be able to recall. The phenomenon of a person remembering things he has not experienced personally occurs when someone unusually close to him is weaving an extraordinary dream, and that dream seems to be transmitted in an inexplicable manner. The vacant expression peculiar to a person lost in reminiscence emphasized the natural lack of expression in Tamao's features, and day by day his languid beauty, like that of a wax doll, became more striking. In exchange, the wax doll named Tamao, by receiving my devoted caresses meant to bring about the revelation of the secret of life, day by day became more sensual.

One night when I was waiting for Tamao he appeared from the core of my anticipation, which was growing stronger every moment. And recently I had been able to dream just as if I were creating the dream through my will. My habit of fantasizing steadily intensified until it began to spread into the realm of sleep.

Ever since I had first explored the organs through touch, one by one, I had been fascinated by that tactile manipulation. I was dreaming of Tamao but, perhaps because the dream was at night and could not involve the use of sight, I related to him only through touch. Yet the strange thing about the dream reality was the fact that I knew Tamao's body very well.

From this nightly experience I was able to understand the extent to which tactile sense comes to the fore when sight is diminished. How amazing that touch can offer almost the same degree of perception as sight.

While my palm was circling on the sleek surface of the lean chest, it searched for and found the nipples that protruded like the tips of needles. They were so tiny that it was hard to tell whether they were there or not, although I had repeated the process many times. But when I located them by both middle and index fingers, they soon began to enlarge. On the stark white skin only the swelling nipples were turning pink; although I could not see this I experienced it through touch as if through sight. When my hand renewed its circling, now moving in larger circles on the spare chest, I perceived the delicate ribs in relief, stretching left and right. The fineness of the skin's texture gave an impression of morbid shivering. My circling palm, moving upward toward the shoulder blades, felt the slender blades and then the lovely rounding of the upper shoulders that alone were slightly fleshy. Since the body was wax, there was no hair, no blemishes, no scars. My palm plunged downward and, with the pleasant sensation of that quick descent, clasped the sharply indented waist. There the torso became extremely narrow, as if constricted. When my hand reached that far, the life in Tamao awakened, becoming like warmth snatched from a burning candle.

The next day again I went to the tearoom in the old building at 3:00 and, as before, Tamao was sitting alone. As I approached he turned his wax-white face toward me. Only when he looked up did his face strain itself somewhere and a steady gaze emerge.

"I wonder what you're thinking about now," I said, sitting down.

How many days had I passed this way, repeating the pattern of solitude at night and Tamao's company during the day?

"I was thinking back on things." Tamao spoke in a courteous tone.

"Yes? About what?" I asked. Night and day were supposed to be linked only by Tamao's ability to recollect.

"Do you know the music 'Love'? It's by Toru Takemitsu." Tamao seemed on the verge of smiling.

He explained that the piece of music consisted of a woman's voice saying "love" and a man's voice saying "love," responding to each other, and this form of exchange was repeated. While the woman or the man continued murmuring alone in a voice varying in volume, tone, and tempo, gradually the pronunciation of "love" rose to a cry.

A shudder passed through me; it seemed that I could not possibly listen to that composition purely as music.

"Were you remembering that music?" I asked. I too spoke politely. Tamao of the daytime was not Tamao of the night. Still, they had affected each other so much that I could hardly distinguish them now. Between reason and non-reason a boundary still existed, and this barely enabled me to make the distinction.

I began to immerse myself in comparing the painting "Love" I had mentioned in conversation the other day, the music "Love" that was now our topic, and the love between Tamao and me. Our love did not seem to resemble either the picture or the music. One could not say it was similar to anything else. If something is truly unique, isn't it likely that, as if exerting a centripetal force, it increasingly resembles itself? Nonetheless, I continued to think about what sort of thing might be able to represent our love. While thinking about that, I realized that the sensuality of Tamao at night suggested a plant. I thought by all means I wanted to find the plant that resembled Tamao—rather, the plant that could replace Tamao. In other words, it was a matter of finding a being that fulfilled the equation, Tamao = plant.

On the round marble-top table between Tamao and me, the lemon of our tea was releasing its fragrance. The yellow color of the fruit was so fresh that the aroma too was given the feeling of yellow. Besides us, the only other guests in the tearoom were a late-middle-aged couple quietly drinking coffee.

"Is there a botanical garden near here?" I asked Tamao.

"Yes. You get off the H train at R Station and take the cable car from there."

"I wonder whether the garden has all sorts of plants," I said, meaning that I wondered whether there was a plant the equivalent of Tamao.

"Since it's winter, I'm not sure . . . ," Tamao replied.

The couple stood up and walked past us, arm in arm as Westerners do. Seeing the darkish spots mottling the wife's cheeks, I suddenly thought of my own age. I was twenty years older than Tamao.

"But I'm sure it's there," I said with particular significance.

"They say that years ago there were about a thousand varieties of plants, so I would think there must be more by now," Tamao responded, sounding strangely knowledgeable.

"Years ago?"

"I've been there to look at the roses. After that I started growing roses at home."

"Did you say 'roses'?"

"May I ask if there's anything troubling you?"

". . . What? You speak so formally, Tamao."

"But you suddenly looked strange."

"When you mentioned roses I felt nostalgic. Odd, isn't it, nostalgia . . ."

Why had I become nostalgic? When I tracked down the reason to the depths of that sensation, I recalled that years ago I had thought of cultivating a garden full of roses, if I someday had my own house. Occasionally one unexpectedly recalls something entirely forgotten.

"Confidants," "White Christmas," "Eden Rose." Even the names of the roses suddenly came back to me.

"Get off the H train at R Station, and then take the cable car, isn't that right?" I said, to make sure.

I thought I would certainly go there in the next two or three days; a cloudless day, transparently clear, would be right.

That night again I waited for Tamao.

Unless he was awakened by my hand, Tamao always remained cold. Starting from the ears, nose, mouth, I coaxed the organs one by one with my hand, massaging many times so the warmth of my hand would soak in; and as I repeated this the life hidden inside Tamao gradually awoke. I came to understand why I had developed a passion for something like a wax doll. The reason is that it is by nature cold. And yet, through my devoted caressing it was possible to draw up the warmth of life from some deep place. Thus it was possible for me to be the activator in an absolute sense. And though Tamao was a wax doll, he was shifting toward something that was not a wax doll. Without ever completing the metamorphosis, remaining always to some extent a wax doll, yet his wax skin glowed with a warm luster. The way it glowed gave a feeling that would have to be called a plantlike sensuousness. But when I stopped stroking Tamao he soon reverted to simply a wax doll.

That night again Tamao awoke in obedience to my skillful hands. The warmth of his organs was like a burning candle, and when this warmth was achieved my caressing was finished. This was always the end.

The last time this process was completed, it occurred to me to apply lipstick to Tamao's lips and thereby add a visual effect to what had been created wholly through touch. The act itself was suggested by a scene in the novel *Haruko,* but that was written from the point of view of the one on whom the action was performed. Not so for me: I would be the one performing the act.

Because I had warmed the cold Tamao, when I brought the lipstick in my hand close to him I felt warm breath softly exhaled from his lips. It was dark and I could not see, but following the contours of Tamao's lips that I knew so well, I painted with thick strokes. His lips were smoother and more supple than my own. The contour of the upper lip formed a distinct chevron. I painted forcefully, and in response to that pressure the breathing became quicker and sharper. The lips were slightly open, the teeth too must have been parted. Beyond the teeth, leading as far as where the life inside Tamao was, I sensed a dark passage, and it was from there that breath emerged.

In this way Tamao was completed and I took him from the bed and stood him on the floor. Because it was a wax doll, simply holding the torso and lifting it was enough. I made him stand with legs apart, arms open to either side, and head slightly raised. Then I moved back five or six steps and admired the figure. Of course it was dark, so what I actually did was to imagine the loveliness of this form: a naked body of pure white wax with only the lips painted red and with the male organs where life seemed to be centered.

The morning I awoke from this dream I felt exceptionally fulfilled.

After some time I felt like going for a walk outdoors. I left the room and walked through the corridor carpeted in deep red. When I reached the elevator, Tamao was there. I noticed something different from usual in his face as he glanced toward me, and I almost exclaimed aloud, but for some reason Tamao went running down the stairway by the elevator.

"Oh!" This time I did speak, and leaned over the railing of the stair landing, looking down. From the fifth floor to the fourth, from the fourth to the third, Tamao's footsteps as he ran down were completely absorbed by the dark red carpet that also covered the stairs, and as I stood above I could only sense his descent.

"Oh!" I spoke out clearly. Was it an illusion, or had I seen just now a lingering trace of color the same as my lipstick at the corners of Tamao's lips?

Perhaps the line between reason and non-reason did not exist anywhere. In this way, while living in reality, I am here, falling through an endless dream.

Wishing to catch Tamao and find out for sure, I followed him down the stairs. Since there was no sound of footsteps I had no idea how far down he had gone. When I reached the first floor, even though it was not yet midday I went into the tearoom where I always met Tamao in the afternoon. He was not there, but the couple I had noticed the previous day were drinking coffee. I felt exhausted and sat down at the table next to them. I ordered a cup of coffee, although it was unusual for me to drink coffee again after having it at breakfast. In the tearoom was a very large grandfather clock that seemed to be quite old. The numbers on the face were written as if out of proportion. It was 10:38. I emptied the coffee cup in one gulp. I expected that to wake me up, but "reality" seemed hopelessly vague, and I had long ago lost the distinction between dream and non-dream.

The woman of the neighboring couple nodded at me and smiled. "You, too, came to see it?"

I looked straight at her, puzzled.

"We came to see it after thirty years, didn't we?" She turned from me to the man.

"Earlier, I didn't agree; it was my wife who felt so enthusiastic. But then . . . I don't know how to say it, but when I got to be this age I thought what a splendid thing it was, and I came to appreciate it."

The man smiled at me as if to complement his wife's smile.

Once again I stared at them, uncomprehending.

"When the violet blooms, that's when I first met you," the woman sang softly.

"To truly understand that, one must reach a certain age. So my wife didn't understand." The man spoke without seeming to seek my agreement.

"You're bringing that up again. That was a young woman's dream," the woman said to him.

"No, not at all. It's an older man who discovers the beauty of a young girl," he insisted stubbornly.

I stood up and, having brought my purse with me, left the hotel directly. I caught a taxi and instructed the driver to go to the cable car terminal near R station on the H line. I had not intended to go there but suddenly I felt like going to the botanical garden. As the cab went along the river, T Girls' Opera House came into view on the side opposite the hotel. Words came to me then that matched what the man in the tearoom had said: It is an older woman who discovers the beauty of a young man.

When I reached the cable car terminal, the clear sky had clouded over and a cold wind had started blowing. Since I had left my room planning just to go for a walk outside the hotel, I was wearing only a dress. I stood there stiff with cold, wondering what to do.

The white light that had wrapped me completely ever since I passed N City while riding the H-line train last month was extinguished in one puff and the dark sky was oozing into me. I was standing on a plateau at the foot of the R mountain range and beyond the streets I could see the sea; it had turned exactly the same color as the dark sky. I was in no condition to search for that which would satisfy the equation Tamao = plant, so I decided to find a cab to return to the hotel. The freezing sensation throughout my body was becoming so unbearable that even inside the taxi I could hardly sit up. I wanted to lie down in a hospital bed, it didn't matter where, and I asked the driver to stop in front of a clinic we happened to pass. However, all the rooms were full. Under the circumstances they let me lie down on a black leather couch placed in the hall. Feeling the cold settling steadily through my body as if I had met an

accident in the snowy mountains and were freezing to death, I fell
asleep.

When I awoke, I was on the same black leather couch, and among
the outpatients coming and going through the corridor the peculiar
manner of one old man caught my eye. He was stooping so low he
was almost crawling, holding a magnifying glass to his eyes with
his right hand and examining the floor as he walked this way and
that. He seemed to be peering through the magnifying glass at the
people's feet. Suddenly I recalled the circles of life and death which
I had completely forgotten for a while; and now that I thought about
it, the old man looked a bit like that fortune-teller. Those who were
destined to die, in whom death accumulated no matter how hard
they tried to live, and those who could not die, in whom life accumulated for some reason regardless of how much they wanted to die—
in both cases, it was hell. I knew that I belonged to the latter group.
Although I had thought I was freezing to death a while ago, I had
awakened again, and there I was, alive. The fortune-teller had told
me that somewhere inside me, unrelated to my will, unyielding life
was swirling, and because the force was excessively strong it pushed
the men I loved into the circle of death. The old man who was walking around examining the floor with his magnifying glass occasionally reached out with one hand to pat the floor.

"What are you doing, sir?" I asked, lying on the couch.

"I'm really in trouble. I lost my contact lens and I don't know
what could've happened to it," the old man replied.

I felt relieved and brightened up a little. Deciding I would return
quickly to T Hotel where Tamao was waiting, I stood up.

As I neared T Hotel, that anxiety I had felt earlier in the morning
recurred, intensified. I had to find Tamao, no matter what. But he
did not show up in the tearoom at his customary time. When I
knocked at his door there was no answer. Oddly enough, I had never
entered his room. I wandered around through the deep red carpeted
corridors of each floor, searching for Tamao. Fatigued from walking,
I went to my own room and waited for the sound of Tamao's steps;
he would pass my room as he returned to his, which was on the
same corridor. The steam radiator was overheating the room, and it
was so sultry I felt slightly suffocated. An aluminum container filled
with water had been placed on top of the radiator to prevent the air
in the room from becoming too dry. Outside a wind was blowing
intermittently, swishing through the pine trees. The whitish riverbank could be seen, the narrow current bleak and clear, and across

the river T Girls' Opera House was in view. I decided to go to
Tamao's room once more. Perhaps I had missed his footsteps because the carpet had muffled the sound. I knocked at the door but
again there was no answer. I peeked into the room through the old-
fashioned keyhole. At the far end of the roundish space visible
through the keyhole, red roses were blooming. It was not the color
but rather the idea of the roses that upset me, as I again remembered that I had once wanted to raise roses if I ever had my own
house—roses such as "Ophelia," "Ina," "Harkness." Why did I
recall in such detail even the names of the roses?

I could not find Tamao that day after all, but once again, as I expected, in my dream I met Tamao of the night.

Before starting to dream, I thought about the equation Tamao =
plant.

Usually people associate sensuality with animals, but for me that
sort of sensuality has no relation to beauty. What I had been trying
to create in Tamao was something that might be called a plantlike
sensuality. Therefore, when Tamao did become sensuous, he should
resemble the sensuality expressed in some plant. What plant could
it be? Tamao is a male, therefore it could not be a flower. Something
that made one imagine green sap, greenish, watery, something like
a leaf or stem—I went on expanding my ideas. Quite possibly leaves
and stems instead of flowers could be sensual.

Suddenly it flashed into my mind: an amaryllis. Then I slipped
into dream.

Through my repeated caressing the wax grew warmer and warmer
and all of Tamao's organs began to awaken. But Tamao would never
act of his own accord. An utterly passive being, he received my
caresses. Then I felt that I had discovered a plant that would be the
equivalent of Tamao, the amaryllis that abruptly sprang up from
the ground in early autumn. Its slippery smooth green stem was
quite sensual. The single stalk with no leaves slid straight up. The
green of the stem looked watery and was heavy as if it contained
oil somewhere. Not yet blooming, the amaryllis was growing out of
Tamao. The bud too was green, sharply pointed, watery, oily. The
supposition that the interior was wrapped in poisonous red seemed
to make the green of this bud even more sensual. Actually, the calyx
sheathing the bud was already splitting and through those gaps a
flickering of red was visible. I wanted to paint such a picture. If I
could, it would be a picture of an amaryllis bud and stem growing
out from between the thighs of Tamao's beautiful nude body.

"Tamao," I called. For the first time sound intervened in my dream.

There was no response, but I was convinced that Tamao of the daytime, not Tamao of the night, was there.

As evidence of that, after I awoke, when I lay idly drifting in the morning sunlight, this time the body warmth of the flesh-and-blood Tamao clearly remained. Where Tamao's head had rested on the bed was a hollow the shape of his skull. Four or five strands of hair had fallen out; I picked up just one of them. I went over near the window and held the single strand to the light. It was chestnut brown and very fine. I pulled out one of my own hairs and held it with Tamao's, studying them both in the light for a while. They were virtually identical.

After breakfast in my room I got dressed to go out and went into the hall. It was a clear day, suitable for riding the cable car to the botanical garden. I had to search for a plant that was much closer to Tamao than the amaryllis. When I found it our "love" would surely be perfected.

I knocked at Tamao's door.

"I'm going to the botanical garden," I said when he opened the door.

"I think even if you go, you won't find anything—since it's winter, I told you." Tamao was so expressionless he could be mistaken for a wax doll.

"That's all right. It's an imaginary plant," I said, undiscouraged. Tamao did not ask about the imaginary plant.

"Today I'll finally finish." He lifted slightly something that he was holding in his left hand.

"What will you finish?"

"Thirty words to go, then I'll have memorized all of 8,000 words. Every day I've learned thirty words."

It was a thick English-Japanese dictionary that he was holding.

"Oh, I see. The national university entrance exams are a week from today, aren't they?"

As if through vertigo I saw in the distance our "love" that would continue nightly even after exam day had passed.

Then I walked toward the elevator. When I turned around Tamao was still standing in the doorway as stiff as a wax doll, looking this way.

The couple were in the elevator.

"Good morning. Are you alone today?" the woman asked; and instead of speaking the man gave me a forced smile.

"I'm always alone," I replied, and walked away.

The peculiarly white light flowing out of the granite soil that spread through the foothills of the R mountains enveloped every step I took. Surely this light that comes not from the sky but from the ground hints at earthly happiness. I stood at the cable car terminal for a while, observing the cloudless sky reflected on the ground and this entire region in particular glittering and glimmering. It was the exact opposite of the way it had been when I stood there the day before.

Only a scattering of passengers were riding the cable car. As it climbed lightly and easily I looked out the window and saw this region favored by white light stretching out in a long, narrow strip. It was distinctly different from the darkish area far beyond. The white light was rising in bursts as if flashbulbs launched from earth into the air were exploding every second.

"Which way is the botanical garden?" I asked hastily when I got off the cable car. There was another cable car farther up the path, I was told, and I had to take that cable car to reach the botanical garden.

Again I boarded the car and it ascended smoothly. There were even fewer passengers than in the first car. Only the sky was in view; this morning it was clear.

"Which way is the botanical garden?" I asked again when I got off the cable car. In front of the park, I was told, was a bus stop, and I should catch a bus from there. During winter the bus left once every hour. When I was sitting on a bench waiting for the bus, the cloudless sky still seemed to be reflected on the ground and a wide band of light was rising from the lower part of the mountain. Neither T City nor N City nor K City was visible, only the plateau at the top of the mountain and the blue sky.

I rode the bus for about ten minutes. One section of the forest of the R mountains had been partially cleared and made into the vast botanical garden. I bought a ticket at the gate. I entered alone, since I was the only passenger who had gotten off the bus. Just as Tamao had said, the flowering trees were not in bloom and the deciduous trees were wintry and bare; even the green of the evergreen trees had darkened—the whole scene was desolate. Even so, the sky was blue, and against that background the dry vegetation had a skeletal beauty. Although occasionally I met people in the garden, the area was so vast that they seldom came into sight.

I walked along while tossing around the notion of a plant that was Tamao. The world of human beings and the world of plants were perfectly parallel, and concealed in this universe somewhere was a plant that was the counterpart of each person. But it might be terribly difficult to find that plant: Tamao became sensual only briefly during the night; therefore the matching plant would also express its sensuality, identical to Tamao's, for only a brief period.

Then, far across this desolate wintry garden I caught sight of a blaze of color. There were many greenhouses arranged in rows, and weren't those roses inside them? My previous thoughts were blotted out and I felt my mind abruptly drawn to roses. I walked quickly toward them.

When I entered the greenhouse the well-tended rose bushes were in orderly rows and the flowers were in full bloom. I went back and forth along the path many times. The colors and fragrances were overflowing and I felt unable to tell one rose from another, but after a while I could study in detail each flower that attracted my attention. I gazed at a dazzling crimson rose with round, thickly clustered petals and read on the sign that its name was "Array." After that I observed a light vermilion flower, voluminous and sedate; its name was given as "Inter-Flora." A scarlet rose with a velvet sheen was called "Red Devil," and a radiant deep red flower was "Papa Mayan." Such subtle distinctions as these were found among the red roses, and they rivaled one another in luxurious beauty. In a corner of the greenhouse was a small shed. When I opened the door I saw some odds and ends of gardening tools, evidently no longer used. I noticed an old sprinkling can and filled it with water. I felt like watering the plants. Rosebushes are especially fond of moisture. I tilted the watering can over the rosebushes one by one and the water streamed out vigorously, soaking the soil at the roots. I moved slowly from the group of red roses to the pink ones. An elegant, creamy pink flower caught my eye and I read its name, "Confidants."

I felt myself expanding in boundless space. The antique copper watering can was heavy in my hand. Morning and evening I water the roses like this, every day. In the morning while everyone is still asleep and in the evening just before I prepare supper, it is my task to water the roses every day without fail. Now it is the hour when the oblique light of the setting sun comes flowing, and that tint makes the coloring of everything most exquisite. In this region the sun sets over the sea, and the rays of light like golden syrup lengthen and linger forever. Leaving the greenhouse, I go to a flowerbed where the rosebushes bear no blossoms yet, and I water them one by one. The glow of the sun shining directly from the west paints the spray of water gold.

Tamao. Looking around, I called my son.

Just then, on the other side of the garden fence footsteps slowly approached, and I sensed someone stopping and standing there.

Pardon me. This is my first time in this area, and I was wondering whether there's a hotel where I could stay, a voice said.

A ghostly woman with disheveled hair stood there.

Well, T Hotel might be nice, if you go to T City, I told the woman.

A Bed of Grass

TSUSHIMA YŪKO

Translated by Yukiko Tanaka and Elizabeth Hanson

Tsushima Yūko (b. 1947) was a year old when her father, Dazai Osamu, a writer of considerable fame, killed himself in a double suicide, ending a self-destructive life that was filled with alcohol, drugs, and sexual promiscuity. While in school Tsushima wrote for *Mita Bungaku*, a small noncommercial magazine. In 1971 she published her first book, a collection of short stories, and after a brief and smooth beginning to her career, she established herself as an important young writer and literary prizewinner. Divorced and the mother of two children, she has continued to write prolifically.

A basic motif in much of Tsushima's fiction is the stifling nature of family and blood relationships. The families portrayed in her stories are often disjointed and supply neither warmth nor support. The young female protagonists who leave such families fail to establish meaningful relationships outside. Another motif that frequently appears in her work is a yearning for the innocence and purity of early childhood, qualities that can be recaptured only in the world of autistic children who refuse ever to grow up. Tsushima's young women, unlike those of Ōba and Takahashi, do not remain in an enclosed inner world but try to cope with reality. For Tsushima this reality, though more dismal than that presented by her contemporaries, exists with undeniable weight and solidity.

"A Bed of Grass" is the title story of Tsushima's fifth collection of stories, which was published in 1977 and won the Izumi Kyōka Prize.

THE SEA looked yellowish green, maybe because my eyes had been saturated with the green color of the grass. When I looked at a photo of the sea a week later, it was a blue color, as it should have been.

"I wonder if it was really this color," I asked Kumi, but she just said "I think so, it was a nice blue," without looking at the photo again.

Everywhere I looked there was grass. The pale green spread thickly in all directions. I have underrated grass until now, I thought. Each time the strong wind changed, we stopped walking and felt compelled to watch carefully the undulation. The long shadows of the waving grass startled me.

I was the one who had wanted to go somewhere wide and open, but as we walked along the ridge I started to feel like complaining to Kumi for bringing us to such a desolate spot. There was nothing taller than myself as far as my eyes could see. Well, there *was* a lookout tower that we had seen as soon as we had reached the top of the mountain. It was a simple structure that looked like a steel pole stuck in the ground. A single bird perched on top of it. It was indeed a bleak scene.

We walked toward the lookout tower on the only path. We could see the ocean on our right underneath the cliff. The sea looked like soft rubber, as if it would bounce us back if we slipped and fell in. We couldn't hear the sound of the waves because they were too far away. This didn't make us feel safe enough to look down from the cliff, though; we were actually too scared to look.

It was difficult to walk upright because of the strong wind that blew in from the sea. It seemed always to be windy there—it wasn't that our luck was particularly bad. Only the sky was perfectly clear.

From the bus stop we had climbed a gradually sloping mountain path for half an hour or so. Halfway to the top of the mountain, the wind had not been so strong and we had felt cheerful. Kumi had even sung a few children's songs with her daughter, Nana. When we reached the top we were going to eat our lunch somewhere, walk along the ridge to the highway on the other side of the mountain, and get a bus back to the station.

Kumi's parents had brought her here once when she was small. She had not seen her father, she said, from that time until she had started junior high.

"He said when they split up that it was for my sake, and when they got back together it was for my sake, too—that selfish man. But the picnic was really nice." Kumi had seemed to be remembering a good time. "It's a neat place. We can come back the same day."

"That's it then, let's go there." I had jumped at Kumi's idea, but she had simply nodded, suddenly looking doubtful.

We had decided two weeks before to go somewhere for a picnic. Spring was near. The sweet daphne were in bloom and the tulip trees had started to open too. Something nice had to happen. We walked around our neighborhood with Nana every evening but that was not quite enough to satisfy the feelings that were bubbling up inside of us because of the warm season.

The night before our picnic I went to Kumi's place and took salted salmon slices, pickled plums, and seaweed for making rice balls. Kumi was puffing on a cigarette, lying as usual on the quilted spread that she rarely put away. She looked at me but didn't smile. Nana was sitting alone at a small table eating a sausage, and came to me shouting "Moun-tain, moun-tain!" when she saw me. She ignored her mother's mood. I made several large rice balls, letting Nana do whatever she could to help me. I felt that any fewer than ten rice balls would not be enough, although I knew very well that we wouldn't be able to eat them all. The number and size of the rice balls alone revealed my excitement about our picnic.

How many years had it been since I had gone on a picnic? The last time probably had been when I was in high school and a friend and her family had invited me to go for a drive to a port to see the foreign ships. I hadn't seen that friend since we had graduated. We went with her father, her younger sister, and a driver; it must have been soon after my friend's mother had died. The driver was about sixty and lived with them. I walked beside him and talked to him most of the time. I have a tendency to get acquainted first with a driver or a maid, or at school with a custodian, and to feel close to them. My mother has always disliked this part of my nature and says that I want to run away from the strong and associate with the weak instead.

Still, I had enjoyed that drive. It had been more than ten years before, and had been March then too. The sea had been rough. My friend had argued most of the time with her father and her sister.

Kumi, who is seven years my junior, would have been in grade school then. Whenever the neighborhood children teased her, calling her "kinky hair" or "curly head," she had tried to hit them with her fists. But Nana, who had inherited Kumi's type of hair, got lots of attention from the adults in the neighborhood because of her Western-style curls.

"People think she is cute now. They made a fuss over me too until I was three or so," Kumi said with a disgusted look each time this happened.

Nana walked by herself until we reached the ridge, but the moment she saw the expanse of grass she wouldn't move.

"I'll leave this brat here," Kumi said, slapping Nana, and walked on. I picked up the sobbing child and followed Kumi.

"She's only two. It's too hard for her," I said.

"She's taking advantage of you," Kumi said, turning around.

"Anyway, please don't make her cry today, since we came all this way for our picnic."

"Come here, Nana."

Kumi took Nana from me and put her on her back. Nana was still crying but soon started to smile at me as I walked behind her. I patted her head.

We walked along in silence until we arrived about noon at the base of the lookout tower. Kumi let Nana down from her back and said, "Want to rest here for a while?"

"Sure, but what about lunch?" As I said this, Nana started to pull at my bag and scream "Lunch-ie, lunch-ie!"

"All right then, let's eat," Kumi said right away.

"This place is no good. We've got to find a better one," I said, taken aback.

The lookout tower was a bare iron frame and didn't look like it would protect us from the wind. The frame was rusty and the ground was strewn with reddish-colored flakes. More than anything, I disliked the bird that circled the tower above our heads. It seemed to have decided that the tower was its territory.

Kumi looked up at the bird too and said, "Don't worry about that bird, there's only one."

"But why don't we go a bit farther, to a better spot?"

Kumi started to laugh calmly, barely making a sound. When she laughed like that it made me feel that I was younger than she was.

"A better spot? What kind of place are you talking about? This place is no good?"

I forced a smile and nodded. I suddenly realized that I had been preoccupied with a childish idea of a "happy lunchtime" and I felt embarrassed but couldn't let go of my expectations. Kumi looked around and said to Nana, "We'll eat lunch in a little while, it's not time yet."

Though she was only two, Nana seemed able to accept schedules; perhaps she had been trained to do so at the day-care center where she had spent most of her days since she was a baby. She didn't cry but simply knit her nicely shaped eyebrows and asked her mother how many more minutes it would be.

Kumi turned to me and suggested that we take a picture. I didn't mind, and went ahead and took my camera from my bag. We hadn't taken one photo that day. I told Kumi to pose. She looked around again and then started to climb the iron ladder of the lookout tower, urging Nana to do the same. The steps were steep and widely spaced, but Nana did not seem scared and started to climb ahead of her mother with agility. Nana was probably afraid only of an unfamiliar expanse of space. Even when her mother fell asleep, drunk, on the street, Nana would crouch down calmly beside her, waiting for her to regain consciousness. She could also laugh in excitement even when her mother pushed the swing on the playground to almost 180 degrees.

"Now look at Auntie, Nana, and smile."

Kumi and Nana turned around and smiled at me from halfway up the steps. I held the camera and quickly took a picture. The edge of Kumi's pink panties and some white skin showed between her tight jeans and sweater. Kumi was plump and had a hard time finding clothes that fit well. I once asked her how much she weighed and was shocked to find out that she was forty pounds heavier than I was. Kumi told me at that time, as if it were a big secret, that in order to raise a child alone one needed that much weight, and that "a skinny person like you could never manage." I thought what she said must be true, so I couldn't sneer at the extra fat around her stomach. I couldn't carry Nana for more than ten minutes, but Kumi could lift her daughter as easily as if she were a rubber doll and carry her on her shoulders or on her back for as long as Nana wanted. Just watching Kumi eat with all of Nana's weight on her shoulders made me feel tired.

For Nana, Kumi's body must have been as big, strong, and dependable as a father's body. Kumi's chest, as broad as a father's, had big breasts, bigger than the other mothers'. As long as she was next to her mother, Nana was bold and rarely cried. She would even tease other children who happened to be nearby, including those who were older than she was. Nana had pulled my hair and pinched my thigh, but this had happened only when Kumi was nearby. Once Kumi had asked me to pick Nana up from day-care. About ten children were running around in a large room, scattering small pieces of paper, and Nana sat alone, looking vacantly around her. When I had taken her hand and tried to get her to stand up, she began to cry, "Where's Mama, where's Nana's mama?"

I took two more shots of Kumi and Nana standing at the top of the lookout tower. Both of them grinned for the picture. The tower wasn't large but must have been five or six meters high. When I looked at the finished photos later, Kumi and Nana's faces were too small to tell what their expressions were.

When Kumi came down from the tower, she took the camera and told me to climb up so that she could take a picture of me.

"Actually I'd like a picture of all of us, but there's nobody around to take it for us."

I fearfully started to climb the steps. Once I had started up, I realized that they were steeper than they had appeared to be from a distance and were difficult to climb. I was anxious. The wind blowing against me seemed to become stronger, as if it would push me and I would fall to the ground headfirst. Between the steps I saw the wind-blown grass, the yellowish-green sea, and the sky with its circling bird. After climbing two or three steps I wanted to go back down.

When I was a child I didn't like playing on climbing poles, wall bars, or even jungle gyms. I was afraid of anything that separated me from the earth. Going underwater was not so bad; there wasn't a pool that was bottomless.

"Stop right there. Look this way. I'll take one." I heard Kumi's voice when I got halfway up the ladder, the same spot where they had posed for their pictures. I tried to look down at them and smile as I'd been told, but no matter how much I craned my neck, I couldn't see their faces. I was holding the pole tightly and in order to see them I would have to relax my arms.

"Come on! Which way are you looking?"

"Come on, Auntie!"

I heard Kumi and Nana's voices. I gathered my courage and extended my arms, peeling them away from the pole, and looked down. I felt a bit dizzy. Their faces looked very small, even though I had climbed only halfway up. The grass whirled around them.

"What's wrong? Don't look like that. Smile!"

I tried to smile. Even Nana was smiling and looked happy, but I couldn't change my expression. I was so scared that my face no longer felt like my own. Their faces were floating in front of me.

"You don't mind looking like that? I'll go ahead and shoot." I heard the clicking of the shutter in the distance.

"I'll take another when you get to the top. Go ahead and climb up!"

Kumi's voice was cheerful. It was strange that I was the only one who was so scared. I couldn't move even a finger.

"What are you doing, just standing there? Auntie's silly, isn't she, Nana?"

"Stupid Auntie, stupid, stupid!"

Kumi and Nana started to laugh. I couldn't move. "Stupid" was one of Nana's favorite words, but even so it sounded too harsh to me then. I was irritated with Kumi because she wouldn't make her daughter shut up. Once Kumi had told me with pride that Nana was exactly like her in her tendency to make fools of others. There was no question that Nana was good at discovering other people's weaknesses. Whenever she found someone she could tease, she was happy and started to yell, "Stupid, stupid!" When she was with her mother she was particularly loud.

"Come on, how long do I have to wait?"

Kumi was starting to sound annoyed. Nana began to run around the lookout tower with both arms outstretched, repeating in a high-pitched voice, "Stupid Auntie, stupid!" I just stood there, looking down at their faces. My throat ached, like it does when you're about to cry. The wind from the sea was too strong. I knew very well that I couldn't continue to stand there like that; no one could rescue me from my stupid anxiety except myself. At the same time, though, I was slowly becoming stubborn.

"I don't care, I don't mind staying here," I'd say. "Why do you two care about me, a person like me? If you want to leave, go ahead and go." I was aware of my silly obstinacy while I was thinking this, and this paralyzed me even more. I knew Kumi would not leave me because of something like this, and I felt ashamed of myself.

When I was small, I often got lost in department stores. I would feel so helpless when I lost sight of my mother that I thought I would never find her. The anxiety of being lost overwhelmed me, and even if I was in a place where she was apt to see me, my fear would send me running in an opposite direction. Then I would tell myself that I was truly lost, had no place to go, and would have to stay there until I died. I would cry as I wandered around the store. Some clerk would always find me and take me home, unharmed. Naturally my mother would be angry because she had been worried. I would not look at her or say anything. It did not occur to me to apologize; instead I would feel annoyed by my mother's scolding. In the end she would start to cry from frustration. Without understanding the situation, the maid and my retarded older brother would defend me and blame my mother, which made her even angrier.

My brother and I would leave our crying mother and go out into the yard to play as we always did. My brother, who seemed both a child and an old man, was my best ally. I could trust him completely . . .

"Are you going to stay there forever?" Kumi shouted, then started to climb the steps. "What's the matter? Hey!" She reached out, grabbed my right foot and pulled it.

"Don't. I'm scared." One shoe came off and fell to the ground.

"Well then, come down, hurry up." Kumi pulled my foot again and started to climb down. I followed her. Once I had started it wasn't difficult. My entire body was stiff. During the short time I had been up there the grass seemed to have grown.

"It's really quiet, isn't it?" I said instead of apologizing. Kumi glanced at me with a thin smile.

We decided to have lunch there. Both the bird and the wind had stopped bothering me. Nana was sleepy and wanted to nurse, and when she was refused, she started to cry. After a while Kumi opened her blouse and let Nana have a nipple, and she fell asleep immediately. Kumi's breast was white and full, and I felt embarrassed no matter how many times I saw it.

"I don't mind things the way they are, I'm used to it," I had once told Takashi.

"What do you mean, 'don't mind'?" Takashi had raised his voice when he heard my words. We were sitting so that we faced each other across his desk. I had already changed into my pajamas, and had to pass Takashi's desk to get to the small, four-and-a-half mat room we used as a bedroom. Takashi had raised his eyes from his book and called to me just as I had thought he would. I stopped and answered him coolly.

I was well aware that my words would make Takashi angry, since he had been saying for some time that the two of us ought to change our arrangement, but I didn't want to conceal my true feelings. The expression "I don't mind things the way they are" pleased me. I couldn't say "I *like* things the way they are," but I was afraid to make the first move to disturb the equilibrium of our daily life. Takashi insisted that my life would be more fulfilling if I lived alone, but I couldn't believe this. Rather than taking such a risk, I preferred to adjust myself to the present situation, stifling as it was, and curl up quietly to sleep, disturbed by no one. As long as I was not forced to leave, I wanted to stay.

Takashi stood up and came toward me. I smiled at him timidly and started to explain myself. Takashi walked around in front of me, looking annoyed. My explanation only made him angrier. Soon I was protecting myself from his fists. Why had he called me over in the first place? We should have kept our mouths shut and ignored each other, I thought. I felt bitter toward him.

What I meant to tell Takashi was that I had lived alone with my mother for a long time after my older brother had died, and I was accustomed to the way we had lived. It is true, I told myself; I am comfortable living this way, with both of us turning our faces away from each other.

I was in junior high school when my brother died. He was sixteen but was still a child. When the funeral was over and our normal life had resumed, my mother and I tried to avoid each other in the house. I felt uneasy being with her without my brother there. His death made me realize for the first time that Mother and I had cared only for him. I had seen my mother existing simply behind my brother, and she had seen me as no more than an ordinary child who was growing quickly and who would soon catch up with him. Both of us had been clinging to him in our own way, but our sadness was not the same. I felt that her sadness was hers alone.

I started to spend most of my time outside the house, staying at my friend's house at night. I was afraid of touching the sadness of my mother, which I could not understand, and so I continued to ignore her. My father had died over ten years before in an accident. I was afraid I would be overcome by the deaths of my father and brother as my mother had been. Ashamed of myself for being this way, I tried to keep my distance from Mother. When I came home after midnight, she would be squatting by the back door, waiting for me. Her figure looked small and dark.

"You'll catch cold, sitting here like that," I would say tartly, but my legs were shaking and my voice trembling. I could not bring myself to apologize to her or speak to her gently. I hated myself and I hated Mother.

On those occasions Mother must have hated herself and her daughter just as I did. She did not cry in front of others when Brother died.

"Waiting like that . . . Did I look lonely, like I was trying to cling to my daughter?" she might have said to herself. "Never. I'm not so weak that I'd make my daughter pity me. It's impossible that I would feel lonely after so long. I don't want her to misunderstand me. I was simply waiting there to scold her."

Until I entered high school Mother punished me by hitting me on my shoulders and back with a quilt flail. I would stand there without crying or apologizing, staring at her face until it became smaller and smaller, as if it were drifting far away from me. I felt like grabbing it and pulling it toward me. Unless I gazed at her face terribly hard, it would seem to shrink and float away into space.

When I started going to high school, I was larger than Mother. I stopped speaking to her altogether, and not being talkative herself, she kept quiet too. Whenever there was a need to communicate, I would write a note and put it by the door of her room after she went to bed.

One morning when I had overslept, I was awakened by what sounded like her screaming voice.

"Beast! This beast!" she screamed and at the same time tore off my blanket. I jumped up and saw her flushed face in front of me. Even though half asleep, I was still ready to defend myself. By then Mother had left the room, and I went back to bed, tensing my body under the blanket. I felt like I had actually grown thick hair and had become a beast with thick nails on the tips of my limbs.

Once, about the same time, Mother had suddenly started to laugh at the dinner table and shouted, "What nonsense, what nonsense!" Thinking that she might come at me the next moment, I waited with my body rigid, still holding my rice bowl. But she began eating again as if nothing had happened.

I continued to stay away from home but couldn't forget Mother. I wanted her to keep living; I wished for nothing else, and yet I did nothing to console her. I kept running away from the sound of her footsteps. I often dreamed that we were walking together on a suburban street on our way to meet Brother. The dream always began with us packing one or two hundred rice balls; both my brother and

I had loved the rice balls Mother made. When I was living with Takashi I often told him about them and made him laugh.

I left home the year I graduated from high school. Mother said nothing. We were both tired of stubbornly living alone while sharing the same house. I didn't see her for the next four years. We talked on the phone occasionally, but she always hung up first, saying she was busy.

Four years later, when Takashi and I visited Mother for the first time, I was six months pregnant. When I told her, she straightened her back and said, "I see. But you know I can't do anything for you, don't you?"

"Of course I do," I said, perplexed.

"Well then, it doesn't matter to me. Is there anything else you wanted to tell me?"

I shook my head. At one time I had imagined that she would take my hand and be overjoyed at the news, and I was angry at myself for having had such expectations.

The baby, a boy, was born in midsummer. I didn't tell Mother about him. That winter he caught the flu and died rather suddenly. If he were still living, he would have been three years older than Nana.

Five years after the baby's death I finally went back to Mother's house. At that time she had a bad cold and had to stay in bed. It was as if she had been waiting for me to come back to get sick.

My sick mother shut herself up in her room and wouldn't let me in, just as she had done in the old days. She wanted her meals left outside the door, feeling, no doubt, that she would rather stay sick or even get worse than let me take care of her. I didn't make any effort to get close to her. I didn't tell her what had happened between Takashi and me, or about my future plans.

I dreamed about Takashi every night in those days. In one dream Takashi came into Mother's house without saying anything. When I told him that he had no business there and asked how he got in, he said, "That's no problem. I have a spare key." I realized he was right, and that therefore he could get to me no matter where I went. In the dream I was accepting this fact.

In another dream Takashi was standing in a glaring flame like Joan of Arc, and he and a strange boy were washing each other. Someone—I couldn't tell who—stood beside me and explained the scene in a low voice. I couldn't understand a word of what he was saying and yet could tell what it was that I was seeing. I was depressed that I had to listen to a lengthy explanation of something I already understood.

For a month or so after I had returned to Mother's house I saw no one. Once I had left my life with Takashi, I realized I didn't have a single friend. Takashi had taken all of the acquaintances we had with him. I stopped working at the company where I had been for seven years and spent most of my time sleeping, leaving the house only to go to the neighborhood supermarket.

Winter was coming. Occasionally I saw a mother and child playing in a children's park across from my house, sometimes even at nine or ten o'clock at night. I watched their shadows from my upstairs room. When I didn't see them I was disappointed, and most evenings I was. The child was always barefoot and wore summer clothes. Her laughing voice was high and clear. When she stood under the street lamp her hair looked silvery and seemed to float. The child's shadow moved incessantly; the mother's, almost never. Her back was stooped and I didn't think she was a young woman. The two were Kumi and Nana.

About the same time I got a telephone call from Suwan, so the following day I took a train and went to the center of Tokyo. Mother's cold was better. Suwan asked on the phone about Takashi, but even I didn't know his new address. There was no reason that I should have known. I had nothing to say to Suwan, but still agreed to meet him the next day, even looked forward to seeing him.

Suwan was waiting for me at a coffee shop, sitting with his knees together and his back straight. There was an empty glass of milk in front of him. His shoulder-length hair had been cut short. As soon as I sat down, I teased him about it.

"Mama cut it. I feel cold," he explained in the awkward Japanese he always used.

"So you've been back to your country, then, even though it's not winter vacation yet?" When I talked with Suwan my Japanese became awkward too, but even hearing myself talk like that brought back memories. While waiting for Takashi to come home late at night, I used to listen to Suwan. He mixed English and Japanese and was sometimes so hard to understand that I felt irritated, but I listened anyway. Occasionally he made comical mistakes and because of them we felt closer to each other. Once, when he had referred to his mother as a "housewife," I misunderstood and thought he had said "house wine," and I visualized her as the owner of a bar.

Suwan could not learn to say my name properly and when he meant to address me as "Onēsan" (older sister) he said "Onisan" instead. No matter how many times I corrected him, he didn't change this habit. He must have found "Onisan" easier to say. I often wondered why Takashi had anything to do with this immature youth, who talked so eagerly about his mother and his school days. Partially because of his language difficulties, he tended to tell the same stories over and over. His pet story was about how he used to carry a knife with him in grade school and how he once tried to attack a teacher he hated.

Every time we met he complained about not receiving a letter from his mother. He said he didn't understand why and worried about her. Each time I responded exactly the same way, saying that his mother was an adult and that no matter how much she loved him, she wouldn't write unless there was something she had to tell him. Adults are busy, I said. Then he would talk happily about how his mother was busy helping his father keep the books for his business, and how much she depended on him, her only son.

After renewing my acquaintance with Suwan, I found out for the first time that this mama was illiterate. His father seemed to have only a grade school education, but they hired three secretaries so they had no difficulty, Suwan said. No wonder he hadn't had any letters from his mother.

"Why don't you send a tape?" I had asked him. He had taken my advice and sent one right away, but there was no answer from her. If she was not used to operating a tape recorder, it might have been more trouble for her than dictating a letter to one of the secretaries. Suwan continued to write a letter every week, but his mother didn't send even one reply. He only received money and a short message from the person considered his guardian in Japan.

I still don't know how Takashi met Suwan. He introduced Suwan to me as a student from Bangkok, but he didn't seem to be studying anything, judging from the fact that he used to spend a lot of time with Takashi on weekdays. His Japanese was too poor for a serious student. When Takashi brought him to our apartment for the first time he said he had just turned twenty. He stayed that evening for only half an hour or so.

Takashi had many friends that he had met in ways I knew nothing about. I enjoyed being given a chance to meet them, but since Takashi didn't actually introduce them to me, I didn't know too much about them. There weren't many that I saw more than once; Suwan was the only one I knew well enough to talk with comfortably. He dropped by quite frequently once he got used to me, in the same way that I went over to Kumi's.

Around the time when I accidentally burned Takashi's thigh, Suwan and I saw each other every day. We took Takashi to the hospital and took care of him together. When his burn had completely healed, Takashi left me. I asked Suwan to keep the things Takashi had left behind when I returned to Mother's house. He seemed to spend the night at Suwan's place sometimes. Suwan cleaned the apartment thoroughly for me. He complained at that time, too, that he hadn't received any letters from his mama. I found myself telling him that she felt so close to him that she didn't need to write letters.

"I came back a week ago. Mama scolded me—'Go back to Japan.'"

Suwan had put on some weight. I remembered that Takashi used to call him a "black pig." After the two of them came back from the public bath together, Suwan used to fix Chinese noodles with lots of roast pork, and the two would face each other and slurp them up.

Takashi would be in a good mood and would tease Suwan, telling him he'd turn into a pig some day.

"Do you know what a 'pig' is? One of those smelly things that oinks." Suwan would say nothing and smile timidly. Takashi would then become irritated with Suwan's smile and would either chase him away or urge the reluctant boy to go with him somewhere. On those evenings Takashi usually didn't come home, and if he did, he would come back just before dawn, dead drunk. I would wait in the four-and-a-half mat room I had taken for myself. I had a bar against the sliding door, and listened to Takashi's rough breathing in the next room. Like a little girl with a large, violent father, I was afraid to be alone with Takashi. I was also afraid of leaving Takashi, even though by then he seemed like a slimy reptile with a long slender tongue and tail. Pretending to be asleep in a room with a bar at the door suited my ambivalent state of mind. It seemed that I secretly wished Takashi would discover the bar, which was as fragile as a fish bone, and break the door open. But about the time I had started putting the bar at the door, Takashi had lost interest in me and didn't attempt to open the door to the back room. He took his bedding out himself and slept quietly.

Suwan told me he had been in his country for two weeks. He wanted to stay there with his mother and she must have felt the same way, he said, since he was good at mental arithmetic and could have helped her with the accounting. An only son, he would eventually inherit his father's business, and if so, there seemed to be no reason for his parents to send him all the way to Japan to study against his will. He was not bright and didn't have any particular talent, so they were wasting their money. He wanted to live a carefree life and enjoy himself—he had no desire to work hard at anything. Suwan had told his parents this, and his mother had listened without a word. She had looked at his long hair and began to question him about how he had been living in Japan. Was he involved with some Japanese girl? Was he associating with some undesirable men from his own country? Was he eating nutritious food? This was all she had to say. His father told him to go back to Japan soon and not worry about money. His mother saw him off at the airport when he returned to Japan, having packed dried meat, bananas, and other food for him. Suwan went to see Takashi as soon as he returned to Japan, but he had already moved. No one was living in his old apartment, and Suwan didn't know Takashi's new address. He had been waiting for Takashi to contact him, but hadn't received even a phone call. He was concerned and, besides, he had Takashi's belongings.

I thought Takashi had forgotten about his things. He must have taken everything he really wanted and didn't care for the things he had left behind.

"If they're a bother, you can throw them away. I'm sure it's all right."

"No, shouldn't throw away," Suwan said firmly.

"I don't think he'll come around to your place."

"Why?"

"I don't know . . . He's like a butterfly, you know."

"A butterfly?" Suwan mumbled, looking stupid. Why should a dull kid like this have to come all the way to Japan to study, I asked myself, and looked away. He had the body of a twenty-year-old, and I felt repelled by him at times. I had an urge, as Takashi must have had, to shout "You black pig!" in his ear and shake his thick shoulders. Whenever I had looked from Suwan to Takashi, I discovered something exceptionally fine in Takashi's ordinary face and body. Takashi had played baseball until he graduated from high school, and his body was firm. When I saw them from behind, twenty-year-old Suwan and thirty-year-old Takashi looked as if their ages could be reversed. Suwan even had some gray hair. Once

I found a long silver strand of hair on the tatami mat while I was cleaning, and after that I resented Suwan's daily visits.

Suwan was not the kind of person one could be nasty to, however. When I saw his smiling face, with its nose that seemed to be melting, I smiled back in spite of myself. When I looked at Takashi's rather sly face, my smile disappeared but I felt safe, as if I had returned to my proper place.

"Yes, a butterfly," I said in English.

"A butter-fly? What is that?"

"It's not a Japanese word . . . Anyway, don't worry. He's not alone."

Suwan opened his mouth, as if to say something, but instead took a breath and shook his head. I could imagine the words he had swallowed: "Onisan is not gentle. She's tough." Suwan had said these words many times, and each time I couldn't help but smile.

When he felt like it, Takashi had used the excuses of a headache or cold to take time off from his work at the university. Because he was in exceptionally good shape, he could afford to enjoy illness. He liked medicine, too. When he took his temperature, he usually had no fever.

"You don't have a fever. Just a hangover, I'll bet," I would say to him. He would answer faintly, "The fever is stuck in my stomach," or "It's coming now." After the baby died I ignored Takashi's fake illnesses. I didn't like to see self-indulgent behavior in myself or in the people around me, and I didn't allow myself to seek sympathy from others, even when I had a strong need for it. Because of the strain this caused me, I resented Takashi, who could act like a whiny child.

After Suwan started coming to our place, Takashi's pretended illnesses happened more and more often. Each time Suwan would fix up a bed for Takashi, sit by the pillow with a serious expression, put a wet towel on Takashi's forehead and feed him oranges and ice cream or prepare a special rice gruel with fresh ginger. I would watch the two without doing anything, and Suwan would reproach me.

"I feel sorry for Takashi. Takashi is lonely," he said.

It was my fault when Takashi's thigh was burned with boiling water from the top of the kerosene stove, although I hadn't intended to do it, and I couldn't stop my legs from shaking with fear when I saw him bend over, groaning. At the same time I heard myself muttering, "It's real this time. You're seriously injured and can moan as much as you want. How does it feel?"

Suwan and I left the coffee shop and went to a bar where I had once gone with Takashi.

"Alcohol. I can't at all. True. No alcohol," Suwan said.

"I can't drink by myself. Come on, you have to," I insisted, and pushed a glass of beer in front of him. It wasn't evening yet, and the bar was empty. The smell of coffee was stronger than that of liquor. One wall was glass, beyond which were some indoor plants. I remembered that Takashi had seemed to like the dark green color of the plants. I ordered a whiskey with water, and drank some.

"I haven't had a drink since I moved. Not a drop," I said. Suwan smiled at me calmly. "It's true. I used to drink a little too much but I never got sick, not even once."

"Onisan can hold liquor. I am like a woman. I am ashamed."

"I can't drink much either. I can't hold my liquor at all. But that day I could take it, for some reason. I was expecting to collapse any time, but my legs weren't even shaky."

"Takashi is strong. Onisan is strong too. I am no good. I'm like a child. Can't smoke a cigarette, either. My friends laugh at me."

"That's all right, your mama is happy," I said. "But I've never heard of a child going to a Turkish bath." The Turkish bath was one of the few jokes that Suwan and I shared. He once had said he liked Turkish baths very much.

"Where can I find one here? I want to go soon. Can you take me some time?" he had asked.

"Well, did you go? How was it? Shall we go together next time?" I had asked him later. When he had first mentioned "Turkish," I had thought he was talking about the country Turkey.

Suwan had said he used to go to a Turkish bath regularly in his country before he came to Japan. A friend of his was the daughter of the owner of a large Turkish bathhouse, and he could go there for free, even though his mama was against him associating with the girl. It was a three-storied building, like a castle, he said. Since it was a high-class operation, it was very clean and had only pretty, gentle girls. Suwan had told me this, but I couldn't tell how much was true. He said he had been going to the bath since he was thirteen.

"Japanese ones are not so good, I think. They're expensive and you might get some disease," I said, not knowing too much about it.

"You mean 'cherry blossom'?" Suwan laughed loudly.

" 'Cherry blossom?' Is that what you call it? I see."

Overhearing our conversation, Takashi had first given me a patronizing look, then tried to draw Suwan's attention to himself by beginning a conversation that I couldn't join or urging Suwan to play cards.

Takashi had taught Suwan to play cards when they first started to spend time together. Suwan learned immediately and became as good as Takashi. I used to play with Takashi every evening when we first started living together, since we didn't know any other way to spend our free time.

One summer Suwan came to our apartment with several of his friends. Their visit was unannounced, and I stood there blankly, not knowing what to think until one of them said, "Don't worry, we'll do everything. Please sit down." He spoke good Japanese. They opened the paper bags they had brought and spread Scotch whiskey, barbecued chicken, skewered prawns, almonds, and watermelon seeds on the table. They got glasses and ice from the kitchen and invited me to join them. Takashi was in high spirits, sitting in the middle of the group, and either teased the young men or gave them some kind of advice.

"The color of your shirt makes you look like a native. Pink and purple make your complexion darker . . . No, if you only study textbooks, you'll never improve. Besides, that textbook is no good. All the expressions are outdated. Actually, being around Japanese like this is the best way. Look how Suwan has improved lately. Don't worry about entrance exams. That university is lenient with foreign students. By the way, that's a nice ring you've got there. Is it a ruby? Can you get them cheap in your country? I thought so . . ."

I went on drinking by myself, looking from one face to the other. I thought Suwan looked best of all, perhaps because I was used to seeing him. He looked the most childlike and, at the same time, the oldest. He sat with a silly smile on his face, drinking coke, the only one who wasn't wearing a ring, who wasn't arrogantly smoking foreign cigarettes, and who didn't seem to quite understand what Takashi was saying. It seemed that he was also the only one who had no Japanese girlfriend. The other young men mentioned the names of Japanese girls now and then.

When Takashi got tired of talking to the young men and began to turn more and more toward the television set, the conversation shifted from Japanese to Suwan's language. Before I knew it, I had drunk half a bottle of whiskey by myself. I kept waiting to get dizzy but in the end the color of my face didn't even change. The drunkenness that should have circulated all through my body seemed to have accumulated in my back.

"I'm surprised. You're strong, Big Sister," a fellow with a gold pendant said to me. Tall and with shiny skin, he smiled agreeably.

"That's right. One or two bottles is no problem. Any Japanese woman can drink that much."

He opened his eyes wide and said, "You're not serious."

"No, I'm not. Come on, let's drink some more."

I went on drinking. The young men kept talking in their own language. Suwan was saying something in a strong tone; his cheeks were flushed. The sound of this language, which I couldn't understand at all, was rather pleasant. I wished that Japanese sounded the same to me. Takashi's words, the words that people at work used when telling me what to do, the words of Takashi's parents—they were all Japanese. This seemed to me a rather strange coincidence. I sang a Japanese song for the young men, and they seemed to be pretending to listen, only to be polite. Takashi told them that it was time for them to leave, and they stood up. It was after midnight when they left. Suwan stayed behind and cleaned up, and I kept on drinking whiskey. After Suwan left, Takashi said, "I'm going to bed. Get out of my way," and I decided reluctantly to go to bed too. My back felt chilled and heavy.

"Suwan is afraid of being left out, even by a bunch of guys like that. I wonder if that's what happens when you live in a foreign country," Takashi said the next morning, as if thinking aloud.

"I guess. It's a shame, since he came all this way to a foreign country." For once I responded to Takashi's comment, trying to match his mood.

Suwan finally finished the glass of beer he had been drinking for over half an hour, and yawned. He looked different when he was with those guys, I thought. He didn't seem to be listening to me, but in fact Suwan and I didn't have much to talk about other than Takashi. When I became quiet, he said "Pardon me" over and over again in a sleepy voice. I started to feel drunk myself.

I suggested that we go and we left the bar. It wasn't even six o'clock yet. I walked with my hand around his plump hip. The wind was cold. Even though Christmas was more than a month away, I could hear the sound of "Jingle Bells." The music wasn't made with human voices or with musical instruments, and when I stopped to listen, I realized that the barks of various dogs had been skillfully combined to make the melody. Big dogs, small dogs, old dogs, puppies—all kind of dogs were barking. I put my mouth next to Suwan's

warm ear and playfully said, "Wan wan, kyan kyan." He smiled
and nodded obediently, and this irritated me. He doesn't even know
that Japanese dogs say "wan wan" when they bark, I said to myself.
I took advantage of the crowded, noisy street and barked again in his
ear, this time more loudly. Suwan kept nodding and didn't say anything. His body was warm no matter where I touched him.

When I met Takashi for the first time, he was wearing a shiny,
slim-cut blue suit that fit his body snugly. It had been seven years
since then, but I could clearly remember the way he had looked at
that time.

I had gone to his office at his university on company business. His
suit was shiny and his hair was too, because of the hair cream he
used. The smallest of all those who were in the room, he acted big
from beginning to end. He was sitting on the edge of the chair with
his legs wide apart and taking me for a student wanting to join the
club he belonged to, he started to tease me.

"You're nervous, aren't you? A graduate of a girls' high school?
Not used to boys, then. Better not overdo."

I opened my bag and silently handed him a paper he had signed
when he rented some films from the library of the small motion
picture company where I worked. The due date for returning the
films had long passed. When he saw the paper he clowned around
with his hands on his head, laughing and saying "You've got me!"
He then showed the paper to the others in the room and they
laughed too. "You've got me" was one of his favorite expressions,
which Suwan learned later and used proudly.

Takashi said then that he would return the films the next day
without fail, and offered to take me to a tavern near the university.
He said it was to show me he was sorry, and putting his arm around
my shoulder, he announced to the others in the room, "Let the two
of us go alone, all right, boys?"

At that time I was certain that I disliked Takashi, but I tend to be
more agreeable to those whom I clearly dislike than to those I like
or don't have a strong feeling about. When I truly dislike a certain
person, I don't show it but still feel guilty; I end up feeling sorry for
them and want to be nice, so I act pleasant. I went with Takashi.

He took me home that night. The following day he showed up at
my company's office to return the films as he had promised. A month
later he moved a bed, a desk, and quite a few books into my four-
and-a-half mat room. By then I felt I couldn't do without him. I was

drawn to his carefree personality that kept me from remembering my life with Mother. I liked more than anything the fact that he had grown up without knowing any of his blood relations. He was adopted, but his foster parents had loved him more than their own son. He had a straightforward, warm feeling toward his parents, just like characters in the stories in elementary school textbooks. He seemed to think that this was one of his virtues.

It took him five years to graduate from the university, and then he stayed on as an assistant to his professor.

"Here's the station. Can you take a train by yourself?"

"I am sorry. I'll take a taxi." Suwan's body was swaying like a goldfish in lukewarm water.

"Can you manage by yourself?" I asked.

Suwan nodded and looked over at the taxi stop. I whispered in his ear, "He has lots of friends and he's busy. He's probably forgotten about you . . ."

"I'll call you again. Is it all right?"

"Of course, but are you sure you're all right? Shall I take you to your place?"

He smiled and said, "No, I can go back by myself."

After I left Suwan I went into the station and looked at the clock. It was five after six. The station was crowded with people going home from work. I didn't want to go home yet but couldn't think of any place to go, so reluctantly bought a ticket and returned to Mother's house.

I found the supper Mother had prepared for me on the table. The table, the tableware, and the food were exactly the same as before. The way I sat in front of the table hadn't changed either. I ate as I always did, looking down with my back rounded. Mother was in the next room unraveling an old sweater while she watched television. She was probably thinking the same thing she always did: "The way you eat makes the food look bad. Eating as if the food tasted good is part of good manners, you know." I was thinking I should have gone to a movie, or maybe called an old friend from work. She probably hadn't left yet. Some department stores were still open . . . While I slowly ate my dinner, I went over the same thoughts I had had on the train.

Once I was home it wasn't so easy to go out again. I hesitated even to make a telephone call. Mother was constantly watching me, and just as in the past, I didn't feel that I could escape her gaze.

This didn't mean, however, that I regretted returning to Mother's house. When Takashi left me I thought only of returning to her. It never occurred to me to remain in the apartment where Takashi and I had lived or to find a new one just for myself. After Takashi told me to leave him alone, I had been waiting for the day when I could go home to Mother's. I didn't want to stop living with Takashi, and yet I was hoping he would disappear from my life through some circumstance that didn't involve my own will. More than that, I wanted to live with my mother again. Mother would undoubtedly criticize me severely for the way I had lived. I didn't want anyone to forgive me for having followed Takashi, and hoped that Mother's brown eyes would remind me forever of my disgrace.

When I got out of the truck I had hired to move my things to Mother's house and opened the door, she stuck her head out from the living room and said, "What are you doing there? Come in and close the door. You're letting the cold wind in."

"But I have some things to bring in . . ."

"Well then, hurry up and get it over with."

I carried various things that I didn't want to throw out upstairs to my room with the help of the truck driver, but Mother didn't come out of her room even once. My kitchen utensils I put in the closet of my room. I couldn't find a place to put the washing machine, so I left it in the garden.

"I don't feel well, so I have to go to bed now. Why don't you go to bed too, instead of moving around and making noise upstairs? You can put your things away tomorrow," Mother told me when the moving man left. I went to the kitchen to fix my supper; I found some eggs and pickles in the refrigerator and ate them with rice.

The next morning Mother came down with a fever. I had told her about my situation in a general way and had asked her with my head down if I could return and live in the upstairs room. This was when I had unexpectedly visited her just before actually moving in. She didn't express any opinion, as usual, and simply said, "If so, you'd better clean up the room today." Since this was a practical suggestion, I did as I was told. I had longed for such a reaction from Mother, and I was pleased.

It was after nine o'clock when we returned to Kumi's apartment from the seashore. Nana had been sleeping on her mother's back. She was cranky on the train; when the train shook, she cried, and when it stopped, she cried. By the time we were about to get off, she had cried so much that her voice was hoarse. The train was quite crowded and we couldn't find an empty seat, so we took turns holding Nana. We were exhausted by our outing and irritated by Nana's incessant crying. Instead of being concerned about Nana's condition, we simply tried to make her stop crying by absentmindedly pinching her cheeks and patting her thighs. Toward the end we didn't even care about making her stop crying.

As soon as we got to Kumi's place we drank some cans of beer we had picked up on our way back. It wasn't very good but I became tipsy almost right away. I drank one can silently and then stood up. I could hear Nana's rough breathing as she slept in a bed fixed up for her in the upper part of the closet. I peeked in at her. Kumi was lying on the floor with her back to me. Nana was lying on her back in a tidy manner, her face dark red. Wondering if she was sunburned, I mentioned this to Kumi. She stood up and looked at my face first, then at Nana's.

"She really is red," she whispered and put her hand on Nana's forehead. "She's hot . . . hot." She turned her head slightly and looked at Nana's hand.

"She's hot?" I touched Nana's cheek. I didn't understand why she was hot. I wanted to go home as soon as possible.

"I wonder what's the matter?" Kumi, who was also tired, stood there looking more bewildered than worried. She was flushed.

"I don't know, but she's awfully hot."

"Maybe it's a cold," Kumi said.

"Gee, maybe so. She may have a cold, but I can't tell. You're the mother, aren't you?" I was annoyed and didn't want to have to stay. Suddenly not only Kumi but all mothers—my mother, Suwan's mother, and the mother that still remained within me—seemed ridiculous, and I felt ashamed. Still, I couldn't take my eyes off Kumi or run away from her room, so I sat down on the floor. I was angry at myself for not leaving in spite of everything.

"A cold, probably," Kumi said. She sat down next to me.

"Hmmm . . ."

"She has a high temperature."

"Maybe so. But if it's late and she's sleeping well . . . I think we'd better leave her like this until tomorrow morning. She's all right, you don't need to worry."

Kumi nodded and sighed the way all mothers do. I felt even angrier but went on talking.

"Even we adults are worn out. She couldn't help it. Someone has to stay with her tomorrow. Can you take a day off? If you can't, I'll stay with her."

Kumi nodded again. "It's not a matter of not being able to. Who wouldn't take a day off for something like this? After all, no one will suffer even if . . ."

"That's good, then."

Suddenly Kumi stood up with a carefree smile on her face and said, "Well then, why don't we drink some more? I'll go get some more beer. You wait here."

While I was hesitating she left.

That night I slept at Kumi's place for the first time. I only had beer but got very drunk. While Kumi rubbed my face and chest I started to cry. I was reminded of myself on the lookout tower that morning; it was as if I were seeing myself in a small illustration in a book. I had no idea why I was crying, and that made me cry all the more. I felt like I had a book in my head that was swollen with water. As the pages turned rapidly by themselves, they dripped water. It was a cheap, incoherent book, and I was in one of the illustrations. I felt I didn't exist outside of that illustration, and I was pitifully small. I resembled something; was it an insect or some kind of lizard or gecko? Kumi wasn't next to me any more but was sleeping in the corner of the room, snoring.

While it was still dark Nana started crying and then woke up every hour until morning and cried for a while.

Only four months had passed since I first began to visit Kumi. It was hard to believe. I felt that I had been listening to Nana's crying for ages and was quite used to it. It was so familiar to me that it made me sort of depressed. The room seemed filled with our three bodies, all slightly feverish and lazily clinging together. I picked up Nana's dirty sock. Underneath it was a half-melted caramel stuck in the tatami mat. A beer can with a little leftover beer and a half-eaten sweet roll were squashed underneath a plastic umbrella that had fallen on the floor. A travel alarm was also lying there on its side, pointing to an odd time. An old-fashioned, twenty-inch color television set was in the corner; it looked impressive but was too large for the room and wasn't working. A pile of clothes was in another corner. You couldn't tell whether they were dirty or clean. The unmade bed had things scattered on it—colored pencils, a cookie, hairpins, tissue paper, Kumi's underwear, a purse. A gold-colored cage with an artificial bird was hanging by the window.

The first time I had gone into Kumi's room I hadn't known where to sit or step. She had simply watched me, as if amused.

"What a mess," I said, being deliberately frank.

Kumi smiled and said, "That's why no one comes near here."

I had spoken to her that day while she was walking with Nana. When I found out that her apartment was behind Mother's house, I was elated. From the entrance to the building I could see the roof of Mother's house. Kumi's room was across from the common bathroom of the apartment building.

After that I went to her place almost every day. I couldn't see Kumi during the day since she worked. Nana stayed at a day-care center. When I saw her at night, we couldn't talk much because Nana would interrupt us and Kumi was tired. Even though we had seen each other quite often, I still felt dissatisfied.

About a month after I got acquainted with Kumi, the telephone rang in the middle of the night. It sounded incredibly loud, jolting my warm body as I lay in the upstairs room. I turned once and then jumped out of bed. I ran downstairs, covered with goosebumps. When I picked up the receiver I heard Kumi's voice amid some bustling noises. The voice wasn't Takashi's; I realized only then that I was excited, even though there was no reason to expect him to call.

When Takashi called it was almost always around two or three in the morning and from somewhere that had loud, cheerful noises in the background. He would be drunk and in a good mood. He wouldn't call to tell me anything but just to share some joke he had happened to think of. Seeing that I was confused and didn't know how to respond, he would give the receiver to a friend or to the women who worked at the bar. They wouldn't know what to say and so would take advantage of being drunk and tell me jokes I wouldn't understand.

"I'm glad you answered," Kumi said. "Could you call this number in ten minutes or so and ask for me? Please. I'm in trouble." She sounded as if she were in a hurry but not drunk. I called the number in ten minutes as she had requested and a young man answered. I asked for Kumi.

". . . Oh, hi! How did you know I was here! I see . . . Are you in a hurry? Okay, then. I'll come right away. Just wait there. It'll be about twenty minutes. See you," Kumi said and hung up.

On my way back to my room I suddenly wondered if she was walking around with Nana at that time of night.

The next day I wasn't sure if I had really talked to Kumi over the telephone. It seemed unlikely, and I started to think I had been dreaming or perhaps had only heard the telephone ring while I was sleeping.

I could hardly wait for evening to come. I could have asked Mother and found out for sure but that seemed unnecessary. Besides, I didn't want her to know about Kumi. I felt guilty when I thought of her eyes watching me go back and forth to Kumi's place. My relationship with Suwan seemed more innocent but actually there wasn't much difference. I knew I was repeating the same pattern. I thought I could hear Mother sighing, "I wonder why you have such a weak character? You always let yourself be pulled toward the weak. Don't you want to learn to stop yourself? You were a mother once, you know. You haven't changed a bit, even though your child died and a man left you. It's disgusting. Your brother wasn't afraid and was good-natured even though he was born with that problem. It's true that the better the child, the sooner it dies . . ."

I left the house without saying anything to Mother, went to Kumi's room and waited for them to come home. Kumi never locked the door when she went out but when she was home she locked it from the inside. Nana had learned this habit and although she always left the door open when she went out, she closed it carefully when she went inside, searching for the door latch. Once Kumi had forgotten to lock the door at night, and a man got into the apartment. She woke up when she felt something heavy pressing against her body. She and Nana screamed, threw things at him, kicked and chased him away. After that, she had once explained to me, she was afraid and was careful to lock the door. I thought of Mother's overcautious way of living and nodded at Kumi's story, thinking about better ways to secure the door. It never occurred to me to doubt Kumi's story.

Kumi and Nana came back a little after six. Nana came into the room first, wearing shoes without socks as usual but bundled up in a baggy parka. When she saw me she screeched "Mama!" She didn't come near me even though I beckoned her. Kumi came in, stooping slightly. Nana clung to her mother and glared at me. I paid as little attention as possible to Nana, ignoring her and smiling at Kumi.

"It's cold, sitting here alone."

"I have an electric heater but I don't know where to put it." She sat in front of the television with her legs stretched out, looked around the room and stared at me. She chuckled softly.

"Hey, today's Christmas. I forgot. You were looking forward to Christmas, weren't you? How should we celebrate?" she asked.

"Today's Christmas?"

"We'll have to have a roast chicken and a cake first. What else? What do you want to eat, Nana?"

"Fish stew, I like that," Nana said, left Kumi's lap and stretched her arms out, jumping up and down.

"Hmmm. Stew sounds good too. What do you say?"

I nodded. I'd given up finding out about the telephone call. It didn't matter whether it was real or a dream. It seemed best not to bring it up to Kumi, who was planning a party, or to Nana, who was excited about Christmas. I remembered that I had told Kumi only a few days before that even though I didn't have any particular Christmas memories, I liked Christmastime more than any other time of the year. As soon as Christmas was over I started to look forward to the next one. I was amazed that I had forgotten what day it was. Dates and days of the week had totally disappeared since I had stopped working. The days had become smooth and flat, and slid along easily so that they passed even when I could think of nothing to do. Being with Takashi had been a kind of work for me. When he disappeared from my life, I realized this for the first time; my days suddenly became shorter, and my evening hours shrunk like a punctured balloon.

I didn't want Kumi to know that I had forgotten Christmas. I told her in a deliberately high-handed tone to clean up the place while I went out to do some shopping, and left without waiting for her to respond. Fortunately I had my purse with me. My discharge allowance wasn't too large, but I still had quite a bit left after I had paid Takashi's hospital bills and my moving expenses. It wasn't enough to rent an apartment for myself, though.

I bought a French wine, a roast chicken with a red ribbon tied around its legs, a cake decorated with Santa Claus and a Christmas tree, and some fish stew. When I returned the room had been tidied up a bit. Kumi was smoking by a table set in the middle of the room. Nana wasn't around, and Kumi said she had gone to meet me.

"But I didn't see her. Is she all right?"

"Don't worry. If she can't find you, she'll be back," Kumi said, taking the things I had bought and examining them one by one.

"But there's a lot of traffic. If you're tired, shall I go look?" I started to stand up.

"Never mind, don't bother."

I looked at Kumi's large bloodshot eyes and sat down. I put six small candles on the cake, and Kumi lit them with her lighter. Then I put the rest of the food on the table and brought two glasses from the kitchen. Kumi sat on her knees and gazed at the candle flames. I stared at her pale, pimply face, remembering the voice on the phone the night before. Her skin was rough and her lips were cracked, but it was still an attractive face. Since it was nicely shaped, sometimes her expressions reminded me of an animal that is always hungry and bad tempered no matter how much it is fed. Her thighs, so plump that it seemed there were no bones in them, looked slightly red as they reflected the candlelight. She was wearing a skirt that night for a change.

"Nana won't die easily. She's like me. Even if she were left at the North Pole, she'd live. I'm sure the two of us will survive." Kumi looked into my eyes and added, "We're different from the rest of you."

Someone knocked on the door. I could hear Nana's voice calling Kumi.

"See? I sometimes wish people would worry about us more than they do."

Nana had some chewing gum in her fist. Kumi went out to pay for it.

By the time the three of us finally sat around the table, the candles on the cake had burned out. Nana wanted us to sing some Christmas songs, so we sang several, then sang "Happy Birthday," repeating it three times and changing the names each time. I took the red ribbon off the chicken legs and tied it around Nana's naturally curly hair. She started to dance. Kumi and I toasted and drank some wine. It was the most expensive wine on the store shelf, but I couldn't tell how good it was. Kumi said it was sour. We let Nana try it, and she drank it as if it were milk. Her face turned pale but she kept dancing as if she were wearing some magic red shoes.

Once as a child I had gotten drunk on plum wine at home and, feeling sick, had covered my head with a plastic bag and danced around like a man from outer space. I clowned around, moving my arms and legs and trying to make my mother and brother laugh. The plastic bag around my neck made me lose my breath right away. The bag was inflated, and I could see the laughing faces of my mother and brother as if through a cloudy white screen. I moved my hand around my neck, trying to untie the string. Even though I was trying desperately to undo it, I didn't want to spoil my audience's fun and continued to dance. I wanted to complete the show and take off the bag easily with a laugh. I was just tearing the bag off with both hands when I fell forward and hit my forehead on the floor. When I came to, my mother was holding me up, an angry look on her face.

"How stupid this girl is!" she said. "I wouldn't let you die in such a silly way." This probably had happened when I was in the third grade.

Kumi and I kept on drinking, watching Nana dance. When the wine bottle was empty we drank whiskey from the same glasses.

After a while Kumi cried out suddenly, "How can you say you look forward to Christmas? It's no fun, no fun at all." Nana stopped dancing, stood rigidly and then fell to the floor. In a second she was breathing regularly and was fast asleep. Kumi put her in the bed in the closet and covered her with a blanket. It was blue with a picture of chicks on it. I had once had a similar blanket that I put in the coffin when my baby died and had cremated with him. I had wanted them to burn the crib with it too. Takashi bought most of the baby things at a department store with money his parents in the country had sent him. Before the baby was born, the department store had even delivered an English-made baby buggy. Large and navy blue, it reminded me of a real carriage. It would have looked nice with white horses pulling it. For a long time I left it out by the stairs because it had been too big to fit through the apartment door.

"Shall we go somewhere? I'll take you somewhere you've never been. I'm getting depressed sitting here like this," Kumi said.

"I don't feel like going anywhere. There's some more whiskey left. It's nice here."

I started to feel drunk for the first time in ages. The orange-colored curtain with the white pom-poms hanging from the hem seemed particularly bright. I wondered if Kumi had made it herself. I grabbed Kumi's legs and made her sit down. She began to gripe.

"Just old people, wherever you go . . ."

"So what do we care? Just being young doesn't mean everything's good, does it?"

"No. And that's why I'm afraid to get old. I'm doing my best to act young, in case you didn't notice. So don't pull at my legs."

"You are young, no doubt about that. Younger than I am, anyway."

"But my body is falling apart fast."

I laughed and said, "You ought to eat healthier food."

Kumi didn't respond. She finished the whiskey left in her glass and ate some chicken, tearing at the meat with both hands. I drank my whiskey and ate the cold stew; some radish slices and burdock root were left. I remembered that my brother and I used to eat the same kind of stew for a snack. The triangle-shaped devil's-tongue had been my favorite then. I didn't remember what my brother's favorite was. The cold radish slices were refreshing when they went down my throat.

Kumi was lying on the floor with her face down, so I lay down next to her, yawning once. I wrapped my legs in my overcoat, smelling a sweet mixture of odors in the room. The beating of my heart vibrated through my entire body. There didn't seem to be a clock that was working in the place, so I had no idea how late it was. In the apartment I had shared with Takashi, there were four clocks altogether—an alarm clock, a round plastic wall clock, a stopwatch, and a digital clock with a radio. In that small two-room apartment you were forced to see the faces and numbers of clocks no matter where you were. The clocks were rarely accurate, each telling a different time, so they didn't serve their purpose. When I needed to know the time I looked at the time reported on the television screen. Takashi took three of the clocks with him, leaving the stopwatch. He liked calendars too and hung them above and beside the desk, in the kitchen and in the bathroom. All of these he took to his new apartment; they had been marked with circles and letters that indicated his plans in detail. He liked to make plans two or three months in advance, even though most of them were never realized. Other than going to the university to do research, he didn't work; he didn't want to do even part-time tutoring, so he had plenty of time, which he spent seeing his friends and drinking with them.

I heard Kumi mumbling something.

"What're we going to do?"

"What?" One of the bamboo leaves painted on the lampshade was much paler than the others. I wondered if it had been that way when it was sold at the store. The painting was cheap, but they looked like real leaves to my near-sighted eyes.

"Are we going to stay like this until morning?"

"It's not so late, is it?" I sat up and poured some more whiskey into our glasses. It was smooth on my tongue, perhaps because it was old whiskey.

"Are you going? Your house is so close, you don't have to sleep here, I suppose."

the clock started to strike. It was midnight. When I lived with Takashi midnight had never seemed late. I went upstairs, fixed my bed and lay down. I could still smell Nana's vomit, the mixed odor of wine that was turning sour, something that smelled like yogurt, and Kumi's body. And there was something else, something I had smelled before. It was the smell of my brother. As soon as this thought occurred to me, I was convinced that I was right. I realized that one is not likely to remember an odor after fifteen years, but I didn't want to question this association. I wanted to consider my brother's smell and Kumi's smell to be the same.

Brother was always dirty. Mother and a woman who worked for us followed him around all day with a damp towel and gave him a bath every night, but it didn't matter what other people did for him because he didn't care about keeping himself clean, and so whenever I saw him, he was dirty. He always had a runny nose and something was always stuck around his mouth. Since he was unable to control his drooling, particularly when he was excited, the edges of his lips were always sore.

His teeth were yellow since he had never learned to brush them. He never washed his hands unless forced and yet loved to use his hands when he played, so they were always grimy and chapped. A mixture of odors floated about when he waved his hand. His wrinkled shirttail hung out of his trousers, and his front zipper was never properly closed.

My clearest memories of my brother are of him after he was ten years old, and particularly when he was about twelve. At that time we liked the same kind of play. I was in the third or fourth grade, and except for the hours when I was in school, almost all of my time was spent with him. I was busier than he was; I had homework to do and had to practice the piano, but he waited patiently for me until I was free. I tended to neglect my duties because I was so absorbed in playing with him. I completely forgot about my teacher, piano instructor, and my mother—who was the worst nagger of them all—when I thought about playing with my brother.

His body had started to mature, and I could feel the change in a certain way, even though he wasn't any taller and his voice hadn't changed. He was still as dirty and sloppy as ever and couldn't speak any better than two-year-old Nana. His body seemed to be surpassing my own childlike body; he became thinner, his bones more prominent, his face longer and darker. His slovenliness was more obvious and his body odor stronger.

What pleased me most was that he wasn't conscious of these changes in himself and remained as faithful to me as before. He had no concept of comparison and continued to believe that I was more beautiful, clever, virtuous, and gentle than anyone else. Sitting on his knees behind me without fidgeting, he listened to me play the piano. I couldn't play very well and always struggled to keep from yawning, but it must have sounded quite marvelous to him. Although I laughed at his gullibility, I also needed the support. I couldn't imagine my future without him.

While I cleaned his nose, helped him eat, and read for him in bed like Mother used to do for me, I thought seriously that I would be perfectly happy if I could always live like this. I knew Mother would die some day and was looking forward to it. I didn't like to see him cry and go to Mother when he hurt himself; I wanted him to come only to me. I wanted his dirty body with its strong odor that I could recognize even with my eyes closed all to myself. We had no rules when we played; we couldn't play with rules, roaming around the neighborhood and going in any place that looked interesting. Once we passed through someone's house without saying a word. We went into the main hall of a temple, the operating room of the hospital, and a high school. We ran around in open lots and cemeteries. When we got tired, we flopped down. We hung from tree branches.

As Brother got older, Mother left us home alone more often. I liked these times best; I felt so free. Since we had no maid at that time, the entire house was ours once Mother had left. We could do whatever we wanted; nothing was prohibited. Overwhelmed by this freedom, we often ended up playing more quietly than we normally did.

Once I thought of taking all my clothes off. This seemed to fit my sense of freedom. As soon as Mother left, I took off everything, including my underwear. I made Brother do the same. Our naked bodies were not particularly strange to each other since we were used to taking our baths together. Still, it felt odd to stand naked in front of each other in the living room in the middle of the day, nowhere near a bathtub or shower and away from Mother's eyes.

I felt weak and fragile. The windows and doors were open and the house felt extraordinarily spacious. I couldn't think of anything to do once we were naked so simply ran through the empty house with Brother following me. We went into the yard and peed. After that we went to the kitchen, found some food, and ate it while lying on the living room floor. We pulled bedding out of the closet and rolled around on it. We pretended to wrestle; Brother was stronger than I was. Holding each other, we fell asleep. He seemed cleaner without his clothes. His chest was broad and soft, and I licked and tried to bite the soft flesh. When I put my teeth on his chest, he started to cry. I changed roles quickly and comforted him, holding his big body on my lap like a doll. This pleased him and he made a purring sound like a cat, and then his penis began to get hard. His penis, his wet lips, everything about him was sweet and fascinating to me. He was like a toy to me and, at the same time, like a fleecy cloud.

The fifth or sixth time we played like this, Mother came back sooner than we had expected and found us. Of course I was held responsible, and we were never left alone again. After that Mother took both of us or just Brother with her. I also had to take a bath by myself after Mother and Brother had theirs. But even so, we were able to figure out ways to repeat this kind of childish play if we wanted to.

Early in the morning on the day after our picnic, Kumi and I took Nana to the hospital. We wore the same clothes we had worn on our outing. It was afternoon when I returned to Mother's house; she had expected me to come back the day before. She said nothing to me, but her entire body eloquently expressed her opinion of me. She seemed to sigh and say, "Who could put up with you when you behave like this? I wonder how that man was able to tolerate you for so many years." Suddenly it occurred to me that she might have been satisfied with me if I had been able to bring my child to her home. I couldn't remember what my child looked like—he would have been five years old—and instead kept seeing Nana's face.

Nana had an acute ear infection. Kumi didn't go to work for two weeks, and shut herself up in her room. She lounged around on the unmade bed and let Nana climb on her back and pull her hair. Kumi kept staring at the ceiling. I had to start looking for a job, and spent the day going to see various acquaintances. In the evening I often saw Suwan and once took him with me to Kumi's room. Kumi was pleased to see us but for some reason she was unusually quiet and focused her attention on Nana. Suwan's Japanese hadn't improved at all so I had to do all the talking, initiating the conversation, responding and agreeing. Of course I couldn't continue this for long, and after an hour or so I urged Suwan to leave.

Kumi then said, "Listen, my birthday's on the sixteenth. Why don't you mark it on your calendar?"

"Gee, that's not far away. We'll have to celebrate. Can I invite Suwan, too?" As soon as I said this, I regretted it.

For about four months I had been going out with Suwan to various places and spending nights at his place, but we rarely spoke about anything except Takashi. It was as if he was with us whenever we met. Just as Suwan couldn't help thinking of Takashi when he saw me, I started to enjoy remembering Takashi's voice as I listened to Suwan talk. Now that Takashi wasn't around anymore, I always remembered him treating me with kindness. Because he wasn't there, he belonged only to me. I didn't want Takashi to meet Kumi, and yet at the same time longed for him to see her. If I didn't think of him, my passion for Kumi seemed meaningless. I wanted to introduce her to him as my new friend.

Kumi was pleased with what I said. "I'll be twenty-two. I don't need to lose hope. Not yet. To hell with work and the people at the day-care," she said.

Kumi had had frequent warnings from both her employer and the staff at the day-care center. She had grumbled more about this criticism since the beginning of April. They said things like, "You're careless about time and the way you dress. You should be more careful for the sake of your child. You should go to bed earlier. If you expect to leave work early because of your child, you ought to work harder while you're here. Instead of eating out so much, let your child have some home-cooking. Can't you at least wear clothes that don't show your skin? You make us feel embarrassed . . ."

"They are only afraid of me because I'm a woman," Kumi told me. "Once I leave this room, I feel like there's nothing but men out there. They think I don't think of anything but men. That's why whenever my eyes meet a man's I'm sure I know what's going on, too. And at night my body feels like . . . what do you call that rock? Yeah, granite. That's right. I feel like I've lost my voice and no matter how they treat me, I don't feel pain any more because I've become a rock. I could even go lie down in the street naked. Yeah, I could. Still, when morning comes I feel fine again. I guess that's because I'm still young. And when I leave this room I feel like saying, 'Who do you think I am? Don't underestimate me. I can take care of a man or two!' " Kumi went on, glancing at Nana, who was pulling all the clothes out of the closet. "I like children. That's why I went ahead and had one, even though her father left me. But it's a different story when it's your own child. Nana never lets me forget how stupid I am and what my limits are."

"But compared to a baby who was born and then went ahead and died, Nana is better off. I've never tried to do anything by myself before, and that's why I don't have anything left."

"Do you think so? You're really nice."

"No I'm not." I was bewildered by Kumi's response and blushed. Kumi looked into my face, laughing a little, and said, "You're always so jumpy. Why are you so timid? I feel sorry for you. I can tell what sort of kid you were, you know."

She then started to tell me about her own childhood. "Thinking back on it now," she said, "until I went to grade school I was almost an autistic child. I sat around tearing paper into strips. That was when my parents were separated. Even now I remember how good it felt to tear a sheet of paper into little pieces that didn't hide anything, like snow flakes. At least at that time I was filled with love, love for myself."

Suwan and I left Kumi's place, went to a hotel in the city center, and stayed the night there. As soon as we got to the room, Suwan fell asleep. As usual I slept next to him as a sister or a sister-in-law. Suwan paid the bill. He had more than a million yen in his bank account. This was the love his parents had given him.

I didn't have a chance to see Suwan again until after Christmas. With only two days left until New Year's, the busy streets were filled with a holiday atmosphere. We met in front of a department store and Suwan asked to go to the top floor so we could eat fried noodles. It was warm there. A few fathers were playing with their children. We tried some electric games, then left the store. Outside it was cold. We went into the underground shopping center and stopped at a coffee shop.

"Is Takashi all right?" Suwan asked his usual question.

"Who? I don't know who you're talking about."

"You can't forget."

"Even if you can't, I can. I used to forget a lot of things when I was a kid."

"Takashi promised me. Next summer we go to my country. Play a lot."

"That sounds nice."

"You come with us."

"If it's just you and me, I'll go. Can I stay at your house?"

"Three of us. It'll be fun."

"Fun?"

"Yes. It'll be cheap, too. The sea is beautiful also."

"Even so, I don't think he'll go."

"He said he wanted to go very much. True."

"You won't take me without him?" I asked teasingly. Suwan answered in a serious tone, "I promised him." I laughed loudly. Suwan smiled back confidently, looking like a silly old man.

I recalled that he had once told me about Pattaya Beach, that he used to skip school and drive there. There were rows of hotels, white sand, blue sea, and groups of almost naked foreigners. Suwan and his friends wouldn't swim there, though; they weren't interested in swimming. Only foreigners and poor kids swim in the ocean and get sunburned, he said. When I asked him what they did at the beach, he laughed and said there were lots of other things to do.

"I love swimming in the ocean," I said. "You rich kids from Bangkok are strange."

Suwan, looking at his own dark-colored hands, said, "You're a foreigner. You'll love Pattaya Beach. Kids in Bangkok aren't kids, they're adults."

A tropical sea, a sea of cobalt blue like those I had seen so many times in photographs. "Pattaya Beach . . . I'd like to go there," I whispered to myself, ignoring Suwan.

I suggested that we leave the coffee shop. At the ground level the sun was behind a cloud and the temperature had fallen. Our breath looked white.

"What sort of place did you used to go to with Takashi?" I asked while we walked along.

"I don't know. Many bars. Takashi's friends' houses, too."

"Was it fun?"

"Yes. Takashi is nice. Has many friends. Everybody likes Takashi."

I nodded at Suwan and grasped his arm. "Your Japanese didn't improve a bit while you were spending time with him, did it? If you don't know the language, that means you're a *moron*."

"A moron?" Suwan repeated the word, still smiling.

"Can we go to your room now? I'm tired." I smiled back at him. Suwan mumbled, trying to say no, and wouldn't start walking. When I stopped a taxi and got in, he did too, sighing. He gave the driver the name of a place I had once heard of.

Suwan's room was on the second floor of an old apartment building, six mats with a sink and a bathroom. As I walked in, the setting sun was casting rays through the window. The room looked bright and neatly arranged. There were some dark pink curtains that Suwan had chosen himself. On the steel desk, the kind that grade school children use, there was a picture of his parents. His bed, stereo set, and a small television all looked brand new. There were some kitchen utensils by the sink, and everything was neat and clean. A flower-patterned hand towel hung by the sink.

Sitting on the bed, I drank some whiskey, which Suwan said Takashi had left. Suwan drank coffee, put some Japanese popular songs on his stereo, and showed me an album with some recent photos. His parents were both slender. There was a picture of Suwan in a high school uniform and of Suwan being sent off at the airport; he was wearing a purplish blue suit and a lei and was smiling shyly. The pictures were amusing and I laughed at everything I saw. Suwan sat rigidly in front of his desk and smiled. I remembered the time we had played with fireworks, and mentioned this to him. We had taken twenty fireworks or so to an empty lot and set them off. When we got back we found Takashi in the room, lying in front of the television set. I also talked about a restaurant we had gone to many times when Takashi was in the hospital. The pork cutlet on rice had been good. We saw a big white cat with silvery gold eyes there and always found some white hairs on the tables where he liked to sleep. Suwan was afraid of the cat and couldn't take his eyes off it while he ate.

He had tried to cheer me up, and would say, "Don't worry. Not your fault. Was accident. You watch your health." In Takashi's hospital room I moved about like a poorly made wooden doll while I helped Takashi change his pajamas or wiped his back with a hand towel. I felt as if my hands and legs would fall clattering to the floor.

Ignoring Suwan's timid request that I leave, I got into his bed with just my underwear on. I was drunk and soon fell asleep. The next morning I found him wrapped in a blanket and sleeping on the floor beside the bed. I had a headache but I got dressed anyway and left.

Suwan called unexpectedly that night. The following day, on New Year's Eve, I went to his place again. We watched a television program and then went out to a Shinto shrine. Both of us were surprised at the crowd; when we returned to his room, exhausted, we drank some whiskey, saying that New Year's Eve was a special occasion. Suwan got drunk right away and fell asleep with a bright red face. I put him to bed and continued to drink whiskey and listen to records. Toward dawn I finally felt sleepy and lay down next to

Suwan, putting my cheek against his soft, plump back and closing my eyes. It was a gentle, broad back. He was sound asleep.

The next day I woke up late in the afternoon. Seeing me awake, Suwan said in a shy voice, "Happy New Year." On the desk I saw some New Year's delicacies arranged in a small wooden box and soup in a pan. I smelled ginger. Suwan had already changed into his clothes and was watching television. I quickly put on my dress and said "Happy New Year" to him.

After the New Year I started to see him every three or four days. We didn't do anything special, just walked around, went shopping, and stopped to have a cup of coffee. We once went to the street where Takashi and I had lived. Suwan and I were equally ignorant of this city, but actually Suwan, who had a detailed guidebook for foreigners, knew more about places to go than I did. Takashi must have told him about some of them. Whenever I suggested going out of town to a port or a nature park in the suburbs, Suwan said he had already been there once or twice. I lost interest in going to such places, and so we ended up walking the same streets we always walked. We sat on benches like an old couple, basked in parks or on the roofs of department stores and listened to each other's old stories.

Suwan talked a lot about his mother, as usual—the mama who took care of him when he was sick as a child, who worried about his health even after he got better, and who wouldn't let him go out of the house. Thanks to her care, he was able to play outside most of the time after he was ten or so. The family had always had enough money. Mama was always busy. Papa was home only when he was working. At night he went to his young mistress's house where he had another son, whom Suwan of course had never met. Once late at night Mama had cried in Papa's office and when Suwan heard the sound from the hallway, he thought at first that she was laughing.

I also told him my childhood memories one after another, choosing only the pleasant ones: Christmas presents Mother gave me, games I played at New Year's, snow rabbits Brother and I made together, snowball fights with our maid and me on one side and Mother and Brother on the other. Mother was the toughest. Then there was skating on the frozen pond. More than once Brother and I had broken through the thin ice and fallen in. In the summer we splashed around in the same pond.

My father died when I was still little, but I don't remember ever having any money problems. Mother's family owned a large kimono business, and they sent us money that Mother invested in stocks. Until Brother died, Mother was probably quite happy. She was able to function as she believed a mother should. She had strength, and because she believed in her own strength, she was gentle. As a child I felt that nothing was lacking in my life. Still, there was a time when I had secretly wished that my father was alive somewhere. Once I had tried to find out about him from Mother and she had scolded me unsparingly. She must have felt that I was disregarding the care she had given me every day and yearning romantically for a father who had died long ago, and that this was a sign of my cowardly nature. I don't know even now if I was a particularly sentimental child or if Nana too, for example, might go through a period when she would have the same longing.

During that winter and spring I saw Kumi and Suwan in turn. I didn't try to keep this a secret, but there was no need to tell one about the other. Neither Suwan nor Kumi wished to expand their circle of friends. They wanted to draw me into their burrows, and I found it pleasant to be alone with each of them in their little rooms. It wasn't that they had no other friends besides me, but they didn't let me meet any of them. I thought this only natural.

"I really helped you out, you know. Have you ever thought how you would've ended up if I hadn't been around? When I first met you I couldn't believe what a wreck you were. You were pale and looked sour. You smoked like an addict. You weren't much to look at. When I saw your dumpy apartment, it gave me the creeps and I wondered what a girl was doing alone in a dark place like that. It depressed me. But you have definitely changed, thanks to me. You're pretty cute now. You should be more grateful." Takashi used to tell me this repeatedly when I was carrying the baby. Each time I agreed with him and said, half jokingly, "You're right, I was disgusted with myself, too, and I'm really grateful." Takashi truly believed what he said, though, and I even thought he was probably right.

I didn't want to lose him because I was going to have his child. I wanted to avoid offending him if I could; since I had started to live with him, I had changed nearly all of my habits, even my taste in clothes. Takashi liked soft, subdued designs. Not an especially rugged man, in fact he was more sensitive than I was in many ways. He arranged flowers himself at home and made sure that the bedding wasn't crooked. Still, I was always afraid of him—I couldn't help it.

I studied his moods carefully, played up to him and laughed. When he was studying in the evening, I tried not to make any noise and ironed his shirts and trousers or did the dishes, deliberately taking a long time.

I didn't expect him to give me his meager income from the university for our expenses, so I used my own salary. Since Takashi was a free spender, my income was not enough for us and we gradually got into debt. Takashi then asked his parents to send money. He had already asked them to pay all the necessary expenses for the baby. I just watched him without criticizing. As long as he was nice to me, I was happy. I expected nothing more from him. He would be in a good mood as long as he had enough time to play and study, if he was respected by people around him, and, on top of all this, if he was blessed with a healthy baby. Takashi had a mirror that reflected a perfect image of himself. This mirror hadn't clouded once, and I kept helping him polish it.

Was I responsible for encouraging this childish young man to remain as he was? I didn't think my timid flattery had much effect, but since I was the person he saw every day, I was perhaps the main support for his happiness. If that was the case, I had to continue to worship him, no matter what I really felt about him. He was my savior, my benevolent father . . .

After the baby who ought to have grown up healthily had died, I started to feel that I had been acting all the time I had been with Takashi. I could laugh with him when his laughter was wholehearted, but I couldn't share his grief. It was impossible to hide the fact that my tears were different from his. Takashi had been an active boy who had had the jungle gym all to himself in the schoolyard. He had been one of the boys who yelled "Stupid shithead, stupid shithead!" when he saw my brother and I pass by. I had been afraid of those boys but at the same time wanted to be included in their group and play with them, even if only once. I had been timid and didn't have the nerve even to approach them; all boys had seemed to me a whirlpool of violence.

I was the first to turn away, not Takashi, and because of this change within myself I started to become more afraid of him.

I kept my promise to Kumi about her birthday, even though I wasn't excited about it, and went to her room with Suwan. She wasn't back from work yet. We cleaned her room, put a pot of primroses we had bought for her on the table, and waited for her return.

She came into the room, panting, and smiled shyly when she saw us. We sat around the table right away and toasted. Suwan put Nana on his lap, saying he loved children. Nana didn't try to run away like she did the time I had tried to hold her. After an hour they had become good friends and were coloring together. Because of this, Kumi and I were able to relax without being bothered, Suwan paying no attention to us, we ignoring him.

Kumi and I got drunk almost immediately, as usual. By the time Nana had fallen asleep in Suwan's arms, we were lying on the floor. I was half asleep but listened to Kumi's thin voice complaining about something: "While I was taking time off from work, my desk disappeared. One morning when I went back, they looked at me in this odd way, like they were thinking 'What did she come here for?' I didn't say anything and wouldn't leave. One of the bosses came over and patted my breast and hip. I knew if I ignored him he would leave me alone without doing anything else, but if I yelled at him to stop and showed that I was really mad, the other men would come over and all say to each other, 'Does she want a man that much, do you think? She's not a woman, she's an animal. Disgusting. I can smell her, she stinks. We don't want our office to be contaminated. Get out of here right now!'

"The day after this happened, though, they were all particularly nice and came over to me and whispered, 'You must be having a hard time, but your kid will get older soon and things will be easier for you.' It sounded like they'd heard this somewhere before. When I heard this, I realized that they were really going to throw me out soon. I didn't want them to, but I hated to cling to such people. So I left the office and came right back to this place. Since they never give me any real work to do, no one suffers when I'm not there. But on the day when they teased me, I sat in the office until closing time. I didn't fall asleep, just sat there like I was dreaming. I wasn't bored. I was sort of in a trance. I didn't see or hear anything."

I just smiled and let Kumi talk without interrupting her, not feeling either sympathy or doubt. Since there was nothing about me that attracted people's attention, I wished I could be conspicuous like Kumi. Even though it was her breasts and hips that caught people's eyes, I didn't think this was so awful. Her fair, soft body must have made everyone feel gentle. I believed this was Kumi's role; I didn't know what my own role was. But even though I didn't know it, I was attached to Kumi.

Kumi and Suwan were standing when I came out of my reverie. She seemed to be persuading him not to leave. I felt too lazy to get up so watched them with half-opened eyes. Kumi grabbed Suwan's arm and pulled him toward me, saying, "Look at this. She falls asleep so easily. Look at that innocent face." I had to pretend I was sound asleep. I couldn't hear Suwan's voice. He probably couldn't understand Kumi's fast speech; I could imagine him standing there with an uncertain smile on his face.

"She says she feels safe here. Isn't she strange? But she's a bit like you. Haven't you ever thought about that?" Kumi's hand stroked my cheek. I could tell it was her sweaty hand. I had to try not to change my breathing. "She's sleeping soundly. Are you sleepy too? It's strange, that you are a foreigner, a person like you . . ."

Kumi laughed so that only her breath escaped. Her hand was moving toward my breast. Pretending that I was really asleep, I groaned softly and rolled over so that her hand slipped away and my back was turned toward the two of them. I thought I heard Suwan's voice but I couldn't check to make sure. I continued to pretend to be in a deep sleep.

Suddenly the room became quiet and I didn't hear anything. I waited for Kumi's voice but she didn't say a word. Instead there was a noise that sounded like something heavy crawling across the floor. I thought I was completely awake, but I must have been half-asleep and thus heard the noise as if in a dream. I would have heard the sounds of Kumi and Suwan leaving if they had gone out, but I didn't hear such noises. After the sound of something heavy being dragged along suddenly ceased, there was a penetrating silence in the room. They had left me. This time for sure I'd been left alone This was what I had feared most, but I didn't think it would actually happen. I felt like holding a grudge against Suwan and Kumi, but even I knew that wasn't fair. I was the one who had fallen into a comfortable sleep first. For no reason I had believed that I was being watched over by two kind friends.

Even though there was no one there to see me, I continued to pretend desperately that I was asleep. I was angry with myself, angry that I couldn't keep at least one of them to myself. This hand, I thought, this mouth, this body—if I hadn't used these to lure those two, I wouldn't have anything for myself. There was no one who trusted me as my brother had, without expecting anything in return. I started to cry, and for the first time I muttered dirty, abusive words at Takashi. I should have said this or that to him, I thought. My body was shaking. I heard words that I had never said before coming out of my mouth, and they felt hot.

I don't know how long Kumi and Suwan had been gone when

Nana woke up in her closet bed and, finding that Kumi wasn't there, started to cry. She saw me and screamed, "Mama, I'm scared! Mama, where are you? I'm scared!" She tried to open the door and run outside. Quickly grabbing her, I forced her, struggling, to the floor. I lay down next to her. Her face was purple; she went on coughing, thrashing her arms and legs, rolling her eyes so that the whites showed, and crying. I didn't say anything and kept holding her down. I could hear people downstairs and next door pounding the ceiling and the walls. I ignored them and let Nana continue crying.

After a while Nana vomited, then fell asleep, moving her shoulders spasmodically. After I put her back to bed, I wrapped myself in Kumi's dirty blanket and tried to sleep. It was unlikely that Suwan and Kumi would return soon. I felt a strange kindness toward the people who had abandoned me . . .

One summer day I invited Suwan to go see a fair. It was soon after he had come to our place with his group of friends. Takashi was attending some meeting and I didn't expect him home until late. Suwan didn't know this and dropped by early in the evening. I offered him supper, but he declined. We watched television. Suwan liked music programs best, and as I watched the screen that showed a stage lit with many tiny electric bulbs, I remembered that the neighborhood shrine was having its festival that day.

"I'll take you somewhere fun," I told him, standing up and turning off the television. If he had been capable of speaking Japanese fluently, he might have found some excuse, but instead found it easier to come with me than to insist on watching television.

I hadn't been to such a festival for a long time. I couldn't recall going to one since my brother had died. Of course I had passed by such fairs but hadn't stopped to enjoy them.

Suwan's expression changed when he saw the acetylene lamps and tiny electric bulbs.

"We have this in my country. It's the same!" he exclaimed. We tried a shooting game and won a stuffed dog, failed miserably at ring toss, and caught one goldfish in the fishing game, but decided not to take it home. We then bought some cotton candy, licked suckers, and drank soda pop. There were lots of stalls but they all sold the same things, and after having tried them all we lost interest in the fair. Leaning against a low fence at the back of the shrine, we watched children playing hopscotch and leapfrog in their summer kimonos.

"The children play the same, too," Suwan mumbled.

"Really? That's interesting," I said curtly. I was starting to feel tired. I had had a busy day at work. The thick leaves of the trees looked strangely transparent and artificial. The children's cotton kimonos were also transparent, the outline of the bodies visible through the cloth. It had been a muggy day with a gray sky.

"About your baby. I am sorry. Takashi told me. It's sad for both of you. Do you not want any more baby?" Suwan whispered.

"I don't know anything about that," I said, getting off the fence with a forced smile. Suwan didn't smile back as he usually did.

"A couple without a child. Lonely. I can understand well. Only child is lonely too. I want a sister or a brother."

"Stop it. You're talking nonsense." If I try to block out Suwan's words, I thought, it means that what he said was true. I couldn't stand to look at his face with its knowing expression, and I raised my voice in spite of myself. He looked down and became silent. This infuriated me even more. I felt angrier because he couldn't snap back at me. I longed for words that would enable us to express our feelings; we both lacked the words we needed for each other. Knowing this was so, I clung to the words that were spoken to me and let myself get upset.

"Let's go back. Unless there's something else you wanted especially to see," I said to Suwan. I didn't hide my anger. He kept looking down and didn't move.

"Are you still sitting there? Okay, then, I'll go back by myself. You know how to get back, don't you?"

A child's cry came from the group of kids behind us. I turned around and saw a girl in a kimono with a pink sash confronting three boys. Her arms were around another girl who had a red sash and was covering her face with her hands and crying. The boys, in ordinary clothes, were looking at the other children surrounding them with uncomfortable smiles.

"I'll see you at our place, then." I started to leave, but Suwan didn't look up. "Is that all right? Something wrong?"

I thought I heard him groan, felt uneasy, and went back to him.

"What's the matter? Something's wrong." I looked into his face. There were tears in his eyes. His lips were pale, and he tried to smile.

"I am sorry. I just . . . toilet. Is there one near here?"

"A restroom—I think I saw one somewhere, but I don't remember where. Can you wait?" When I understood the situation I was no longer irritated with him. Suwan's eyes looked too childlike.

"I will go back with you."

"But are you all right? Do you have some pain?"

"I am all right. Better go back." Suwan started to walk, doubled over. I ran to him, put both arms around him and looked about me. I didn't know what to do. If he had an accident now, he would be terribly embarrassed. It would probably take longer to find a rest-room than to go back to my apartment; it would take about ten minutes if we walked slowly, I thought. He couldn't rest here anyway. There might have been a first aid tent somewhere, but I wasn't sure. My arm around him, I decided to head back. We left the shrine and walked slowly, stopping frequently so that Suwan's stomach wouldn't be unnecessarily upset.

Suwan didn't seem to be able to see or hear. I too felt that I was drifting in a thick, milky-colored mist. It was a long walk. I was reminded of my baby's body. The room had been filled with a yellow glow; I could see nothing else. When he was shown to me for the first time, his body was red.

I didn't want Suwan's sympathy; I had never wondered what it would have been like if my baby had lived. A part of me had definitely been killed when he died. He was too young to leave any memories, his body too fragile for me to feel an attachment to it. Takashi had cried for a long time beside me, his crying sounding like the buzz of an insect's wings. I couldn't remember much else. It seemed a dream that I had once had a baby. Because it was a dream, it has faded away, I thought. Takashi had still accused me of being careless three years after the death of the baby.

"You may be right," I had said, "but since he's already dead please don't say anything." Takashi had cried. Unlucky child, unlucky father. Only the mother wouldn't cry.

Suwan was able to manage until we got home. As soon as we arrived, he ran to the bathroom and stayed there, coming out half an hour later with a red face. Takashi wasn't back yet. I suggested that Suwan rest for a while, but he wanted to go home. He said he often had stomach problems. Whenever he ate something he had never tried before, his stomach hurt. Even when his mama got angry or the doctor scolded him, he still had a stomachache. I then understood that the suckers and pop had been the cause of his trouble. It seemed like a childish complaint for a twenty-year-old man, and after he left I realized for the first time how funny it was. Chuckling to myself, I felt a certain closeness to Suwan. I noticed when I went to the bathroom later that a roll of toilet paper I had just put out was almost gone. When I looked carefully, I saw that the tile floor was slightly soiled. I was still cleaning the bathroom when Takashi came back.

As I had expected, Suwan and Kumi didn't return the next morning. I waited until almost noon, then took Nana to Mother's house. Mother remembered Nana; Kumi had been living in the apartment building behind Mother's house for two years, so she must have seen the child several times. Even if they hadn't lived so close by, they would have caught Mother's attention. Their clothes and the way they walked were sloppy; only their eyes were strangely sharp. They were always roaming around together, both with the same kinky hair.

"This child is as pale as a gourd. It gives me the creeps. Not the child. You, I mean."

This was all Mother said. I didn't feel like explaining. I didn't let Nana in the house but left her in the yard to play by herself. She had been crying continuously since morning, but when she was left alone in the yard, she ran around frantically, calling for her mother. Sometimes she stopped and looked around. I watched this from the veranda. When she wet her pants, I hesitated a little but still didn't let her in the house. I couldn't resist the temptation to frighten Nana as much as possible.

"Your mommy would never abandon you, never. You don't have to call her like that. What are you scared of? After all, she can't run away from you." Nana was screaming at the top of her lungs and finally started scratching the fence and banging it with her whole body in an attempt to escape. I was confused and couldn't think what to do for her. I felt a chill and kept staring at her. Sensing someone behind me, I turned around and saw Mother. She was sitting on the floor, her back straight, her eyes closed. Her hands were trembling in her lap. I went outside. Holding Nana's burning body in my arms, I stood up and went back to Kumi's place.

Kumi came back in the evening, looking the same as she always did and smiling pleasantly at me. I couldn't say anything to her, so left immediately. Nana had fallen asleep after all that, making noise through her stuffy nose.

"I would have liked to see your baby after all," Mother said that evening in a low voice while we were at the supper table. She was looking down.

"Yes, I wish you could've seen him," I said quickly, embarrassed by this unexpected conversation.

"Takashi came," Suwan said. Suwan's room was stuffy. It was raining outside. "Said he wanted to go to my country."

"What did he really come for?"

"I don't know." Suwan was sitting on the floor, looking at a record jacket with a picture of a smiling Japanese girl with short hair and bangs. I looked over his shoulder at the jacket; I was familiar with it since he only had a few records. He had more than ten cassette tapes, which he listened to more often than the records. They were of popular songs from his country that I didn't like, so when I was around he rarely took them out.

"How was he? Changed much?"

Takashi and I had separated six months before. I couldn't believe that was all it had been. At the same time, even if it had been ten years or a week I would have felt the same. Either way, I told myself, time doesn't pass as quickly as one wishes. I had never wanted to know about Takashi's day-to-day life after he left me, but I would have liked to ask him how distant he felt from me. I still dreamed about him, though less and less, and each time I felt awful when I woke up. There was a dream of him, his mother, and me walking along a country road. We seemed to be going to get the baby's dead body. In another dream Takashi and I were going to look at an apartment we wanted to move to, and in another dream we were going to a swimming pool. Takashi was standing with Nana on his shoulders in front of a large fountain. He said he had to find some red worms that were supposed to be in the water . . .

Suwan shook his head. "Takashi left without staying long. He didn't tell me anything. Said nothing."

"What about his things?"

"Said they're mine. I gave him money."

"To him? Of course he took it, didn't he?"

"Yes."

"How much?"

"Fifty thousand yen. I don't need it."

"You're rich, that's why."

Through the window I could hear the voice of a mother scolding her child. "Go on, don't get in that puddle! I said don't!" It was quiet in the apartment building. Since I had started to visit Suwan regularly, I hadn't seen any of the other people who lived in the place. Suwan stood up and opened a sliding door a little, but the air was still and muggy.

"I gave Takashi money always. Takashi liked my money very much."

"I see. He left without staying?"

Suwan nodded, picked up a piece of gum that was on the desk and put it in his mouth. I took one for myself. I had changed the bank account Takashi used to withdraw money from when he and Suwan went out a lot. Takashi had said nothing about the change and seemed to be borrowing and spending as he had always done. He couldn't have continued to ask for money from his father in the country. Takashi was popular with people both older and younger than he was, so he must have been able somehow to manage to borrow money by giving a good excuse whenever necessary. I suspected that he had been using Suwan. At the same time I couldn't quite believe that he would do such a thing. I thought instead that Takashi wanted to show generosity to Suwan and would pay for him even if he had to borrow money from someone else. Takashi enjoyed being generous and the students in his department liked him because of it.

Takashi was once asked to marry the only daughter of a rich man and become an adopted son. The rich man told him he wouldn't have to work for the family business but would be free to pursue his own interests.

"For some reason I didn't take this offer and chose you instead," he said. This was his favorite anecdote; it might have been true.

His professor seemed to trust him. After the baby was born, Takashi took me to this professor's house for the first time. I was amazed at the witty way Takashi had handled himself then, and how relaxed and pleased the professor had seemed. They seemed to be close enough to understand each other's feelings by merely looking at each other. I sat rigidly and stared at them.

"Sickening . . ."

I could remember the sound of my own voice as I said this word. It had been slow and high-pitched. After I said it, I was frightened by the implications and felt like I had been awakened by my own talking in my sleep. I hoped no one had heard me. I was holding Takashi's and Suwan's underwear, wrapped up in a damp towel. The two of them looked like two young birds in a nest, with feathers that were still wet. Suwan was red-faced from the bath and was smiling. He and Takashi had spent over an hour there; Takashi had come back first, carrying nothing, and then a few minutes later Suwan came in with a large plastic bag of underwear wrapped in a towel. He was also carrying the plastic wash basins. Takashi went directly to the cupboard, humming, and took out a whiskey bottle. Water was still dripping from his wet hair.

I asked Suwan at the door, "Would you even wash his dirty underwear if he asked you to?" Without responding to my question, he smiled faintly. His wet hair was tied back with a black ribbon like an American Indian. Until then Takashi had always let Suwan carry most of their things, with the exception of his own dirty underwear and wet towels. Takashi used to throw these down at my feet when he returned from the bath.

"Hey, what are you doing there? Who is sickening, anyway?" Takashi said and poked my back. I was standing by the door, not knowing what to do with the dirty underwear I had snatched from Suwan's hand. I threw what I was holding to the floor, went into the room and sat in front of the heater. I turned the television off. I had been watching a sports news program that I didn't really care about. Takashi followed me into the room and grabbed my shoulder.

"Get up. I said get up."

I stood up. Suwan was still standing in the doorway.

"You fucking idiot. You don't know what you're saying." Takashi's right hand hit my face. It didn't hurt so much, but I stepped backward in fear of second and third slaps. "Don't you underestimate men!"

Bumping the heater with my heel, I lost my balance. There was a kettle on the top with boiling water. "I have to be careful," I said to myself, and two words flashed through my mind—"fire" and "burn." A burn would be more likely than a fire, I thought the next moment, then fell on my back, my body twisting, and flung both arms in the air. The kettle fell off and I heard Takashi's low cry. It reminded me of the cry of someone in sexual ecstasy. I could see nothing but the white steam. Suwan rushed in, screaming in his own language.

I gave Takashi some sedatives and helped him to bed. Suwan was crying.

"No letter from Mama," he said.

"You must feel lonely." My eyes met his. I started to laugh. Suwan shrugged his shoulders and laughed in a girlish, husky voice.

The open lot was about twenty minutes' walk from Mother's house. It was in an old residential area, but there was a brand-new condominium across the street.

"Sometimes this gate is locked, as if someone happened to remember," Kumi said as she pushed the old wooden door that was wrapped in barbed wire. The gate and fence were high, and no one would have guessed that there was an empty lot on the other side. Kumi had discovered it when she and Nana were walking in the neighborhood one day and Nana happened to push the gate.

Suddenly the scenery became green. Nana seemed to remember the place and ran into the grass without hesitation. For a moment I felt that my body had shrunk to the same height as Nana's. It was a realm of grass. It seemed that anything that might stop the growth of the grass—the wind, the cold—was forbidden to enter this world. The rain that had fallen the night before made the grass shine. I felt the warmth from the grass on my cheeks. The stalks of grass that had grown two or three meters tall had vines wrapped around them, making the shapes of tunnels, men, and animals. Several evergreen bushes stood on the other side of the waves of grass, and some sparrows were chirping on the top branches.

Looking closely, I found that I was standing on a stone path that was covered with low vines. It must have been the path that once led from the gate to the house. I turned around and whispered to Kumi.

"We're supposed to go this way, right?"

Kumi looked up at me and nodded. Nana's voice echoed as she called to Kumi. I couldn't see her but the voice came from somewhere nearby.

"Mama, Mama!"

"Nana, Nana!" Kumi called back in a high-pitched voice. I looked around, holding my breath. Kumi's and Nana's voices rang loudly through the empty lot. I felt that they might awaken something that was asleep somewhere in the grass.

"You go first," I said to Kumi and went around behind her. Laughing, Nana emerged from the grass on the right and disappeared into the grass on the left.

"Are you scared?" Kumi asked.

"Of course I am."

"You're sneaky."

I didn't respond. Instead I gently pushed her back. She turned around, looked at me, and gave an exaggerated sign. I was flustered and smiled back.

"Let's go. You said there's a pond, didn't you?" I asked.

Kumi sighed again and started to walk, her back hunched, her legs dragging. The path was a gentle S-shape. Nana occasionally appeared and then disappeared again.

I began to regret that I hadn't told Kumi when I met her earlier that I was busy and couldn't go with her. But if I had turned her down, I would have regretted it even more. I couldn't turn her down; I was afraid of her blank stare. It was Saturday, and I had just come home from work. It had been two weeks since I had started to work on a part-time basis. I had gone to this office once a month when I had worked for the other company, so I didn't feel much tension. Once I was used to the work and the routine of commuting, I went straight home after work, had supper with Mother, cleaned up, and went to bed early. I had returned to almost the same life I had had with Takashi.

Although I hadn't discussed it with Mother, I intended to live with her indefinitely. When that seemed to be possible, I felt content. I stopped going to Kumi's so often. If she wanted to see me, she could easily come to my place, I said to myself. Even when I felt like visiting her, it seemed like a bother and I kept putting it off. I couldn't talk with her easily any more. She seemed to resent me for not accusing her of having spent a night with Suwan. I continued to see him as if nothing had happened. She seemed to feel that I had amused myself with her body by manipulating Suwan into having a relationship with her. I thought I could hear Kumi saying, "You think you can do anything you want to my body!" her whole body reproaching me.

If I had been even slightly guilty of this, I could have laughed at her accusation right away. I myself didn't feel quite comfortable about what had happened between Kumi and Suwan. All I could do was to treat them as I had before. I couldn't say that they had betrayed me, so I could do nothing but pretend that I knew nothing, not wanting to lose both Suwan and Kumi. I pretended that I didn't understand Kumi's accusation.

Several days after Kumi's birthday, she suddenly told me that she had found a lover. She wanted to go see him and asked me to watch Nana. I did as she asked. She came back after being away for two nights and said, "He threw me out. I came back since I had no place else to go."

Another time, a bit later, she told me that someone had arranged for her to meet a man who was interested in marriage.

"They're trying to make a fool out of me," she said. "What do they mean, 'arranged marriage'?" They want to put me somewhere so that they don't have to see me. If I'm such an eyesore, they should just say so."

She seemed to be taking days off from work without notice more often and had stopped taking Nana to day-care. Once Nana's teacher came to inquire, and Kumi said she chased her away.

"She was shocked when she saw my place. She must be telling everyone about it now," Kumi said.

In addition to these changes in Kumi, Suwan suddenly went back to his country in June. He didn't tell me about his plans until a week before he left, when he said shyly, "It's better I stay with Mama. Mama's lonely. Me lonely, too. I am no good at anything."

He didn't take the university entrance exam in March as he was supposed to. For the first time he told me that Takashi had recommended that university; I could guess that Takashi had reassured Suwan that he would write a recommendation letter and would help him study. Suwan had obviously been relying on Takashi, and had no doubt written to his mama that he would get in. His parents had even sent him the money for the tuition. But Takashi had left that university some time before, and Suwan didn't know where to find him.

"Me a university student . . . sounds strange. I help Papa's business with Mama. Don't want to become great person." Suwan's Japanese hadn't improved at all. He would probably forget all of what he had learned once he returned home.

I went to see him off at the airport with his friends and waved furiously until one of the friends told me that Suwan couldn't see us from the small airplane window. He couldn't even see the deck where we were standing, the friend said. Suwan's airplane was blue.

On the last night together we hadn't done anything special. We played on the bed as usual, tickling each other and pretending to wrestle. Before that we cooked dinner together, making up some recipes with tastes we both liked. It wasn't much different from other meals we had cooked. Some nights I held him in my arms on the bed and sang Japanese lullabies to him, and on other nights he held me and cried, drunk, for no reason. We only kissed once, but we were both embarrassed and burst into laughter.

"Why don't you go with him? You wanted to swim in that blue ocean," Kumi said in a severe tone when I told her that Suwan was leaving. She had finally called me, her voice sounding far away. "You're the one who's crazy. Do you hear? Not me; don't get it mixed up. I don't care what you say. It'll only let everybody know that you're the one who's crazy. You'd better think about it."

The next day I went to Kumi's. Kumi and Nana were not there. I waited for an hour and left. Two or three days passed and I still didn't see her. Then late one night Kumi called.

"You're still up. Sorry. Well, I just wanted to check on you. Someone from my office went to you and asked a bunch of questions, right? No? That's funny. I thought I heard that they had. Strange, really odd."

I finally went to Kumi's room again. It was a Sunday morning. The door was locked. I knocked, but there was no reply. Since the door was locked from the inside, they had to be in the room. I kept knocking on the door and called Kumi's name. I called louder and louder, and suddenly the door opened. Kumi was standing there with only her underwear on. Nana was hanging onto her waist. I lost all my strength and leaned against the door. Someone was in the room, sitting by the window with his back to the door. It was a bald man. Even though it was only logical that it wouldn't have been Suwan or Takashi, this seemed odd to me. While I was looking blankly over Kumi's naked shoulder, she banged the door shut. A moment later I heard her locking it.

I hadn't seen Kumi since then. She had called me often, though, and accused me of being a spy, a traitor, an informer. Before I thought to be concerned about her condition, I became irritated. I listened to what she had to say without responding. While I held the receiver and listened to her, I found myself feeling resentment toward Takashi, wanting to direct all of Kumi's anger toward him; when I thought of him, Kumi became me, and I became Kumi.

After I stopped going to Kumi's place, I became afraid of running into her on the street. I was avoiding her at a time when I should have been closer to her. I thought I could feel Kumi's sweaty body on my skin and I loathed it.

One day I saw Kumi standing at the gate of Mother's house. She was alone. I must have looked nervous and startled, and she began to laugh. She looked haggard and wore torn jeans and a tight red T-shirt. She seemed to have gained some weight. Her lips and fingernails were painted red; I had never seen her with red lips.

I spoke without looking at her, telling myself to try to have a normal voice, a normal expression, and normal gestures. The more I tried, the more difficult it became. I knew that Kumi couldn't have failed to notice my effort, and this was precisely why I had to continue to smile even though I knew it would annoy her.

"Haven't seen you for a while. Where's Nana?"

"Playing. Over there." Kumi pointed toward the children's park. I couldn't see Nana.

"You look better than you did when I saw you last."

She stared at me without a word. I ignored her reaction and went on.

"You should take Nana to day-care. It's better for her. I'm working now, although I'm still in my trial period. Are you going to work every day, too?"

Keeping her eyes on me, Kumi shook her head.

"You're being lazy. You lose money when you don't go, don't you? It's been hot and humid lately. You have to be careful not to feed Nana something that's spoiled." While I was talking I started to laugh, realizing how ridiculous my words sounded. "You have to say something. I feel weird. What's the matter?"

". . . An empty lot," Kumi mumbled wearily. Not understanding what she meant, I repeated her words.

"An empty lot. You wanted to go and see it, remember? I'll take you there now. You're not busy this afternoon, are you?" she said.

"Now?"

"Yes, right now."

"How far is it?" I had not forgotten about the empty lot. It was large and had a mucky pond in the middle of it. I remembered how eager my voice had been when I had asked Kumi to take me there the first time I had spoken with her. If she remembered that time as I did, I felt I couldn't possibly get away from her. I had been too eager then to excuse myself now by saying that that had been a long time ago

"You'll go even if it's far, won't you?"

"Well . . ."

"Wait a second, then," Kumi said and ran toward the park. I heard her calling Nana. I didn't move and waited there for the two of them.

We didn't speak until we arrived at the empty lot. Kumi, who was walking ahead of me, didn't turn around even once.

The day when I had met them for the first time, Kumi and Nana were watching ducks that were kept for advertising at a supermarket. Every time Nana extended her hand and tried to grab a duck's neck, Kumi pushed her hand away. They did this over and over without a word. I stood by them and said to Nana softly, "Cute ducks, aren't they?"

As I said this, Nana's eyes became larger so that the whites stood out, and more creases showed on her face. I was reminded of a dog.

"Cute ducks, aren't they?" I said again. I was at a loss and instead of saying anything else, I put my hand on Nana's head and stroked her hair. Suddenly she jumped up and sprang into her mother's arms. Kumi noticed me then, stood up and faced me. Her eyes were the same as Nana's.

I didn't know what to say and just stood there. Adjusting Nana in her arms, Kumi picked up her shoulder bag from the ground and walked away with a long stride.

"You stupid, drop dead!" Nana yelled from her mother's arms, her eyes shining. Kumi stopped walking. At the same moment, Nana's plump body fell to the ground. When she began to cry loudly, Kumi ignored her and started to walk away alone. She didn't look at me, the one who had caused the trouble. I wasn't used to crying children, and without thinking I ran toward Nana and picked her up. I was always frightened of children's crying since I felt I would start crying too. Nana's body was soft and hot. I didn't know if all two- or three-year-old children were like that. I wanted to hold her but felt a certain repulsion.

Kumi turned toward me and made a motion of bowing only after she had put Nana on her back. She did this in a careless manner, but I was happy to see it because it gave me a chance to hurry and get close to her. I told her that I had seen them playing several times in the park and explained the location of Mother's house. Kumi knew which one it was. She said she passed it every morning on her way to work. Since it was such an old house, too quiet for anyone to be living in, she had once peeked in through a hole in the fence, she said.

"All I saw was weeds. If it's an empty house, we'll go look around in it sometime, I thought. Then a few days ago I saw a light upstairs. I was really disappointed."

When I found out where Kumi lived, I asked her if I could go back with her.

"You haven't done your shopping yet."

"That's all right. There's nothing I have to have right away," I said and suggested that we keep walking.

Kumi seemed to have taken on my bright mood. Her mouth lost its sharp expression and she smiled. I realized then how young she was. My first impression had been that she was two or three years younger than myself, but when I looked closer, I saw she was still a child. I became even more cheerful.

I told Kumi how much I had enjoyed exploring empty lots with off-limits signs when I was a child. I had imagined that I would find a rotten corpse somewhere, as well as different kinds of insects, snakes, and things like that. I was scared and yet couldn't resist looking into every corner of the lot. I felt that the place was all mine, and that something either terrifying or marvelous would happen there. While I roamed around with such fantasies, I forgot all about time. Among the wildly growing grass I would see the scene of a murder, a naked man and woman, and the ghosts of a woman or a child. There had been quite a few large empty lots in the neighborhood several years before, but most of them were taken up with apartment buildings now. The land Kumi's apartment building was on must have been one of those empty lots where I had once played. So was the spot where that house was and where the bank was. Even though I had never found anything in these lots, I had a special feeling toward them.

Kumi had said she knew of only one lot that was still empty. It was very large and had a muddy old pond. Some fish seemed to live in the water, she said. No one seemed to have been there for ages. Every time she went there, she had a vague urge to kill someone, she said. Not that there was any particular individual whom she wanted to kill, but when she was there, she felt like hitting someone with a rock. She would throw the body into the pond. She wanted to see the body start to rot and watch what the water did to it.

"I want to go there too," I had said, grabbing her arm tightly without meaning to. Kumi promised she would take me soon.

"But I can't promise you that I won't kill you there."

"Suit yourself. I'll come back to you as a ghost, then." We laughed together cheerfully. I was thinking then about Takashi, gazing at his long narrow back, then throwing many invisible knives into it. I could sense the warmth of the transparent blood that spurted from the wound.

While we were talking we reached Mother's house. I didn't want to leave Kumi. I stood there looking at her but couldn't say a word. Then she asked if I wanted to go to her place; I was glad and went with her.

I stayed at her place until suppertime. We talked about all kinds of things, constantly interrupted by Nana's various demands. Kumi talked as if to herself. I had to ask questions frequently and have her explain. When I found this too much of a nuisance, I would let her go on without interrupting her. She would then mumble, "Why do you say that?" or "That's odd. Do you know him too?"

I hurriedly said, "No, I don't know him. Who is he? Someone at work?" Kumi would return then to her soliloquy. If I would have let her, it seemed she would have been able to keep talking like that until nightfall: a jazz club where she used to go when she was in high school and a black trumpet player she was mad about; the fellows she went to the club with, one of whom had been thinking of moving in with her. He stopped coming to her room about the time Nana started talking. Whenever Kumi had sex with him, Nana would wake up and call "Mama!" at a crucial moment. Those guys were all too young, she said. Even so, she was always amused by his surprise when Nana screamed.

The narrow pebbled path became wider. Nana was sitting on a rock, waiting for us. It must have been part of the front garden at one time and was the only dry spot. There was a low mound of lawn to the right. Some hydrangea were blooming in front of it; each cluster was almost thirty centimeters wide.

"You can see the pond from there," Kumi said, pointing toward the hydrangea.

"You can't get near it." I pushed back the hydrangea bushes and looked down. I saw a steep green slope, and at the bottom of it there was a black patch of water that looked small enough to hold in one's palm. It was the shape of a gourd. It was as if I were looking down at a lake from the top of a hill. Standing at the edge of the cliff, I couldn't tell how high it was. I saw an old pine tree by the pond—it must have been at least ten meters tall—that looked smaller than the hydrangea. I could see that the surface of the pond was covered with lotus leaves. I gazed at the view below, amazed. I couldn't tell how big the entire lot was; it might have been as large as 3,000 square meters, much bigger than I had expected. There was a white building beyond the trees surrounding the pond.

Looking at the ground where I stood, I noticed some narrow stone steps leading down the cliff. They were covered with a mass of tall weeds, and it seemed they would be impossible to descend. If I missed a step, I would tumble down the long slope all the way to the bottom, and it would be nearly impossible to climb up again. The ripples on the surface of the black water frightened me even more; the water looked like the back of some mysterious creature. This garden reminds me of an anthill, I thought.

"Well? Do you like it?"

Before I answered Kumi, I stepped back a little from the edge. She was crouching alongside, looking up at me.

"You and Nana came here alone? Weren't you frightened?"

"If I had known what it was like, I wouldn't have come in, but once you are here, you get used to it. We haven't come so often, though. The last time we were here was six months ago."

Nana was collecting pebbles and putting them into her skirt. I sat on the ground and leaned on the rock. The soft rays of the sun felt pleasant on my skin. I felt as if I were on the deck of a sailboat. Kumi offered me a cigarette, and I began to smoke.

"Someone must know about a lot this size. If we ask someone in the neighborhood, we'll be able to find out who it belongs to."

"I guess . . ."

"We can look at an old map, too. Anyway, it's true that something you've never dreamed of can actually exist. Don't you think? You know, I was surprised. I felt like I was having a bad dream." Small insects were flying near my eyes.

"It's not a dream."

"Of course, I know it's not. If I had come here when I was a child, I wouldn't have been able to get back."

"Why?" Kumi's voice was sharp.

"Because I couldn't have resisted going down to the pond over there. This must have been an empty lot since then. I didn't know about this place, even though we roamed all over. I'm glad I didn't know about it."

"I'm not sure about that. You say so now but you never know." Kumi picked a pebble up and threw it down. I couldn't hear the sound of the water. It must have dropped into the thick grass. I stared at Kumi for a moment and then looked away in a hurry.

Nana wanted to go to the toilet.

"Go on, you can do it yourself. Doesn't matter where," Kumi said.

When Nana walked away toward the gate, she threw down all of the pebbles she had collected. I heard birds chirping somewhere. They sounded strange.

"But that's not it."

"What?"

"That's not it. It's the breast. It's too big."

"What are you talking about?" I whispered, perplexed. Kumi suddenly raised her voice.

"Shut up. Don't interrupt me. Chasing me this far." She seemed surprised by her own voice and lowered it, turning around. "He can smell out things like this. Must have been some special network for information. I can't believe it. Really ridiculous. A bad dream. No, it's not a dream. Always like this."

I couldn't respond.

"Say, I'm sure you don't remember this but you once told me that you wouldn't mind if I killed you. Do you really mean it? Will you let me kill you?"

"Of course not," I said with difficulty, pretending Kumi was joking. Nana came back, and I called to her. "Did you pee all right?"

Nana made a face, turning her back to me. Kumi burst out laughing. I was relieved and laughed too. Nana, a few tiny branches stuck in her hair, sat on Kumi's lap.

"You were scared. I couldn't seriously talk about dying, killing, and things like that. You ought to be ashamed of yourself."

Again, I didn't know how to respond.

"You're disgusting and sneaky too. It gets to me. But you are my pet. Hey, look at me. Don't be nervous."

As I turned my face toward Kumi, she grabbed my bangs and pulled them. I tried to pull myself away, but both my neck and wrist were in her hands. I gave up and let all my strength go. Kumi then began to shake my body in a big motion, her eyes wide open. Nana, who was between Kumi and me, thought we were playing some kind of game and started to giggle. I let Kumi do what she wanted and didn't say anything. After a while she loosened her grip suddenly and sighed.

"That's right. What is important is a certificate."

I looked up in surprise and stared at her face. Her lips were cracked and dark red blood was oozing out. Some of the lipstick had rubbed off.

"That means going to school and studying." She gave a long yawn. A few drops of tears appeared in the corner of her eyes. At that moment Nana jumped at Kumi, laughing. Kumi fell on the ground. Nana climbed up on Kumi, grabbed her hair, and pretended she was riding a horse. She kicked her mother's chest, yelling "Giddy-up, horsie, giddy-up!" I heard Kumi moan, and grabbed Nana's arm and pulled her down. She bit my hand, and I kicked her as hard as I could. She cried loudly. Putting my hands over my ears to block out the sound, I turned around to look at Kumi. I had been crying without realizing it.

Kumi smiled at me and tried to pull herself up by holding onto my ankles. Since she did this suddenly, I fell, face down, on top of her, as if I were embracing her. Neither of us moved for a while. I felt the heavy beating of Kumi's heart in my body. Nana's crying gradually became weaker, sounding like the crash of waves, just as the wind blowing in the grass did. I stroked Kumi's hair. She was still. I kept my eyes closed and continued to stroke. Soon I heard her regular breathing. I fell asleep too.

I don't know how long we slept. Feeling chilly, I woke up. Nana was sleeping by herself, curled up by my feet. It was a tiny body. I felt as if I had discovered her size for the first time.

I went home, carrying the sleeping Nana and resting my cheek on her head. I wondered what sort of excuse Kumi would give me when she came to pick Nana up. Nana was heavy. I was full of love for that heavy body.